Richard Capell was born in Northampton in 1885. He was music critic for the *Daily Mail* between 1911 and 1933, and for the *Daily Telegraph* between 1933 and 1954. He served in both World Wars, being awarded a Military Medal in 1916, and working as the *Daily Telegraph* War Correspondent in World War II. As well as writing *Schubert's Songs* he is the author of over two hundred translations of Schubert's song texts and was the editor of *Music and Letters* from 1950 until his death in 1954.

SCHUBERT'S SONGS

RICHARD CAPELL

UNABRIDGED

PAN BOOKS LTD: LONDON

First published 1928 by Gerald Duckworth & Co Ltd
Revised edition published 1957
This edition published 1973 by Pan Books Ltd,
33 Tothill Street, London SW1

ISBN 0 330 23775 6

Printed in Great Britain by
Richard Clay (The Chaucer Press), Ltd, Bungay, Suffolk

CONTENTS

AUTHOR'S NOTE

THE standard Life of Schubert is Sir George Grove's, in
' Grove's Dictionary of Music and Musicians ' (all editions).
The documents are collected in Otto Erich Deutsch's
' Schubert : die Dokumente seines Lebens und Schaffens '
(Müller, Munich). I have also made use of certain bio-
graphical particulars in Walter Dahms's ' Schubert ' (Schuster
& Löffler, Berlin, 1912), and of the catalogues and paradigms
in ' Die Lieder Franz Schuberts,' by Moritz Bauer (Vol. I
only, Breitkopf & Härtel, Leipzig, 1915).

The songs, to the number of 603, were edited by Eusebius
Mandyczewski, and published in the ten volumes of Series
XX of Schubert's Collected Works (Breitkopf & Härtel,
1894-95). All but half a dozen are also to be found in the
twelve volumes of Breitkopf & Härtel's Popular edition, in
which chronology is not strictly observed, the songs being
assembled for the convenience of different types of singers.
The seven volumes of Max Friedländer's edition (Peters,
Leipzig) contain 433 songs, including several from the operas.
The order is no order at all, but sheer haphazard. The
advantage, however, of two different transpositions of the
first three volumes is offered to the amateur. English editions
of Schubert's songs do not observe chronology, and sometimes
even detach and scatter the songs of the two cycles (e.g.
Boosey's) ; they reprint again and again an arbitrary and
hackneyed choice of songs, and they contain English versions
that are usually flat and sometimes inept. Admirable versions
of the songs are, however, to be found in ' Schubert's Songs
Translated,' by A. H. Fox Strangways and Steuart Wilson
(Oxford University Press, 1924).

R. C.

PREFACE TO THE SECOND EDITION

THIRTY years have passed since this book was first published,
and although they have seen an enormous increase in the volume
of musicological studies and the birth of a new, more scientific
approach to problems of musical style and psychology,

'Schubert's Songs' remains a uniquely illuminating essay. Richard Capell was in fact ideally equipped to understand Schubert's music, and especially the Schubert of the songs. His wide culture, literary as well as musical, enabled him to see not only Schubert's music but the poems of his choice in a perspective both European in range and historical in depth ; but it never destroyed the simplicity and immediacy of his feelings. A witty and urbane manner concealed from those who did not know him well a quite extraordinarily youthful heart and the least sophisticated of emotional natures ; and these qualities in him responded instinctively to the inexhaustible youthfulness, the inimitably natural tone and gait of Schubert's music. Time and again in these pages the critic's accurate, dispassionate judgment of a song is suffused by the poet's sympathy. For that Capell was himself something of a poet is abundantly clear from the paraphrases of song-texts with which the text is strewn, from countless turns of phrase and from his immediate grasp of a poem's character and individuality. His attitude towards Goethe may have been only just this side of idolatry and he clearly gauged the very different absolute status of the majority of Schubert's poets—he makes an illuminating comparison between German literature and English music—but he accepts Mayrhofer and Müller, Jacobi or Kosegarten for what they meant to Schubert himself ; and the book owes its unique character to this gift of imaginative sympathy, this ability to convey to the twentieth century English or American reader the emotional world of a divinely gifted but very imperfectly educated Viennese youth in the opening years of the nineteenth century.

He had another qualification, too, and a rare one in a writer, which gives an unusual interest to this book. It is implicit in the dedication, where the name of H. J. Kimbell is coupled with that of the author's youngest brother, who has kindly explained for me the conjunction. ' In the early " twenties ", he writes, 'Richard had singing lessons with Julian Kimbell and although he never became, or pretended to be, a singer, the technical knowledge that he acquired made him an unusually capable critic of singers. This interest in singing, too, probably increased his interest in Schubert. Certainly his translations of the songs show a recognition of the singer's technical difficulties in such a matter as that of giving him the most grateful vowels on awkward notes '. In fact, although 'Schubert's Songs' is meant for every music-lover and has nothing to intimidate any reader with an elementary technical knowledge of the art, it is in a sense addressed especially to singers. Not only are there frequent hints on interpretation. There are in many cases suggestions of the type of voice, even the character of the singer, best suited to an individual song and pleas for the adoption of some special favourite into the all too restricted Schubert repertory. The figures quoted on p. 63 for the sales of the different volumes of the Peters Edition suggest that there has been a marked revival of interest in Schubert's lesser known songs since 1928, when this book first appeared. Whether this was in any degree due to Capell's advocacy would be difficult to say ; but it will be surprising and disappointing if the appearance of this new edition does not further stimulate the interest of a new generation of singers.

Richard Capell died in 1954, leaving no more ample material for this new edition—which had been vaguely discussed but in no way decided upon—than could be contained in the margins of his own annotated copy. Remarkably few changes have been necessary and for guidance in this matter I have relied on two Schubert scholars, both friends of the author's and well acquainted with his opinions as well as with the latest discoveries concerning dates, attributions and the like. Professor Otto Erich Deutsch, of Vienna, is known as the author of the monumental ' documentary biography ' of Schubert, which appeared in English in 1946, and of the Schubert Thematic Catalogue (1951), as well as editor of a number of the composer's hitherto unknown works. Mr Maurice Brown is an English scientist-musician and a Schubert-scholar of long standing, whose book 'Schubert's Variations' appeared in 1954. All the factual alterations introduced in this second edition are due to one or other—often to both—of these authorities, and my part has been nothing more than that of a collator. Occasionally there were hints in Capell's annotations that he might have wished to expand his treatment of some particular aspect of Schubert's art as a song-writer, but this was manifestly impossible in the circumstances. Changes of opinion, too, were inevitable over the course of twenty-five years. Mr. Maurice Brown has kindly communicated a passage from a letter written by Capell in April, 1947 where he says that ' there are some things in the book that I cannot explain to myself—my underrating *Im Freien, Heimweh* and *Vor meiner Wiege* '. Occasionally I have thought it better to remove a passing reference to the singers of thirty years ago, whose names will be no more than names to the present generation. But when the mention of a still famous artist in connection with a song—such as the approval of Chaliapin's singing of *Ständchen*—throws light on the song's character, I have let the reference stand.

For English-speaking Schubertians Capell's translations of the songs are only second in importance to the present book. None of these were published in 1928, but a complete list of those made over the last twenty-five years will give the reader some idea of the persistence and ardour of Capell's devotion to Schubert. All the following are published by Messrs. Augener of London :

1.   The songs of *Die schöne Müllerin* complete except for *Ungeduld*.

2.   The songs of the *Schwanengesang* complete.

3.   Twenty-one songs of the volume ' 24 Favourite Songs ' (Augener) — *An die Laute* (The Cither), *Auf dem Wasser zu singen* (Barcarolle), *Du bist die Ruh'* (Love's Peace), *Erlkönig* (The Erlking), *Die Forelle* (The Trout), *Frühlingsglaube* (Healing Spring), *Geheimes* (The Secret), *Gretchen am Spinnrade* (Gretchen at the Spinning Wheel), *Heidenröslein* (The Wild Rose, *Jägers Abendlied* (The Ranger's Love), *Die Junge Nonne* (The Young Nun), *Lied der Mignon* (Mignon's Song), *Lob der Tränen* (Praise of Tears), *Des Mädchens Klage* (The Broken Heart), *Rastlose Liebe* (Tyrannic Love), Romance from *Rosamunde*, *Schäfers Klagelied* (The Forlorn Shepherd), *Sei mir gegrüsst!* (Love is all!), *Der Tod und das Mädchen* (Death and the Maiden), *Der Wanderer* (The Wanderer), *Wanderers Nachtlied* (Day's End).

4.   Six songs from *Die Winterreise* :—*Die Krähe* (The Carrion Crow), *Der Lindenbaum* (The Linden Tree), *Die Post* (The Post), *Das Wirtshaus* (The Inn), *Mut* (The Challenge) and *Der Leiermann* (The Hurdy Gurdy).

5.   The following isolated songs: *Am Bach im Frühling* (By the brook in spring), *Am Feierabend* (Day's Work Done), *Am Fenster* (The Old Home), *Am Flusse* (Writ in water), *An den Mond* (The mourning moon), *An die Musik* (To Music), *An Schwager Kronos* (Postboy Kronos), *Bei dir allein* (Thou alone), *Das Lied im Grünen*, *Das Zügenglöcklein* (The Passing Bell), *Der Musensohn* (Wandering Minstrel), *Der Neugierige* (The Questioner), *Der Schiffer* (The Boatman), *Der Wanderer an den Mond* (Address to the Moon), *Die Sterne* (The Stars), *Dithyrambe* (Dithyramb), *Grenzen der Menschheit* (The Confines of Man), *Gretchens Bitte* (Gretchen to the Mater Dolorosa), *Gruppe aus dem Tartarus* (Tartarus), *Horch, horch die Lerch'!* (Hark, hark the lark), *Im Abendrot* (Sunset Glory), *Im Freien* (Love in starlight), *Im Frühling* (Love in April), *Kriegers Ahnung* (Eve of Battle), *Lachen und Weinen* (Laughter and Sighs), *Liebesbotschaft* (The Lover's Messenger), *Nacht und Träume* (Night and Dreams), *Prometheus*, *Sehnsucht* (The Poet in winter), *Seligkeit* (Earthly Paradise), *Trost* (His Consolation), *Vor meiner Wiege* (The Cradle), *Wiegenlied* (Cradle Song), *Zum Punsche* (Punch-bowl Song).

London, *February* 1957

MARTIN COOPER

PREFACE TO THE THIRD EDITION

The opportunity has been taken to correct a few literal errors. Of the Capell translations listed on p. x., all those under headings 1 and 3 remain in print; also *Der Lindenbaum*, *An die Musik*, *Der Musensohn* and *Horch, horch die Lerch!* These are all now published by Galliard Ltd.

London, February 1973

MARTIN COOPER

I

SCHUBERT'S SENTIMENT

THE mere look of a composer's pages is characteristic. The first glance at Schubert suggests a rippling movement, and by the side of the rippling a flowering. Or it is the opening of a window—the air is stirred. Hardly anything else in music is so natural as his babbling semiquavers, his streams of triplets, and accompaniments of repeated chords. In Schubert such things are not mechanical. They have at once the variety and unsurprising naturalness of moving water and springing herb.

There is no avoiding the thought of nature—nature at the springtime of the year—in connexion with Schubert. Never was another musician so young. All his songs, as for that matter everything he wrote, are the song of youth. Poets have told of times when youth had the world to itself. The shepherds in Theocritus and the story-tellers of the ' Decameron ' live in a radiant society unshadowed by the dread wisdom of age. But Theocritus and Boccaccio were wise compared with Schubert, who knew nothing but the rapture and poignancy of first sensations, the loss of which is the beginning of wisdom. The poets have had to invent worlds unworldly enough to allow youth to wonder, love, and suffer purely youthfully ; but such a world was naturally Schubert's. It looks as though there had never been such an emancipated generation, for others are consciously emancipated, and betray in their rebellions the weight and influence of their elders ; but Schubert (whose art came to him almost by instinct, and whose masters hardly made the attempt to teach him anything) was unaware of age and its self-protective irony, its analysis and repressions. He seems never to have felt quizzical elder eyes upon him. One would say that everyone in his circle was young, and more—such is his innocence and his defence-lessness against pain—that, even so, there were few in that circle. In a crowded circle there would have been some wise youth spreading that ironical and critical word of which there is no trace in Schubert.

Imagination, then, insists on putting Schubert—the Viennese Schubert—in a pastoral scene. In cities youth is old before its time. But we never hear in Schubert the sharp tongues, the rapid wit, and multifariousness of the streets. The poets, when they have wanted to isolate the idea of youth, have invented Arcadias, where their young people could be sent off, out of sight of experience, to keep sheep and be their very selves. All pastoral poetry is an attempt to separate, seize, and conserve life's hour of hours, the May morning, the 'age between sixteen and three-and-twenty,' which Shakespeare's disgruntled old shepherd wished that youth would sleep out. The poets know that everything that comes after is a declension.

It is not that the May morning is regularly sunny. But in the wildest of spring tempests it is none the less spring. To live is to suffer ; but youth can afford suffering, and in a way enjoys it. Schubert is more often than not plunged in woe, but at that age, when to live is to enjoy, the worst is bearable, and the pangs of rejection, bereavement, or whatever, are strangely revelled in. Its sorrows are a luxury compared with the later sorrow that is feared, in the light of the experience that life has no longer the resilience once never thought of as possibly failing. 'If youth but knew !' Yes, but the very point is that youth's beginning to know is the beginning of the end. Most Arcadias are hopeless attempts at retrieving the past—a past so lost that such pastoralism is a byword for artificiality and spuriousness. Schubert's Arcadia is different. It simply is his whole known world, from which he never conceives of an escape. It is his reality, and he reveals unconsciously the sweetness of the woes of his young life. That is only to be appreciated by comparison, in the course of the disillusionment of time.

So there is no bitterness in Schubert. He simply wails when he is hurt, almost like a child. It is still all too fresh for him to have thought out his resentment. He believes himself to be suffering as much as can be, but the hurt is not really so great when it first comes—it seems to be accidental and not in the nature of things. For Schubert has everything to find out for himself. That is why we cannot help thinking of him as the shepherd, fluting away his young days in a grassy solitude. His tunes come to him of themselves, and as for his feelings, they are at the mercy of the moment's event. His friends in the valley, ' many a rose-lipt maiden and many a lightfoot lad,' are no more apprehensive than he, and no more prepared against the hurts of experience.

This pastoral fancy of ours refuses to be banished, in spite of the risk of setting up the image of a china Corydon in the place of Schubert's quivering flesh and blood. To account for all his generous guilelessness, an extraordinarily simple society has to be made out. We know how in the peasant's lot age comes with suddenness and there is a singular gap between young folk and parents. In Schubert's world elders are simply disinterested in the young folk's nonsense, and hence the freedom of all the artless and extraordinarily innocent love-making, which never knows the fear of elderly ridicule. Schubert's immediate and uncensored feelings are his world, and there is no one at hand to hint at triteness in his wondering exclamations at the moonrise and the nightingale's song, or ludicrousness in the constant exhibition of his heart on his sleeve.

His simplicity, which we shall have to call a German simplicity, could not have been tolerated in a sophisticated society. In Schubert it was passionate and divinely expressed; but not even the chance of one day producing a Schubert could induce the polite world to listen encouragingly to all the uncritical sentiments of its adolescents. In circles of taste and leisure, where sentiment has been a great deal considered and discussed, the form of the expression, the wit and ingenuity that are put into it, are, it is found, that which is capable of variation and entertainment ; while the simple tale of calf-love would, if its utterances were made public property, have a terrible monotony from generation to generation, and make mountains of bad verse. It is not only that. In society one cannot go naked, and the passions have to conform to the general rule. The more urbane one's life, the more important do clothes become. Courtly singers up and down Europe had for seven hundred years been analysing and describing with a thousand artifices the very sentiments which Schubert without a suspicion of irony recognized only as the tender offspring of his own heart. Crude sentiment is more than likely to be tiresome in society. Man has, in the interest of his fellows, learnt to temper his sincerity with irony and with humour. This affection of love, in particular, can play havoc if left to run wild, and all sensitive civilizations have hedged both its practical and artistic expression round with elaborate conventions. It is a simple error to overrate the quality of sincerity. Like any other, humour or whatever, it is not an absolute value but depends on the person. Take our English singers. That sincerity of Schubert's, which we appreciate as one of the most beautiful flowers of the human mind, what destruction might it not have worked if it had been forcibly planted on Dowland or Purcell ! It would have been the enemy of elegance and courtly compliment, of graceful meiosis or hyperbole, and all flavour of irony. And all there would have been to it, the child of genius being subtracted, would have been a rustic uncouthness.

Schubert was never a courtly singer. When opportunity offered him the place of one, he took it with a bad grace and escaped from it as quickly as possible. He simply sang for himself and for any of the ' golden lads and girls ' in his alley who cared to listen. Another age would have left his songs unrecorded and his name to be forgotten. Luck gave him more than that. He was not an obscure peasant ; he belonged, as it happened, to the middle class, the class that is literate without being urbane. The blind fate is perpetually being reviled that struck Schubert down at thirty-one. In fate's favour it might be admitted that we are fortunate in possessing Schubert's music in a more satisfactory form than traditional song.

Schubert was the first considerable musician who belonged to that modest rank of society and always remained of it. We have to look outside music—to Villon and to Burns, say— to find other artists in a comparable situation. The known musicians down to his time took their tone from their social superiors. Even Beethoven began by being courtly. Schubert was the first of the great middle-class German composers of the nineteenth century. His station was the humblest of any. The music of Mendelssohn, Schumann, and Brahms is full of a dense domestic affectionateness. Family feelings are more thought of in such circles than anywhere else. So far from there being any need felt for a polite disguise—for here the whole social sphere is practically only a family affair —a constantly intimate and genial tone is kept up, and it always seems to be somebody's birthday. Schubert is rather nearer to the peasant and, by so much, is freer of family ties. His feelings, we may say, are rather for his friends than his relations. He roams at will. He recognizes the obligations of domestic attachments no more than the obligations to be sociable and amusing. The duty of being of an affectionate disposition, which is often felt to lie heavily on the music of Schubert's followers, did not exist for him. Never was there anyone more tenderhearted, or less critical of the impulses of his heart.

He roamed the streets and the fields, and we know in what moods. He wondered at the stars, he blushed when he caught a girl's glance, he sank into rich melancholy at the sound of the bell that told the death of an hour, and at the sight of the sunset that marked off a lost day from the tale of days which, with the best will in the world, he, being young, could not but believe to be unending. He came back from every wandering as innocent as before. He suffered keenly but not intolerably. He had a response to everything from the fund of a nature generously sweet. Not very common and not very rare, perhaps, is Schubert's adolescent purity of character—guileless, unaware of cynicism, incapable of cruelty. But it was, we should say, unique in an artist so possessed of the very highest gift of expression. Other young lives come and go with inappreciable profit. Schubert's transparent art miraculously preserves the image of his beautiful and unconscious youth. He died, and will never grow old.

II

SCHUBERT'S POETS

SCHUBERT set to music the best poetry that came his way. He did not perhaps go far out of his way for it, but the old saying that he could set a bill of fare to music is beside the mark. Schubert took to poetry with simple earnestness and enthusiasm ; and although he often set feeble verses, there was nearly always something in them that appealed to his feelings. Poetry meant more to him than to any German musician before him—more, perhaps, than to any of the musicians who had come between Dowland and him. He lived in a group of poets and painters whose passion for music he returned with a passion for their arts less intense only because there was not such another as Schubert among them. Schubert's poets, then, for what they were worth, helped to make him. We see him quivering with responsiveness and filled with song when they touch even weakly on a theme that is dear to him—the stars, the hills, and moving waters, the throes of young love, the pity of death, the glory of the bardic calling. The verses of his poets are something more than an excuse for his melodies. He paid them a regard that resulted in a demand for a new style of singing. The singer who is indifferent to Schubert's poets cannot tell the whole tale. A more literary turn of mind is required than for the adequate singing of Handel, Bach, Haydn, or Mozart. The difference is clear in comparing Schubert's songs with those of the musician to whom, of the four mentioned, Schubert came nearest—that is, such songs in ' The Magic Flute ' as *Ach, ich fühl's*, and *In diesen heil'gen Hallen*. The latter we generally call ' Qui sdegno.' This shows how little the words, their sound and sense, amount to in our idea of the music. Schubert had a simple but clear view of the poetry he wanted for his music. The innuendo in the saying about the bill of fare is that, out of the abundance of his music, he set any text that happened to lie in his way, quite uncritically. How little true that is can be seen from the fact that tradesmen's catalogues were, after all, as accessible to Schubert in 1820 as they were in 1920 to Darius Milhaud, who actually did choose to set a nursery-gardener's price list. The text of seventy-one of Schubert's songs is by Goethe

—Goethe, the overtowering poet of German literature. There are not nearly so many settings of any other poet's work. Schubert's texts are by more than ninety different writers. These include all but a very few of the noteworthy German poets he could have known. By some accident he set no verses by Eichendorff, the pleasing lyrical poet whom all the world knows through Schumann's songs ; and it was by accident that he luckily alighted, only a little before his death, on half a dozen of young Heine's lyrics, to the great enrichment of music. If a great deal of the verse in Schubert's songbooks is naïve and poor, the reason is in part to be found in the fact that German literature simply had not the provision to supply the child of genius. To put it roughly, German music is a gift to the world comparable with English poetry; while German poetry has pursued a career—spasmodic, often disappointing and sterile—similar to that of English music. True, the name of the illustrious Goethe alters the balance. Our music has, of course, had no such universal genius.

Between the misty middle-ages and the generation before Schubert's own there were virtually no German poets. The sixteenth and seventeenth centuries were blank. Then came Klopstock (1724–1803), a kind of spurious Milton, whose hexameters are hated by schoolboys. Schubert in his youth (1815–16) drew on Klopstock for thirteen songs, of which *Dem Unendlichen* is the most considerable. A contemporary of Klopstock's, J. P. Uz (1720–1796), wrote rococo verses in imitation of Italian and French poets. Schubert set five of his poems, putting a countrified charm in place of the rococo style in which he could not deal ; but these songs are not outstanding. A rather similar poet, J. G. Jacobi (1740–1814), provided Schubert with verses for seven inconspicuous songs, and one on whose stream he is safely sailing to immortality : the *Litanei*. C. F. D. Schubart (1739–1791), a minor poet, musician, and revolutionary, enjoys similar fortune. He wrote *Die Forelle*, and among one or two other pieces set by Schubert, *An mein Clavier*. When we hear this delicate little song we may give a thought to the music-loving, luckless poet who was imprisoned for ten years in a Würtemberg fortress on account of inadmissible political opinions.

Before we come to Goethe there are two or three more of Schubert's minor poets to be mentioned who were born about halfway through the eighteenth century. L. H. C. Hölty (1748–1776) died at the age of twenty-eight of consumption. Though Schubert set twenty-three of his poems,

it is rather through Brahms's settings of *Die Mainacht* and
An die Nachtigall, that his memory is kept green, for
Schubert's music for the same poems is slighter and is practically unknown. Hölty was a precursor. Roses and spring,
the nightingale and the moon, started within him simple and
melancholy thoughts and limpid verses of the sort that was
the rage in Schubert's own day, to which his career and his
art, both so pathetic, should have belonged. Schubert's
Hölty songs, like most of his settings of these early poets,
were written in his youth (1813–16). One is the little masterpiece *An den Mond*. Matthias Claudius (1740–1815) wrote
verses in the vein of folksong. Of Schubert's twelve Claudius
settings two are extremely celebrated (*Der Tod und das
Mädchen* and *Wiegenlied*).

Two noble and literary brothers, Christian and Friedrich
Leopold, Counts zu Stolberg, were friends of Goethe's.
The latter (1750–1819), the translator of Homer, Plato, and
Ossian, wrote seven poems that were chosen by Schubert.
No one who has tried to make an English version of *Auf dem
Wasser zu singen* can think greatly of him as a poet, but the
world may be thankful to him for having prompted Schubert
to such a song. Between June and October 1815 Schubert
set in his simplest style, in strophic form, twenty-one poems
by L. T. Kosegarten (1758–1818). Seven of these were
written in one day, October 19. Kosegarten was a North
German country clergyman. His respectable Muse incited
Schubert to the composition of no song that is generally
remembered. *An die untergehende Sonne* (composed in
1816–17) is superior to the rest. Friedrich von Matthisson
(1761–1831) was another respected but inferior poet whom
Schubert took up in his young days (1813–16). None of his
twenty-five Matthisson songs is of the first order. *Adelaïde*
only hints at Schubert's true quality ; it cannot compare
with Beethoven's celebrated setting. A fancy typical of what
may be called German Valentine verses is expressed in
this poem, when the lover declares that the flowers growing
on his grave will possess the singularity of blossoming with
the name ' Adelaïde ' appearing legibly on the petals. From
another minor contemporary poet of the older generation,
the Swiss J. G. von Salis-Seewis (1762–1834), Schubert, in
1815–17, selected thirteen poems. Most of these songs
count as less than secondary in Schubert ; but there is a
fourteenth Salis song, *Der Jüngling an der Quelle*, composed
in 1821, which is, in the shortest and simplest of forms,
grace itself.

We come to Goethe. It is as though German poetry had suddenly grown up. All Schubert's earlier poets, and most of the later ones, too, look schoolchildish beside him. To come into touch with him through Schubert (we are not pretending to a larger survey) is to recognize a prince of men. One thing was not at all foreseen, even by Goethe—Goethe, who was almost all-knowing—and that was how much, not perhaps the fame of his poetry, but its dissemination and popularization, was to be due to the song-writers. So far from imagining his glory—the most glory that any man of letters, living, has ever enjoyed—shared with a Schubert, he did not recognize Schubert's existence. The songs were sent as offerings to the altar at Weimar, where the ageing Goethe was (while still falling in love) living half-deified. They were not acknowledged ; and none of the throng of inspiring genies that wheeled invisible about the incomparable sage and bard whispered to him that through this Viennese bohemian's music and not otherwise would Goethe's poetry reach masses of the earth's population for whom without it Goethe would be nothing but a name.

Schubert and Goethe should have met, if only for picturesque-ness' sake. Goethe was very nearly a prince, Schubert very nearly a beggar. The gods had showered on Goethe every gift of understanding and expression, not to speak of person and fortune. Schubert was almost grotesque. There were days when he went hungry, and he died of typhoid—the disease of the unwashed. Schubert never even dreamed of most of the worlds in which Goethe's spirit roamed. Yet it is not certain that Goethe is everywhere even an equal part-ner with Schubert ; for there are probably, outside Germany, numbers of persons who have counted *Geheimes* and *Heiden-röslein* as lifelong friends, without once asking who the poet was.

If Schubert and Goethe did not meet in the flesh, in per-petuity the two go on arm in arm, and picturesqueness is not lacking. What is so much to be appreciated in Goethe, especially when we come upon him after all the little girlish poets, is that he had sensibility, no man more, and at the same time he did not suffer himself to be its victim. Admir-able sage, whose mind for all its wisdom could remain a field of dewy poetry ! Admirable poet, whose sentiment could stand the full light of the intellect and not wither !

How does Schubert bear himself in such company ? Walk-ing by the great man's side, the child of genius does not necessarily take in all he is saying. Not all, but enough.

The poet speaks, and in the other and not less divine nature
the lilt of a dozen words and the sense of one have engendered
a new being. Schubert cannot attend to every hint that
Goethe drops. All would be excess when a single one can
do so much. Schubert paces on with the new sounds delightfully dancing in his mind, and turns to pay attention again
when the speaker's tone changes. That is as much as to say
that verse has to live on terms with Schubert's melody. In
that rapture there is no question of following the implications
of every word.

Verse started in Schubert a music that led a closely associated
but still an individual existence. There was a more equal
union in his art between melody and poetry than has been
found in any song-writing since Dowland. In courtly
eighteenth-century song the words were a peg for the music.
But the dawning of a new German literature—the event of
Goethe's and Schiller's fame—meant a new relationship.
Observe how deferential Mozart suddenly was when he set
Goethe (*Das Veilchen*). The great poet himself most approved
of Zelter's settings, in which music is relegated to a humble
place. Schubert's was not Zelter's way. Nor was it his
way to hug the words of his text one by one with the intensity
of later song-writers. Often he makes the effect of carrying
hard words and dark sayings away in a rush of sweetness
and ecstatic animal movement. Or a hint of tenderness
is expanded by him into an effusion. This is not to say that
he misunderstood the poem. Who can talk of misunderstanding when such a sister-poetry has been evoked ?

What poetry, and Goethe's in particular, meant to Schubert
is realized if the Goethe songs are put against the rest. There
are, we have said, seventy-one of them. Goethe's range
of ideas, his brilliance, his brains, are seen to hoist Schubert
up. What would Schubert be without *Prometheus, Grenzen
der Menschheit, Ganymed, An Schwager Kronos*, the ' Faust,'
the ' Wilhelm Meister,' and the ' Divan ' songs, *Der Musensohn, Wanderers Nachtlied*, and *Erlkönig* ? Still, of course,
the beloved musician ; but an altogether humbler figure.
Schubert's Goethe-music is exceptionally vivid and varied
and grand. The sturdiness and buoyancy of certain of the
poet's love-lyrics make for a refreshing tone in a music which
may at other times be felt a little too freely sympathetic with
moping and forlorn passiveness. Not an exact counterpart
of the poetry is to be looked for in the music. It is not so
much that the concentrated sense of a Goethean phrase
is translated, as that that aspect of it is rendered—softened

and spread and tinted—which most readily catches the mirror
of the musician's temperament.

Schubert set to music forty-two poems by Schiller (1759–
1805), eight of them more than once. *Gruppe aus dem Tartarus*, composed in 1817, is Schubert at his very best. It
is among his grandest masterpieces. Other Schiller songs
have characteristic beauties ; but certain ones are relatively
dull, and between them, as a collection, and the Goethe songs
there is hardly a comparison. In his young days Schubert
was nearly as assiduous towards the one poet as the other,
but nearly all the Schiller songs were written before 1818.
There were none at all after 1823. Goethe's attraction was
more powerful and lasted longer. In 1826 Schubert was
composing repeated settings of *Nur wer die Sehnsucht kennt*,
a poem he had first tried in 1815. As a boy, Schubert wrote
music for enormously long stretches of Schiller's verse. *Die
Erwartung* is a cantata rather than a song. Ballads such as
Der Taucher and *Die Bürgschaft* are like whole operas reduced
for performance by one voice and pianoforte. Both the form
and the text of these compositions were suggested by J. R.
Zumsteeg (1760–1802), a friend of Schiller's, who had
enthusiastically set many pages of his poetry to music which
Schubert closely studied and imitated. In the wonderful
year 1815 Schubert wrote fifteen songs to texts by Schiller,
but just twice as many Goethe songs. Schiller's attraction
seems to have dwindled after 1817. In the remaining years
Schubert set only seven of his poems. The last was the
fine, spirited *Dithyrambe* (1823).

On the whole the association was disappointing. Faith in
Schiller's poetry was almost like an article of religion in
German-speaking lands at that time and even after. He
was apparently one of the first poets known to the young
Schubert. And again and again we see the musician returning to the charge—only to be put off by something in Schiller
that was prosaic and frigid. What indeed is a Schubertian
to say if not that Schiller seems, on the strength of the songbooks, to miss the lyric note ? His subjects are abstractions ;
there is no seizing and fixing a particular moment's vividness.
Edifying principles are no compensation in a poet for a dullness of the senses. Schubert gives the impression that
Schiller was not a true lyric poet. That he was a great man
is clear, or he would not have been so taken up by Goethe.
He is celebrated as an historian and æsthetician. The
German people are said still to delight in his dramas.[1] But

[1] Librettos drawn from which entomb some fine operatic music by Verdi.

his lyrical poetry appears to be earnest and eloquent without magic—that is to say, not really poetry at all.

He was a conspicuous author of those ballads, imitated from Percy's Reliques (1765), which were the rage in literary Germany at that time. The movement was begun by Herder (1744–1803) in the intention of linking the new with medieval German literature. (Herder's translations from Percy included ' Edward,' which Schubert set as *Eine altschottische Ballade* in 1827.) It produced masterpieces from Goethe, as witness *Erlkönig* and *Der König in Thule* ; but, from everyday writers, masses of sham chivalry and wan fairy-tales. The hold such things have on Germans is shown by the fact that 150 years after Bürger's ' Lenore ' Schönberg was working on a similar theme in his ' Gurrelieder.'

More interesting, if less ambitious, was the poetry based on lyrical, not narrative, folksong. In 1805 there appeared a collection, called ' Des Knaben Wunderhorn,' edited by Arnim and Brentano, of anonymous rustic verse ; and this inspired Wilhelm Müller (1794–1827), the poet of Schubert's ' Schöne Müllerin ' and ' Winterreise.' Müller, who was the father of Max Müller of Oxford, was not quite the simple soul his verses might lead one to suppose. His extreme naïvety was somewhat affected. At its best his writing was pretty and touching, but in its innocence it could sometimes be absurd. If we think of a real peasant poet, let us say Burns, Müller looks childish. There are some unfortunate fancies in the Schubert lyrics. The despairing lover who complains that the jackdaws threw snowballs at him from the eaves ! That he had not the spirit to pick up his hat when the wind had blown it off ! The happy lover who designs his sweetheart's name on a garden-plot in mustard and cress ! The brook's request for the miller's daughter's handkerchief to cover the eyes of her drowned suitor ! The Schubertian will, for all that, keep a soft spot for the amiable author but for whom we should not have had the two inestimable song-cycles. Müller, with his suggestions of waterside greenery embowering an idyll of lowly love, and again, of the frost-bound countryside, the frame of a more desperate passion, tapped a well of musical poetry in Schubert. We cannot be Schubertians without being a little Müllerian also. The unsympathetic say that Müller's situations and sentiments are as cheap as a chromolithograph. That is not fair. His little verses are shapely, they are limpid, and they have a singing quality. Schubert fell in love with their tender spirit. We must take the period into account. There was nothing ridiculous thenadays in being soft-hearted and woe-begone. If anyone was of his period it was Müller, who enlisted as a youth to fight Napoleon, wrote poetry, loved a maiden who turned nun, and died young. Apart from the two cycles Schubert wrote one other song in which Müller's verses were used with others by Wilhelmine von Chézy—*Der Hirt auf dem Felsen*. This extended composition in his opera-tic manner, with clarinet obbligato was designed for the intelligent Berlin soprano, Anna Milder-Hauptmann, who had taken up his songs with enthusiasm and to whom he dedicated the second *Suleika song*.

Two constituents of German romantic poetry—fabricated medievalism and the songs of the peasantry—have been mentioned. Both, and the second particularly, appealed to Schubert ; a third, the new Catholic spirit, rather less. He composed a good deal of sacred music, but it contained no specifically mystical note. The religious spirit in which Schubert's music abounds is the simple and wondering pantheism proper to a child of nature. God is the stars, the mountains, the seasons, and the flowers ; God is the link between us and nature ; God is the rapture we feel in our communion with her : that sentiment is lavishly and variously expressed in the course of the songs—with splendour in *Die Allmacht*, with humility in *Grenzen der Menschheit*, with hushed awe in *Im Abendroth*. Schubert's God is sometimes music (*An die Musik*), sometimes love (*Du bist die Ruh'*). He is beauty ; and to meet beauty with beauty is for Schubert the equivalent of prayer. Like the juggler in the story, whose prayer was to juggle before the Most high, Schubert offered up the most beautiful Schubertian melodies. In this sense a piece like the *Ave Maria*, which would be out of place in a conventional liturgy, is sincerely devotional.

Novalis (1772–1801) was the typical German romantic-mystical poet, both as man and as artist, for his short life was compounded of frustrated loves, unearthly aspirations, and tuberculosis. He was not unknown to Schubert, who drew on him for *Vier Hymnen*, *Marie*, and *Nachthymne* (1819–20). It was, however, left to Hugo Wolf many years later to complete the romantic movement by finding the full musical expression for the tribulations and ecstasies of romantic mysticism. Schubert seldom leaves us so cold as by a song like his *Pax Vobiscum*, whose peace is altogether too easily obtained, leaving an impression of something like sancti-moniousness. And yet—incalculable spirit !—he did at least once compose a page instinct with Christian suffering and

sympathy. This is *Vom Mitleiden Mariæ* (F. Schlegel,
1818). It is a day worth remembering when one first comes
across such a piece as this in the less frequented Schubertian
tracts.

This Schlegel, Friedrich (1772–1829), was—like his brother,
August Wilhelm (1767–1845), the translator of Shakespeare—
one of the authors of German romanticism, a movement
that had its origin in Bürger's 'Lenore' and Goethe's
'Wilhelm Meister.' Both brothers are represented in Schubert's songbooks, the younger one more fully. Neither was
by any means a great poet, and when a Schlegel song of
Schubert's is exquisite (as several are), the poet scores as
much by luck as judgment. Who could have guessed that
such a vague fancy as this of the younger Schlegel's, 'Study
the stars, and life's little difficulties will all dissolve,' would
call forth music of the grace and tenderness of *Die Sterne*,
in which, indeed, a heavenly body seems to point the way
to bliss? The sixteen settings of this author in Schubert
are very diverse. They range from the enormously long,
landscape-like song *Im Walde* to *Das Mädchen*, a perfect
example of the Schubertian Valentine. The melodious
Fülle der Liebe, and *Die Rose* and *Der Wanderer*,[1] which are
exquisite, are other songs with which Friedrich Schlegel was
so fortunate as to become associated. The best known of
Schubert's ten settings of the elder Schlegel [2] (which include
three translations from Petrarch) is *Lob der Thränen*, which
is facile, easy-going Schubert. One or two others will carry
his name along safely—thus the impassioned serenade *Sprache
der Liebe*.

As the chord of spiritual asceticism, so the heroic chord was
hardly touched by Schubert. He set in 1815 a number of
poems by K. T. Körner (1791–1813), but most of these
songs remain in obscurity. Körner's was the voice of German
patriotic youth in the painful period of Napoleon's advances
and retreats. He himself died a soldier's death, after blowing
bugle calls in verse. None of Schubert's settings of Körner
is well known, and they are as a set possibly the least interesting
in all the volumes of Schubert. One is a lullaby. Others

---

[1] The text of the earlier and more famous *Wanderer*, Op. 4, was by the
perfectly obscure G. P. Schmidt (1766–1849), of Lübeck. Schubert is said
to have found the poem in an almanac.
[2] The text of the two charming songs, *Delphine* and *Florio*, Schubert's
Op. 124, composed in 1825, was erroneously ascribed to Schlegel in the first
edition of 1829, an ascription which Peters's edition repeats. The pieces
were incidental music written for a play, 'Lacrimas,' by Wilhelm von Schütz.

are love-songs. *Auf der Riesenkoppe* is an enthusiastic address
to mountain scenery. The best of the war-songs, *Gebet
während der Schlacht*, is an imploring cry; and we are
reminded of the tremulousness and pathos of Schubert's
music elsewhere in times of peril—in *Kriegers Ahnung*, for
instance, where the warrior on the eve of battle allows himself
a perfect crisis of homesickness—and again in *Schiffers Scheidelied*. The warlike virtues, it is clear, left Schubert unmoved.
He comes nearest to the heroic strain in songs that exalt
poetry and the poet in defiance of the philistines and the fates.
Another of Schubert's poets who died young, younger than
Schubert himself, was E. K. F. Schulze (1789–1817), nine of
whose poems he set. Best of them is the exquisite *Im Frühling*. Schulze's life was overshadowed, in the true romantic
way, by a tragic love-story. A reminiscence of this is *Tiefes
Leid*, Schubert's setting of which (1826) foretells the heartache
of the next year's 'Winterreise.' It was Schulze's fortune to
be encountered by Schubert in 1825–26, years in which hardly
a line he wrote is negligible.

An outstanding German poet of Schubert's generation was
J. L. Uhland (1787–1862), whom we know through Schumann,
Brahms, and Strauss. Schubert left only one Uhland song—
the endearing *Frühlingsglaube* (1820). Uhland's poems were
published in 1815. They often sound the anti-Napoleonic
bugle and drum. Schubert had, we have said, no particular
answer to that summons. A few more years, and there
would surely have been more Rückert songs by Schubert.
Friedrich Rückert (1788–1866), orientalist and poet, published
a book of lyrics in 1823, and in the same year Schubert wrote
four of his five Rückert songs. All five are in his richest
vein. They are: *Sei mir gegrüsst, Dass sie hier gewesen, Du
bist die Ruh', Lachen und Weinen*, and *Greisengesang*. Near
in spirit to these passionate and many-coloured songs are
Schubert's settings, two only, of poems by Count Platen
(1796–1835), the celebrated master of the German sonnet.
Platen is thought of as a well-regulated and rather cold
'Parnassian' poet, but Schubert's Platen songs, *Du liebst
mich nicht* and *Die Liebe hat gelogen* (1822), are of an extraordinary emotional intensity. Friedrich de La Motte Fouqué
(1773–1843), who was a typical German romantic for all his
French name, appears insignificantly in Schubert. The
best of the five La Motte Fouqué songs is *Der Schäfer und der
Reiter* (1817).

Schubert set in 1827 two poems by Friedrich Rochlitz
(1769–1842), *Alinde* and *An die Laute*. Both are slight but

charming.[1] Rochlitz was an enlightened music critic and for many years editor of the Leipzig *Allgemeine Musikalische Zeitung*. Beethoven esteemed him and hoped he would write his biography. The author's name on another simple song, *Hippolyts Lied* (1826)—Johanna Schopenhauer's—is also rich in associations. Johanna (1766–1838) was the mother of the philosopher of ' Die Welt als Wille und Vorstellung ', but the poems in her book are, by her own account, the work of Friedrich von Gerstenbergk. Of another rather trifling song, *Hänflings Liebeswerbung* (1817), it is perhaps worth mentioning that the author, Friedrich Kind (1768–1843), wrote the libretto of *Der Freischütz*. Carl Lappe (1773–1843), another minor poet of the romantic movement, was rescued from obscurity by two settings of his verses by Schubert—*Im Abendrot* and *Der Einsame*, both of them famous songs. Lappe was a pupil of Kosegarten's ; a schoolmaster, and later in life a recluse. The four Alois Schreiber songs are not quite of that quality, but they are good enough to safeguard Schreiber's name. The most popular is the pretty *Blumenbrief*. Schreiber (1763–1841) was an historian and professor of æsthetics at Heidelberg and later at Karlsruhe.

We come to the poets of Schubert's own friendly circle in which practically everyone wrote verse, himself included. It has to be admitted that very few of the members had talent. There was much activity, much goodwill, and a certain naïvety in the way in which they poured out trite and tearful rhymes. Viennese society had only lately taken to literature. Vienna had no literary history. Its music was its sole distinction. The handsome barocco style of its architecture was borrowed from Italy. The meagreness of Austrian letters has been put down to the Hapsburg censorship, which was medieval in severity ; but nor was there any considerable school of painting. ' Music,' remarked the eighteenth-century traveller, Riesbeck, ' is the one art for which the Austrian nobility displays any taste.'

For the results of their cultivation of that taste the world is indebted to that bygone nobility. They made possible the achievements of Haydn, Mozart, Beethoven, and (less directly) Schubert too. Vienna had become in Schubert's

---

[1] They appear in the collected works among the songs of December 1816, but the MS. is dated 1827 (see ' Nachtrag zum Revisionsbericht,' Breitkopf & Härtel). They were first published as Op. 81 in May 1827, together with *Zur guten Nacht*, for barytone solo and chorus, the text of which was also by Rochlitz.

day a city of music-lovers. His circle was not one of professional musicians. These were rather few among the
bohemians, burgesses, gentlefolk, painters, actors, and civil
servants whose scribblings were usually feeble, but who had
only to know Schubert to appreciate him. For various reasons
Schubert's lot was none too comfortable even in friendly
Vienna, but it is only fair to his friends to imagine what it
would have been in contemporary London. Here would
have been no chance for him at all. We shall then incline
to tenderness towards the host of Schubert's admirers who
pressed upon him their innocent rhymes and egged him on—
him all willing—to compose more and more songs.

The pre-eminent man of letters in Schubert's Vienna was
Franz Grillparzer (1791–1872), who was a dramatist first and
foremost. Schubert knew him through his friends the four
Fröhlich sisters. Anna taught singing at the Vienna Conservatorium, Josephine was an opera singer, Betti was a painter,
and Kathi was Grillparzer's fair friend. The poet lived for
years in the sisters' house and died there. The whole family
were musical, and they sang Schubert's songs before any
were published. Grillparzer himself was a pianist, and
there is a flattering account of his improvizations by the
novelist Caroline Pichler, who also figures among Schubert's
poets. Grillparzer's works include a set of verses which
describe his Kathi's listening in entrancement to Schubert's
music. For all that, there is only one Grillparzer song in
Schubert—viz. *Berthas Lied* (1819). The ascription of *Blondel
zu Marien* (1818) to Grillparzer in Peters's edition is erroneous.

More noteworthy is the *Ständchen* (1827) for barytone and
men's chorus. Anna Fröhlich has left an account of the origin
of this piece—how, to celebrate her friend Gosmar's birthday,
she wheedled the poem from Grillparzer, and turned to
Schubert for the music. Leaning against the piano he read
it through to himself once or twice, breaking off to exclaim
on the beauty of the verses. Then after a while of staring
at the page he declared : ' I have it ! It's done already ! '
Three days later the completed manuscript was in her hands.
Schubert rearranged the men's chorus for women's voices.
The piece does not fall within the province we have chosen,
but the anecdote interestingly shows us Schubert under the
influence of poetry and (to the meagre extent in which that
mysterious act, so much more mysterious in his case than in
most, is visibly demonstrable) in the act of composition.
The 1828 cantata, ' Mirjams Siegesgesang,' was also written
to a text by Grillparzer.

The tale of Schubert's Viennese poets is very much a
domestic one. It should properly begin with Josef von
Spaun (1788–1865), one of the first of Schubertians. There
is only one Spaun song of Schubert's, *Der Jüngling und der
Tod* (1817), in which is quoted the famous ' Death ' theme
from the Claudius song, *Der Tod und das Mädchen*, of the
same year. But indirectly we owe a good many more songs
to Spaun. He was the elder schoolfellow of Schubert's at
the Stadtkonvikt who provided the small boy with music-
paper, the lack of which was holding up his composition.
Spaun remained Schubert's friend all along, though as a
civil servant in the Lottery Department he was for some
years (1818–26) absent in the provinces. At the Konvikt he
had been an elder brother. Later on wherever he went he
championed Schubert. In Vienna he talked of him in
society and introduced him here and there, notably to Matthäus von Collin, and through him to Caroline Pichler and
Pyrker.

This Collin (1779–1824) was a brother of the better-known
H. J. von Collin (1771–1811) for whose ' Coriolan ' Beethoven
wrote the overture. He was tutor to Napoleon's son, the
Duc de Reichstadt. Through the musical parties at his
house, where Vogl sang, Schubert became known to the
fashionable world. Of the half-dozen Collin songs the most
famous is *Nacht und Träume*, which was composed in the
year after Collin's death. There are also the pathetic *Wehmuth*
and the singular ballad *Der Zwerg*. *Epistel : Musikalischer
Schwank* (1822) is an elaborate operatic address from Collin
and Schubert to Spaun, reproaching him for remissness in
letter-writing. The fun lies in the misapplication of a serious
style rather than in any attempt at parody on Schubert's part.
His humour was too innocent for that. Schubert was high-
spirited, but not humorous in the full sense. His susceptibility to pathos had no such defence. He possessed nothing
nearer to humour than good humour.

Franz von Schober (1798–1883) was so good a friend to
Schubert that his poems must be forgiven him. The elegant
young man may be seen in Kupelwieser's portrait in the Vienna
Schubert Museum—all but his legs, which Bauernfeld records
were somewhat bandy. Persons still alive have seen him as
an old man in Dresden. Schober was born in Sweden. His
circumstances were easy, he was well connected, a man of the
world. It pleased him to dabble in all the arts and to live
romantically. In imitation of Wilhelm Meister, he acted
for a time in a travelling company. The young Swede (whose

mother was Austrian) was a student at Vienna University in 1816. Having been introduced by Spaun to Schubert's music, he sought out the composer, who was then, much against the grain, teaching in his father's school. Through Schober, Schubert and his songs became known to the opera barytone Michael Vogl (1768-1840), who was to be a great friend of the man and a champion of his art.

Vogl is depicted by everyone as a distinguished and delightful person. He had come up to Vienna in his youth to read law. Through his friend Süssmayr (Mozart's Süssmayr) he was attracted to music and the theatre. He was said to read philosophy in his dressing-room. When he met Schubert his operatic career was coming to an end. Schubert started him on a new career, one that has preserved his name. Spaun has left a record of their first meeting. Schubert introduced him first to the Mayrhofer *Augenlied*, then to *Memnon* and *Ganymed*. Vogl was guarded to begin with, and rather on his dignity before the insignificant-looking little composer. He soon warmed up generously. Later on they were to spend summer holidays together. Vogl sang the *Erlkönig* at the Kärntnertor Theatre in 1821, at the concert by which Schubert's fame was first spread beyond private circles. The association had more than an external bearing on Schubert's art, or so we may suppose when we read that, long before their meeting, the schoolboy Schubert, hearing Vogl at the opera in Gluck's ' Iphigenia in Tauris,' longed to ' fall at his feet to thank him for his Orestes ' ; and further that one of Vogl's mottoes as an artist was, ' If a thing is not worth saying, it is not worth singing.' Their meeting was engineered by Schober. This enthusiastic friend also provided Schubert with lodging at times in the composer's bohemian years, and we can only suppose that he opened his purse to Schubert too, or there are periods when the musician's existence becomes inexplicable. He was evidently agreeable. Schubert showed a lively affection for him all along. The letters they exchanged were pitched in the emotional tone of the romantic period. The song *Abschied* (1817), Schubert's only setting of his own verse, was composed on the occasion of the friend's departure for a year's absence from Vienna.

Schubert set a dozen of Schober's poems, the first, *Genügsamkeit*, in 1815, the last, *Schiffers Scheidelied*, in 1827 ; and in 1821-22 he complaisantly accepted the friend's impossible opera libretto, ' Alfonso und Estrella,' which took more than thirty years to reach the stage (Weimar, 1854). To Schober, Schubert on his deathbed addressed that letter

of November 12 which can never be read without harrowing
—the letter that begins : ' I am ill ; I haven't eaten a thing
or drunk for eleven days,' and asks for something to read,
some more Fenimore Cooper. Universally known among
Schubert's settings of Schober is *An die Musik* (1817), which
perpetuates the generous friendship between the composer
and the young dilettante. *Viola* and *Vergissmeinnicht* are
flower-songs, both enormously long. Schubert poured out
music in the endeavour to float his friend's floral fancies.
Pilgerweise of the same year (1823) was more tractable. *Am
Bach im Frühling* is a beautiful little Schober song of the
early period. But the friendship of these two was luckier
than their actual collaboration.

For us the most important of Schubert's Viennese poets
was Johann Mayrhofer (1787–1836). If Schober liked to
pretend to be a character in romantic fiction, Mayrhofer all
too much resembled one in earnest. Melancholy had marked
him for her own. In song after song there transpires the
frustrated poet's weariness of life, his distress, his ever-present
vision of the abyss—the abyss into which he was one day to
throw himself in suicide. We know him from Bauernfeld's
description : ' gruff, sickly, and irritable—deep, and full of
ideas—never laughing or joking, disdainful of women and all
frivolity—whist his sole amusement.' This singular, moody
man shared his lodging for some time with the ebullient
Schubert. Mayrhofer was a civil servant, employed in the
Censor's office. He had been educated for the Church, and
then had thrown up theology for the law. He came to know
Schubert through Spaun in 1814, the year of the first Mayrhofer song, *Am See*. A few more songs followed in 1815,[1]
then in 1816 a long series, and in 1817 more still. The Mayrhofer song, *Erlafsee*, was Schubert's first published composition (1817). Some of the finest songs of the collaboration are
dated 1820. After 1824 there were no more. Mayrhofer
and Schubert shared the lodging in the Wipplingerstrasse for
two years (1819–20). There are numerous accounts of it—
by Josef Hüttenbrenner, who lived in the same house, by
Bauernfeld, and by Mayrhofer himself in the affectionate
memoir he wrote after Schubert's death. It was humble,
not to say squalid. The arrangement came to an end, says
Mayrhofer, on account of ' the comings and goings of streams
of friends and acquaintances ; illness ; and a changed outlook

---

[1] The two stage pieces written by Mayrhofer and Schubert also belong
to 1815—a ballad opera, ' Die beiden Freunde von Salamanca,' and an
opera, ' Adrast ' (fragment).

on life.' Mayrhofer continued to belong to the Schubertian circle.

There are forty-seven Mayrhofer songs. The finest is *Memnon*:

> ' Memnon's image, in ancient story, uttered at the rising of dawn its one glad note, after a night of sighs.
>
> ' Day is breaking, and I, the poet, am dying—the poet, whose heart's wailing has seemed mere music to the world. Dawn, goddess ! my last word is for thee. Take me into thy radiance. Open to me a world that this world is not.'[1]

Some such expression of homelessness on earth and of longing for escape occurs again and again in Mayrhofer's poems. No sentiment of the sort was natural to Schubert ; but in his music he extended to his friend, as it seems, a kind of sombre compassionateness which gives a peculiar quality to the best of the Mayrhofer songs. Even in a poem in which the speaker is the sun—*Freiwilliges Versinken*—Mayrhofer's tone is darkling. The sun departs gravely for unknown regions, and leaves earth a legacy of night. And Schubert obediently depicts, in a magnificent piece of music, the most veiled and least flamboyant of sunsets. The unhappy man was not a good poet. Grillparzer summed up his verses rather severely to the effect that they always seemed either to be awaiting completion by a musician's melodies or to be reminiscent of the melodies of previous poets. That is not enough to account for the disappointing result of much of his collaboration with Schubert.

Great and original poetry is frequently not apt for a musical setting ; and it is certainly not the only sort that is apt. There is no possible music for some of the best pages of the English poets from Donne to Shelley and onwards. The reason is that music, while it can go with words to any depth of thought or feeling and surpass them, is foiled by rapidity and intricacy of verbal play and the multitudinous and subtle associations of words in the older literatures. If Schubert could so light-heartedly tackle the greatest of the German poets, it was because Goethe was using a young language and his words were simple, for all the depth of his nature. It was the luck of the German musicians that the finest of their writers should still have been primitives, and could blandly and repeatedly utter with the merest of first intentions such words as ' Sehnsucht ' and ' Frühling '—pluck them, so to say, like berries from the bush, and roll them on an unsated

---
[1] Freely rendered.

tongue—a sort of juvenile joy unknown to our poets, who for generations had not been able to go a-maying so irresponsibly. We remember how incompatible Wagner felt his forest-murmurs and valkyries and dragons to be with the urbane French tongue. Frequently, indeed, his text was simply onomatopœic.

No contemporary German poetry was too great for Schubert, but often his lesser poets were, we have seen, good enough ; and perhaps lesser but still good poetry is the sort which generally is most apt for music. But Mayrhofer seems not quite to have achieved either a poetry of large ideas or one of small shapes pleasingly finished. Grillparzer was rather out when he suggested that Mayrhofer's verses only needed music. Both his more and his less ambitious pieces are often seen to hamper Schubert by a certain vagueness. The happy particulars on which Schubert seized in Müller and the definiteness of mood and situation in Rückert, Platen, and even in the humble Lappe are lacking. Schubert often had to do the best he could with Mayrhofer's general indication of gloom. Let us look at *Sehnsucht*, Op. 8. The poet's first quatrain tells of spring and of the lark's triumphant clarion, sounding winter's defeat. Schubert takes up the idea rapturously. Spring dances in his tune, and the lark trills. But himself, the poet goes on, is sterile, and none of his desires can be fulfilled on an earth so hostile to ideals. He must take wing with the cranes to a more kindly land. Schubert is visibly dashed by this development, which disparages the spring he has just evoked so brilliantly, and confuses the image in the mind by a departure of migrants in the very season of arrival. He does what he can for his friend's inconsolable melancholy while not convincing us that he finds it reasonable. The song tails off. For all that, we should be inestimably poorer without the Mayrhofer songs. In several of them we see Schubert grappling with new problems of scene and sentiment. Some are of remarkable breadth and fine, sombre colouring. Now and then one is a gem. The best of the Mayrhofer songs are : *Memnon, Orest auf Tauris, Der entsühnte Orest, Freiwilliges Versinken, Sehnsucht, Der zürnenden Diana, Heliopolis* I and II, *Der Sieg, Auflösung, Abendstern, An die Freunde, Auf der Donau, Philoctet, Am Strome, An die Dioscuren,* and *Nachtviolen.*[1] Perhaps the only widely popular Mayrhofer song is the cheerful *Alpenjäger*, Op. 13.

[1] *Der Gondelfahrer* (Mayrhofer) for men's voices and pianoforte is excellent Schubert.

There were other old Konvikt schoolfellows, beside Spaun, whose verses Schubert set at different times. They were: Albert Stadler, Josef Kenner, Franz von Bruchmann, and Johann Michael Senn. The Bruchmann songs are the best. All five belong to a good period (1822–3), and are considerable. The first is *Schwestergruss*, the last the charming barcarolle *Am See*. *An die Leyer* is the most popular. *Im Haine* is a graceful and *Der zürnende Barde* a spirited song. Bruchmann was the son of a well-to-do burgess family, at whose house ' Schubertiads ' were often celebrated. The two Senn songs, *Selige Welt* and *Schwanengesang*, belong to the same period. Senn, a Tyrolese who was reading law at Vienna, was a more considerable poet. He incurred the suspicions of the political police, and was banished to his native province. The three Kenner songs (1815) and the three Stadler songs are hardly conspicuous. Through Randhartinger, another of his Konvikt comrades, Schubert knew Count Louis Széchenyi, a scion of the great Hungarian family, two of whose poems were set in 1817—*Die abgeblühte Linde* and *Der Flug der Zeit*.

Caroline Pichler (1769–1843) has already been mentioned. She was a fashionable and prolific novelist whose works were collected in sixty volumes. Schubert's three Pichler songs are not very noteworthy. He met in the same circle the poet and prelate Johann Ladislav Pyrker von Felsö-Eör (1772–1847), who in 1818 was Bishop of Zips, in 1820 Patriarch of Venice, and in 1827 Archbishop of Erlau. He was the author of three epics. Schubert dedicated to Pyrker in 1821 his Op. 4—three songs which included *Der Wanderer*. In the summer of 1825 when Vogl and Schubert were holiday-making together they met the Patriarch at Gastein, where he had founded a hospital for invalid soldiers ; and there Schubert wrote his two Pyrker songs, *Das Heimweh*, a long cyclic piece, and the famous hymn *Die Allmacht*. The Patriarch of Venice felt, so it appears, a romantic love for mountain scenery. Another of the more aristocratic Schubertians (whom we see as the composer's lively well-wishers, only rather put off by his extreme distaste for any formal society) was Baron Franz von Schlechta, an official at the Finance Ministry and the father of a celebrated orientalist. Schlechta turned journalist on Schubert's behalf, and poured out praise of his music in the Vienna *Konversationsblatt* after the production of ' Die Zauberharfe ' at the Theater-an-der-Wien in 1820. There are six Schlechta songs. *Auf einen Kirchhof*, dated from 1815 and *Widerschein* from 1819. The fine song *Des Sängers Habe* is dated 1825, the popular *Fischer-weise* 1826.

Johann Gabriel Seidl (1804–1875) was a country school-master, numismatist, and poet, who won a State prize for a set of verses for Haydn's Imperial Hymn. Most of Schubert's Seidl songs, which are all interesting, date from 1826. They include *Im Freien* and the beautiful *Zügenglöcklein*. Schubert dedicated the ' Vier Refrain-Lieder,' which were published in August 1828, to the poet. This set deserves to be better known. The last song of all, *Die Taubenpost*, is a setting of a poem of Seidl's. Four of the earlier Seidl songs, includ-ing *Wiegenlied*, were issued as Op. 105 on the day of Schubert's funeral.

There are eight Leitner songs, all of Schubert's latter period, and containing such delightful pieces as *Drang in die Ferne*, *Des Fischers Liebesglück*, and *Die Sterne*. Carl Gott-fried von Leitner (1800–1890), who was born at Graz, was a poet of some little note. His first verses, published in 1825, earned him the appellation ' the Styrian Uhland.' His themes were those of a provincial romanticism, which Schubert, as he makes plain, found charming.

It does not appear whether Schubert came personally into touch with Jacob Nicolas, Baron von Craigher, the author of *Die junge Nonne*. Schubert first in 1824 set Craigher's trans-lation of Colley Cibber's *Blind Boy*, and in the next year *Todtengräbers Heimweh* and the supremely celebrated *Junge Nonne*. Gabriele von Baumberg was another of Schubert's more obscure Austrian poets. The five Baumberg songs all belong to 1815. They are insignificant. A number of writers are represented by a single piece in Schubert's song-books. Thus J. F. Castelli (1781–1862), a playwright of a somewhat lowly order, to whose libretto Schubert wrote the one-act operatic piece, ' Die Verschworenen,' in 1823. The only Castelli song is *Das Echo*. The Hüttenbrenner song, *Der Jüngling auf dem Hügel*, would not be worth mentioning if it were not for the associations of the name. The poet, Heinrich, was one of three brothers, Anselm (1794–1868), Heinrich, and Josef, who came of a well-to-do family of Graz. Anselm was a good musician, a pupil of Salieri's, through whom he knew Schubert. A strong friendship grew between them, and Josef (who was Mayrhofer's neighbour) was even more devoted. The brothers' name is immortalized by their friendship with Beethoven, who died in Anselm's arms.

Eduard von Bauernfeld (1802–1890) is represented by one

smallish song, *Der Vater mit dem Kind* (1827). He is remembered as having been one of Schubert's intimates in the
latter period—a lively, scatterbrained youth, one imagines—
a Murgeresque bohemian, who later on wrote successful light
comedies in the French vein. In his middle life he set down
with a light pen some memories of his happy-go-lucky youth,
which give vivid sketches of the Schubertian circle. He was
introduced to Schubert in 1825 by the young painter, Moritz
von Schwind. He could talk, joke, play the piano, and drink.
The three became inseparables. Schwind was eight years
younger than Schubert, whom he had known well since he
was seventeen. Bauernfeld gives us a doubtfully accurate
picture of the three as sharing one another's lodgings, clothes,
and purses—which often meant Schubert's purse—of unflagging activities and spirits, of talk and of merry-makings to
all hours of the night. We read him with a certain discomfort,
for while the Rodolphe and the Marcel of the party leave us
indifferent and are free to any recklessness they choose, we are
too fond of the Schaunard not to fear a hint that he is playing
fast and loose. The romantic young Schwind's letters[1] indicate
the emotional pitch of this trio. In the last two years of his life
Schubert began work on an opera libretto by Bauernfeld, 'Der
Graf von Gleichen.'
Before we come to the poets of Schubert's 'Schwanengesang' there are some of his translated texts to be named.
These are from Italian and from English, and there are also
a number of settings of Italian texts. *Verklärung* (1813) is
a setting of Herder's version of Pope's 'Vital Spark of
Heavenly Flame.' It is very early Schubert but still of real
interest. Schubert's note-values do not quite fit Pope. It
would be worth editing the song in that sense. In 1815–17
Schubert composed music for long stretches of 'Ossian.'
There are nine of these songs, including a fragment, and
nearly all are on an heroic scale. Ossian, a supposititious
Gaelic bard of yore, was more or less the fiction of James Mac-
Pherson (1736–1796). He had a fantastic vogue throughout
Europe in the latter eighteenth century. 'Ossian,' exclaimed
young Werther, 'has quite superseded Homer in my heart.'
There were a number of German translations, the first in
1764. MacPherson may be said to have invented the Celtic
Twilight. He was one of the authors of romanticism. His
landscapes are without detail, his personages lack all the lesser
human characteristics, in especial a sense of humour. All
things in Ossian drift on a tide of grandeur and gloom ; but

[1] Quoted at length in Karl Kobald's ' Franz Schubert ' (Vienna, 1928).

this flux was felt by many at the time to be a relief and a refuge
from the eighteenth century's primness, and the refugees were
all willing to fill in the details of MacPherson's wild and wan
characters from their own ardent minds. As musicians are
wont to do, Schubert came upon the literary wonder rather
late in the day, but he must have been much taken, to judge
by the energy with which he threw himself into his Ossianic
scene-painting. Colley Cibber's *Blind Boy* in Craigher's
translation has been mentioned. The three Shakespeare
songs came together in 1826. The translations were by
different hands—*Hark, Hark, the Lark* (' Cymbeline '), by
A. W. Schlegel ; *Who is Silvia?* (' Two Gentlemen of
Verona '), by Bauernfeld ; and the drinking-song, *Come,
thou Monarch of the Vine* (' Antony and Cleopatra,' Act II),
by Ferdinand Mayerhofer von Grünbühel. The first two are as
well known as anything in Schubert ; the vigorous and very
C-majorish drinking-song less so. It should be more sung,
especially since the music fits the English text. As also to
Hark, Hark, the Lark, a second German stanza was added
to *Come, thou Monarch* after Schubert's time.

Schubert's songs from Sir Walter Scott were composed in
1825 (seven) 1826 (one) and 1827 (two). The solo songs from
' The Lady of the Lake ' are : Ellen's songs, *Soldier, rest* and
Huntsman, rest from the first canto, Norman's song *The heath
this night must be my bed* and Ellen's *Ave Maria* from the third,
and *My hawk is tired of perch and hood* from the sixth canto.
We hear a good deal about these Scott songs in Schubert's
letters written during the happy 1825 holiday. Vogl apparently
sang Ellen's and all ; and everyone fell in love with the music.
Artaria of Vienna bought the seven ' Lady of the Lake '
songs for the equivalent of £20, which to Schubert was
exceptionally handsome payment, and published them in the
spring of 1826, in two volumes, as Schubert's Op. 52. Also
composed in 1825 were settings of *Hail to the Chief* from
the second canto of ' The Lady of the Lake,' for chorus of
men's voices, and the Coronach *He is gone on the Mountain* from the third canto, for women's voices. In 1826
Schubert set the king's song *High deeds achieved*, from ' Ivanhoe.' It was published by Diabelli in March 1828 (Op. 85 and
86). Annot Lyle's song *Wert thou, like me*, from ' A Legend of
Montrose ' and Norna's song *For Leagues along the Watery
Way* from ' The Pirate ' appeared as Op. 85 in the same
month.

As well as settings of A. W. Schlegel's translations of sonnets
by Petrarch, composed in 1818, Schubert wrote at different

times a number of Italian songs, most of them on texts by Metastasio. Some date from his Konvikt days, when they were written for Salieri's inspection. Four considerable Canzoni date from 1820, and three bass airs, Op. 83, which were written for the great Neapolitan Luigi Lablache, who sang much at Vienna in the 1820's,[1] belong to the last period.

Two of Schubert's poets were peculiar to the last year of all —Ludwig Rellstab (1799–1860), and Heinrich Heine (1797–1856). Rellstab, the son of a music critic, was himself the music critic of the Berlin *Vossische Zeitung*, and also a copious novelist. He visited Beethoven in 1825, to propose himself as his collaborator in an opera. After Beethoven's death some of Rellstab's verses were found among his papers, and these Schindler handed over to Schubert. There are ten Rellstab songs by Schubert. The seven which form the first part of the ' Schwanengesang ' are universally known. It appears that the unfinished *Lebensmut* was to have been the first of the ' Schwanengesang ' set. As it stands it is a simple strophic song. Schubert may have dropped it because the reckless gaiety with which he launched out on Rellstab's first stanza was difficult to modify appropriately as the poem went on. It remains a captivating page. *Herbst* is another of the more unfamiliar Rellstab songs, and the third is *Auf dem Strom*, with horn or violoncello obbligato, which was composed in haste for performance at Schubert's concert on March 26, 1828.

Rellstab's talent resembled more or less that of a great many ebullient young bards of the day, and Schubert's Rellstab songs, among which *Liebesbotschaft*, *Ständchen*, and *Aufenthalt* are pre-eminent, show no special departure. Heine was different. He was clever. We have not thought of any other Schubertian poet as that. Germans frequently become ruffled by the foreigner's overrating of Heine. It is no good ; we cannot resist his special spice—that of the self-critical sentimentalist. He came, of course, of an old race. His forms were those of the simple Müller, which he perfected. But the liquor which he distilled into them had a new taste, being delicately flavoured with the least drop of wormwood. Heine was, in fact, intensely civilized. Even when the picture he evokes is ridiculous (as, for instance, that of a fir tree which yearns for the company of a palm) he is saved by the suggestion of a parody at the expense of his more naïve contemporaries. The ' Buch der Lieder ' (1827) came out in time—if only just in time—for Schubert. There are

[1] He was, like Schubert, a torchbearer at Beethoven's funeral.

six Heine songs in the ' Schwanengesang,' every one a master-piece. Heine gave Schubert what so many of his rhymesters had failed him in—a precisely indicated scene and sentiment, and the essence, not the froth, of poetic contemplation. Schubert's response in that last August affords the final wonder of his life. Not that Heine struck him as amusing ; he evidently struck him by the intensity of the feeling and experience in those artless-seeming, artful lines. Schubert's imagination seized on the hints of scenery ; his sympathy overflowed at the other's confession of pain. He was with it all richly appreciative of the poet's concentration, which came as a challenge to him, the exuberant, a challenge that he rose to and encountered superbly. There was, after the Heine songs, no saying what Schubert could not have done. But he died in the following November at thirty-one—six years after Shelley, who was thirty, and seven years after Keats, who was twenty-six. He had known nothing of them who were, alone of his generation, his true peers.

If we attempt a synopsis of Schubert's relations with the poets, we see him engaged at first with minor eighteenth-century poets and with Schiller. To them at the end of 1814 is added Goethe, whom he draws on enthusiastically in 1815 and 1816. The minor eighteenth-century poets are still very freely used in these two fruitful years, and a start is made on the works of his Viennese contemporaries. From now on, for some years, there are many Mayrhofer songs, and the names of the Schlegels occur frequently, while the attraction of the eighteenth-century poets decreases. There are very few Schiller songs after 1817. Goethe is almost neglected for a time, but a return is made to him in 1821–22 with dis-tinguished results.

For two poems in Goethe's ' Westöstlicher Divan,'[1] *Ver-sunken* and *Geheimes*, Schubert writes an intensely concen-trated music, and in this style there are the wonderful Platen and Rückert love-songs of 1822–23. The form and the packed contents of these lyrics prepare Schubert for the Heine songs of his last year. Meanwhile he comes, in 1823, upon Müller's versified village romance, in his music for which he sums up in the most finished form all his more homely and countrified types of expression of the previous decade. He returns to Müller in 1827 ; and the style of the ' Winterreise ' is that of ' Die schöne Müllerin,' enriched and ensombred by passing time. Meanwhile, in the 1820's,

[1] The text of the two ' Suleika ' songs from the ' Divan ' is ascribed to Marianne von Willemer, Goethe's fair friend of the period.

Schubert sets the fluent romantic verses of Viennese friends and other contemporaries very freely, and often in a loose and expansive style that is particularly characteristic of these years. After 1826 there are no more Goethe songs. There was plenty left in Goethe for Schubert to do, and if he had had the time he would assuredly have gone back there. There was a world of things left for him to do. He can be imagined in the 1830's engaged with Eichendorff, Uhland, Mörike, and going deeper into Rückert and Heine. But the time was refused him.

III

SCHUBERT'S STYLE

THERE is in Schubert no bad music—which is not to say no inferior music. For he wrote with style. He had, even when he was least vividly himself, an admirable pen.

What are the conditions of bad writing by considerable men ? The first is a laboriously-acquired and uncertain grasp of the language employed. Another, a lack of delight in the sheer means of expression ; again, a mind naturally incommunicative and unsupple. And another, a straining beyond the fair sweep of the writer's experience and imagination.

Let us observe how Schubert was favoured by nature and grace. Music was virtually his mother tongue. The first pieces, *Hagars Klage* and the rest, at the beginning of the collected edition of the songs, were composed when he was fourteen. They are not absolutely interesting, but the boy who wrote them had unmistakably a grasp of style. They are fluent ; they are as correct as Zumsteeg's pieces on which they were modelled, and quite as vivacious ; and while on general lines they follow the exemplar, they are not mere imitations.

The music which Schubert so early wrote and thought in as glibly as in the language of speech was a local and contemporary idiom. The musical world was Vienna. Of its three divinities, Mozart had not long been dead (1791), and was a living memory for any number of persons ; Haydn lived on for twelve years into Schubert's life ; and Zeus himself was present on the scene, in the person of Beethoven, down to 1827. Music at Vienna was a small Hellenic city-state, extremely busy and in the closest touch with heaven. Its practical history was only a generation old. Such a composer as Handel was rather vaguely thought of as an archaic Titan. As Egypt to Greece, so was Italy to this young state—the immemorial fount of art and learning, now appearing somewhat distant and desiccated. We whose music is a monstrous empire that has embraced Moscow and Madrid and as greedily annexes provinces in time as in space, are farther from Schubert's world than was Hadrian's Rome from the Athens of Erechtheus. Let us imagine, if we can, a young English composer, working between 1911 and 1928, for whom music for all practical purposes was what had been composed in London since about 1870. His lot would at least have been less confusing.

The most beguiling music in the Viennese air was that of the symphony, sonata, and quartet. The opera remained largely in Italian occupation, but it could boast Gluck, Mozart, and, later on, Weber. Then there was the popular music of streets, taverns, and dancing places, which was certainly affected by the native idioms of the Hapsburgs' non-German subject peoples who have always been numerously represented at Vienna.

All these are among the elements of Schubert's music. They are to be called constituents rather than influences : his words and elements of phraseology, so to speak, and not his matter. If he writes a ländler or waltz, as in *Hark, Hark, the Lark*, it is indisputably his own ; but only a Viennese, and perhaps only a Viennese of about that time, would so instinctively have set a song of Shakespeare's to a ländler tune. Similarly, the suggestion is often conveyed of the Adagio of a string quartet—but a Schubertian Adagio— as, for example, in *Litanei*. The setting of Schiller's *Sehnsucht* is made of what looks like the material for a pianoforte sonatina. The operatic scena (Recitative, Andante, Allegro) occurs principally among the earlier songs—e.g. Schmidt's *Wanderer*. Folksong is suggested again and again.

Almost the last place in which to find the sources of the Schubertian river is the German song-writing before his time. It has been said how he modelled the long, cantatalike pieces of his youth on Zumsteeg (two or three of whose compositions Mandyczewski conveniently prints in a supplement for comparison). This was clearly a sort of exercise on Schubert's part. It has to be remembered that the vast editions of his works are due not to the composer's choice, but to the postmortem publication of all the masses of his papers. Even so, only a few of his hundreds of songs show a direct relationship to the work of such men as Zelter, Zumsteeg, and Reichardt. The true Schubertian song had no palpable ancestor. It was the assemblage by some unexampled magnetism, in a fortunate hour, of all the fiery particles of poetry and music that were in the air.

German song had not had a very wonderful history down to Schubert's time. The courtly Italian school had hardly ceased to reign at Vienna. Handel and Mozart, great masters of a vocal style, were half Italianate. The typical achievements of the Germans had been in instrumental music. They had had no school to compare with the English lutenist-singers, and no one like Purcell. But then came the new German poetry, and, above all, the splendour of Goethe. What Schubert had in common with a few minor composers who a little before his time had gone in for song-writing was—rather than points of musical technics—an attraction to poetry such as Bach and Handel, Haydn and Mozart, it is perfectly obvious, hardly dreamt of. We say Mozart ; and at once have to admit the exceptional, the unique *Veilchen* (Goethe), a piece which, without being exactly Schubertian, deals with German poetry in a new and exquisite way, and which sets us wondering how Mozart, if he had lived, would have responded to the strong new literary currents of the nineteenth century. He would still have been less than sixty at the time of *Gretchen am Spinnrade* and *Erlkönig.* Haydn's best songs, on the other hand, happen to have been the English canzonets he composed in London in 1792.

Beethoven's songs include some precious chips from the workshop. Even he, the unliterary, the almost illiterate, was affected by Goethe's glory. Once, now and then, by sheer musical thought, he made a superb song, like *Wonne der Wehmuth*, his share of which is noble out of all relation to the tearful text. And still more rarely he was captivated by a poem almost to a Schubertian degree, and set pianoforte and voice collaborating towards a new effect of picturesque-ness. Our example must be the ' Flea ' song from ' Faust,' a brilliant and astonishing piece. It is too much of an exception to have a real bearing on Schubert's case ; but it does show what currents were in the air.

There are one or two curious parallels between Beethoven's songs and Schubert's, apart from their choice of Goethe's poems. It seems strange that Schubert should in his youth (1814) have tried his hand at Matthisson's *Adelaïde*, after Beethoven had set the poem once for all in his noble, classic fashion. Perhaps this falls within the same category as the Zumsteeg exercises. It is more curious that Schubert when he was twenty-five should have set Sauter's *Wachtelschlag* in a not very dissimilar style from Beethoven's song of more than twenty years before. The quail's jerky call haunts both songs. Beethoven renders it thus :

and again :

Schubert's quail sings in 6-8 time :

and again :

The tracking of reminiscences is apt to be a petty sort of criticism, and Schubert as a matter of fact affords it singularly little scope. If one or two points are raised here, it is not in any spirit of disparagement. The intention is to suggest that Schubert did not take over the song as a certain and special form, but swept into his association with the poets all the music that was prompted within him. His art was one of extraordinary variety and freshness of shapes and colours, which were demanded of his musical faculty by his keen appreciation of the poetic scene and action that were to be illustrated. The charm of the man lies in the generous response he was perpetually making to the appeal of nature and of the human affections. The glory of the musician is the unfailing alchemy with which he transmuted, Schubert-ized, what we have called the music in the air. Considering what were Beethoven's powers, innovations, and prestige, the wonder is that Schubert was not more impressed by him. Really he was hardly impressionable at all. His mind refused to be stamped on ; instead, it absorbed, and what it absorbed fructified. The theme in *Der Zwerg* is only in that way related to the motto of the C minor Symphony :

and later :

Another example or two will show how Beethoven pervaded Schubert's air, and at the same time how Schubert had but to breathe to render the air his very self. Thus he takes up, in 1815, a poem 'To the Moon.' It is clear enough that verbal associations set in movement tones and harmonies reminiscent of a certain Sonata in C♯ minor of some fifteen years before :

The process is carried on in a region of the mind that is certainly not conscious. Nothing in Schubertian biography is more familiar than Spaun's account of the furious composing of the *Erlkönig*. The poem (and this was far from being his only experience of the sort) took possession of the composer in a positively supernatural way. Before Schubert's incomparable achievement, at which astonishment never fails, we could indeed believe anything about it rather than that it was consciously elaborated from a suggestion culled from Beethoven. At the same time, the evidence would have to be almost supernatural that would convince us that Schubert had never heard 'Fidelio'—notably the duet 'Nur hurtig fort' in the dungeon scene :

But such textual approximations to Beethoven in Schubert
amount to hardly anything. The real bearing of Beethoven's
art on Schubert is a more general question. Beethoven's
restlessly and profoundly ranging mind opened up new worlds
of music. He pointed to dozens of strange ways which
those with the strength could explore further for themselves.
Many of his indications meant nothing to Schubert, who never,
for instance, adopted the Beethoven scowl. Beethoven's
general significance lay in his sense of an illimitable universe ;
depth beyond depth. His nature, more complex and
variegated, included among much else a certain Schubertian
element of rapturousness and sacred exhilaration. What
Schubert first of all gathered from his example was the
endlessness of possibility. The next thing was, with his
special and delightful faculties, to pursue the suggestions of
himself in Beethoven, those moments in the other's music
to which he had such a natural affinity that a movement like
the Allegretto of the seventh Symphony is felt to be positively
Schubertian.

* *
*

Schubert's dramatic songs are very considerable, but the
most part of his songs are of a certain meditative order.
In them he is not addressing the world ; he is finding things
out for himself as he goes his lyric way, and turning them
over for his own charmed gaze. Concert songs are rare in
Schubert. He himself, we know, gave but one concert in
his life.
One does not read lyrical poetry to a crowd. And extemporizing on the pianoforte is naturally a private entertainment.
(There was in Schubert's day even a fashion of extemporizing
publicly : to be taken as an outward sign of the widespread
domestic habit.) In the early days of the pianoforte, fingers
must always have been tapping and sounding in the exploration
of the new keyboard's possibilities.
The Schubertian song was not what other songs had been,
but was the outcome of a delight in the new poetry and the
new instrument. In effect, it combined the reading of verse

and the practice of music within the most exclusive of conditions—within the room of two or three intimates, and
possibly indeed of the utterly solitary. The Schubertian
song is the thing we know, first from the impulse received
by its marvellous author from Schiller's and Goethe's
lyrical works ; and secondly from the suggestions that
arose in the course of the wanderings of his fingers over
the keys.

Music is first of all sound. Only after a singular intimacy
with the reality is it possible to reach the point of conceiving
an ideal soundless music. There is no example of a musician
who was deaf in youth. Music is not invented in a vacuum.
A musical thought has, as progenitors, feelings and sounds.
There is a sort of puritanism that would prefer all such
things to be the offspring of sheer internal logic, like the
' Art of Fugue.' But the Bach who in his latter days composed the ' Art of Fugue ' had long before—having hands,
feet, ears, and an organ—cut into a virgin forest of sounds,
straining logic beyond all precedent. A hint at a line of
argument must suffice here ; one would suggest a long interplay between musical minds and the promptings from the
instruments at hand, particularly the keyboard instruments,
and most particularly the equally tempered ones, which
could at last give into one man's grasp all the kingdoms of
the world of music for the toy of his solitude. Bach at his
organ, Beethoven at his pianoforte did certain things, so we
are suggesting, on lines on which they would hardly have
written before. And so with Schubert ; in whose pianoforte
writing we again and again see, it can hardly be doubted—
in many characteristic figures of broken chords, for instance,
and especially, of course, in the so personal, fresh, and delightful courses which his modulations take— the immediate
outcome of his hours of vagrant improvisation. When a
piece of Schubert's begins like this :

or this :

he cannot but be imagined as abandoning himself to the
direction, indeliberate and indefinitely foreseen, but safely
to be counted on as happy in the event, of fancy's interplay
with the effects of the roaming and modulatory hands.

Beethoven was the grand exploiter of the pianoforte's
sonority and eloquence. By his pianoforte improvisations
he formed his style and was helped to find out his own
thoughts. Since then the instrument and the facilities it
affords have been so much abused that we cannot easily
realize the charms it had in its young days. How effective
they were is seen by the eclipse of the wiry, glittering harpsichord. The over-used pianoforte is now often reproached
for being cold and colourless and percussive, but it must have
seemed thenadays a miracle of warmth and rich singing
quality. The harpsichord had made much less of a pretence
to sing, and its *p* and *f* were mechanical. Its displacement
was unfairly complete, but we have to imagine what it must
have been at that period to discover a keyboard instrument
with a ' soul.' (The clavichord had had a soul, but only
a very little one.)

The early pianists in their beguilement flattered the sounds
they made. Beethoven's pianoforte music is full of horn
themes, timpani strokes, and string passages. The pianoforte
could just hint at such things. It was playing a curious part
in music in Schubert's time. The suggestions which it
gave to the improvisers (who need not be thought of as ever
denying themselves the luxury of the diminished seventh)
were immediately worked into the writing of instrumental
music, and were developed a little later into Wagner's
wondrous enharmonic style. But if Beethoven and the
rest were so influenced in their general writing, they necessarily
had to think, when making music for the pianoforte, of the
sounds of the more real of musical instruments. There is
a measure of reality in the pianoforte, but always in its music
there is—more or less, according to the composer—something else, which let us call an oblique representation. Piano-

forte music veers between a genuine sensuous communication
and an idea of music, an abstraction. The voice, the violin,
the clarinet, or whatever, has unmitigated reality. Each is
solely itself, concrete music, with no capacity of representing
an imaginary music ; while pianoforte music is more often
than not something else in short score.

For all that, it would be an impropriety to orchestrate
Beethoven's pianoforte sonatas—'the abstract joy, the half-
read wisdom of dæmonic images '—or Schubert's lyrical
songs ; and for a reason beyond the difficulty of orchestrating
them congruously. It is that although the music was frequently conceived by the aid of more or less unconscious
thoughts and memories of the tones of real instruments, the
expression is so very much the affair of one contemplative
and concentrated mind, or a pair of chambered collaborating
friends, whose closing of their outer door is the opening of
the inner world of this music.

The composer of such music is the pianist. Beethoven
admits a violinist on occasion, Schubert a singer, out of
friendliness : except for which the violin sonatas and the
songs might often have been made into pianoforte music
pure and simple. If the composer is satisfied with the
suggestions of reality which his ten fingers can evoke, he has
no essential need of the accompaniment of voice or fiddle.
The real gain is the friendly communion.

Therefore to refer to the pianoforte part of Schubert's songs
casually as the accompaniment is to invite misunderstanding.
To refer to it as such with an inflection of disparagement is
an impropriety too obvious to be mentioned if it were not
at the root of the unsatisfactoriness of many concert performances. Even without any such error in the first step of
the approach, there is no overrating the difficulty of the
problem. The crux lies in this, that pianist and singer are
on different planes. For the moment the question is not of
Schubert's openly dramatic pieces, like *Prometheus* and *Der
Kampf*. In his typical lyrics the pianoforte makes an
imaginative reference, and the singer when he is introduced
into the music must also, if by a different way, appeal to the
imagination. He has to lead us not to himself but to something through himself. The sound of his voice can only be
actual ; he has, however, the resource of saying as well as
sounding. The most direct and physical effects of singing,
then, are to be withheld. The way to sing Schubert's songs
is a contained way. Not the singer himself is involved in
the described passions.

At the same time the expression must not seem rehearsed. One must every time be, as it were, stepping delicately and wonderingly in a world of unexplored feelings, and not of represented adventures. Not the first reaction to reality is sung, but its reflection in imagination. The singer is not to act as someone else, and yet is utterly to forget to be himself, so sunk is he to be in the evocation. Singing thus, he addresses us indirectly, and an appeal so modified harmonizes in a way with the reflection of a reflection in the pianoforte's music.

This is not to exaggerate the delicacy of his engagement; for indeed no other sort of music is so rarely given to perfection, and the habitual listener comes to the conclusion that listening, or at any rate cold-blooded listening in a crowd, is not the true approach to Schubert's songs. And as for the singer, the deeper he goes into this world of poetry the more courage must he feel he needs to play his part. He must exert himself towards an ever superior purity of tone, sensitiveness of line, and spiritual concentration when he hears all the inner music and not merely the cold sound of the instrument in Schubert's exordia. Take any one of a hundred :

or :

This is no deterrent. The life of art is full of such tempting impossibilities.

The starting-point for the endeavour is a state in which technical mastery and the production of appropriate tone, acquired in years of singing music of the direct kind, are second nature : the state in which the mind is free to be engrossed by the poetic vision.

The singer is for convenience' sake called ' he,' though the

quotation in B*b* minor just above introduces, of course, a
female voice, and there are a number of Schubert's songs
that can only be sung by women.   There are still more which
can be appropriately sung only by men.   Why this ' can
only,' if the lieder-singer is to aim at being a reflecting instrument that suggests more than it can tell, and is not to be seen
as a dramatic personage ?   Well, he is unceasingly man-
œuvring for advantage against actuality ; and it is not good
sense to ask to be extra-handicapped.   The curious thing
is that women may venture fairly safely on some of the men's
songs, while the other way about is an impossibility.   Even
so, it is as well to be cautious.   According to existing manners,
there is something comically improper in a woman's singing
Rellstab's *Ständchen*, with its imploring invitation to the
person above to join the amorous serenader in the garden.

The special demands of Schubertian technics are that the
singer shall be most feelingly aware of the pianoforte part
and shall most feelingly think of the words.   The alliance
with the instrument is not hard and fast—it is a different
case from, let us say, the great arias in Bach, where the
principle is a theological obedience to the dogmatic letter.
Everything in Schubert's art reposes in an understanding
between friends.   The very melodiousness is lost in an
unbalanced performance, say, by a masterful and showy
singer and an effaced pianist.

Schubert's melody was from the first irresistible.   Schubert
and melody—it is a truism, the two are almost synonymous.
But in a great number of Schubert's songs the vocal line is
not self-supporting.   A professional paradoxist might dis-
parage his gift of melody by isolating a given line.   The life
of his melody is again and again found to depend on associated
figures and harmonies.   Schubert constantly suggests to us
that the whole conception was one ; and sometimes as good
as asserts that it could not have been otherwise.   Such an
air as *Totengräberweise* (1826) could not have been thought
of otherwise than harmonically :

(Andante.)

and so on to a D minor cadence before a return is begun
towards the final E major.   The vocal line in Schubert is

in any number of songs a wonder of invention, shapeliness, and grace ; but to name one of his songs brings to mind not just that, but a general view—not alone the carolling miller but also the tumbling water and the wheel, not only the cry of the Erl-king's prey but also the terrible galloping and the tossing of the eerie branches on the fatal ride, and so on with hundreds of Schubert's musical scenes.

Often when there was no call for the picturesqueness of which he has such an extraordinary command, the vocal line was made to bend to the influence of the harmonic instrument its associate ; so in *Stimme der Liebe* the voice's rising minor sixth in the fourth bar, its drop of a diminished fourth in the fifth bar, and its subsequent movement (from the original B*b*) into F*b* are a harmonist's music. Such things were to lead to the characteristic vocal writing of Wagner and Hugo Wolf.

*   *

*

Schubert's song-writing represents a special agreement between music and verse not quite like any known before or since. Classical music never attained to his close terms with poetry. The later romantic music was to become more intimate with the poets even than Schubert's was—and, indeed, to the point of subserviency. Schubert's song-writing was in general a rendering of the mood of his enthusiastic reading. It was not a style of point-by-point illustration. But Schubert had eyes, he glanced rapidly, and he took in the main features of a poet's scene as no musician before him had done. The metre or the shape of some key-phrase in the text engendered the cell of a melody ; and a hint of landscape, of atmosphere, or of an accompanying movement or gesture, struck his fancy and started in him picturesque musical figures of a unique vividness.

The action of literary influence had existed from all time in music ; what was new was the degree of Schubert's free naturalism. Bach's music, of course, and Handel's, is full of derivations from the authors they set. The outcome was highly formalized in the stately manner of the time. Neither of those great men possessed literary taste ; but again and again their melodies and recitatives make the impression of being a kind of sublime extension of the sound of poetic speech. The sound of words, and hence, too, the sense, are indeed to be reckoned as the more or less distant kinsmen of musical tones, and not alien allies. How would great poetry have fared in Bach's and Handel's hands ? The problem

did not arise, since their country was devoid of poets ; and
Handel, in all his years in London, cultivated no feeling for
English letters, and consequently never approached the
sensitiveness and subtlety of Purcell's arioso style.

Goethe came, and made all the difference to music. Mozart
and Beethoven occasionally set his poems (e.g. *Das Veilchen*
and *Wonne der Wehmut*), but Schubert was almost Goethe's
offspring. Of a boy with a genius for music and a bent for
poetry, Goethe, one day in 1814, suddenly made a man—
the day (October 14) when the seventeen-years-old Schubert
composed *Gretchen am Spinnrade*, and so composed it that
we cannot believe he could have done it better in 1828.
Let us remember how modest and tentative was all Schubert's
instrumental music at that time and for long after. Dozens
of the most admired songs came before he was fully himself
in symphony, quartet, and sonata, in which his first memorable
attainments were the unfinished C minor Quartet of 1820
and the unfinished B minor Symphony of 1822. There are
abundant records to show how Schubert was accustomed to
be seized and transported by the chance reading of a poem—
Spaun's account, for instance, of the inspired creation of
Erlkönig. We know how he lived among versifiers, and
himself attempted once at least to put one of his deepest
experiences into rhyme. It is our advantage that this passion
of Schubert's should have rendered to the language of
music, as he had learned it, such new, living forms and
glowing colours ; and also that it was not, for all his
transports, a disintegrating passion—that music, after all,
came first.

Admirable works were built on different bases before and
after. The beauty of the agreement which he reached does
not invalidate the grandeur of eighteenth-century formalism,
any more than Schubert's art was impaired by the engaging
subtleties of the song-writing of a later generation for whose
taste his style was not nearly literary enough. The time came
before the end of the century when such a practice of
Schubert's as his repetition of every one of Goethe's lines
in the course of a song (e.g. *Wer nie sein Brod*) seemed
intolerable. Well, Wolf's concentration and exquisiteness
are good ; and so also the freedom and eager stride of
Schubert's musical movement. Later still, certain broken
songs from which the literary conscience has worked to expel
songfulness have made Schubert's style often look simply
reckless—recklessly musical. Music after all was the channel
of Schubert's mind, a broad main stream which took in

swelling tributaries but remained master of them all. For his time he was singularly susceptible to extra-musical influences ; but we at the distance of a few generations see how far he formalized these influences. He, ' le plus poète,' was too much the musician to be diverted into any not recognizably musical way. His ordinary working methods were thoroughly traditional—and traditional even, in some of the early pieces written during pauses of his inflamed fancy, to the point of quaintness and primness. Witness the setting of Goethe's *Sehnsucht* of December 1814, in which a swift, anapæstic lyric has all the wind taken out of its sails by Schubert's succession of demure little recitatives and coy warblings. At the other end of his career, there is the astonishing *Doppelgänger*, in which the word is closely hugged from line to line, giving the casual listener the impression of the loosest sort of dramatic arioso, but in which there is an underlying plan of four-bar phrases, of the utmost terseness, that calls to mind the classical passacaglia.

The tune in Schubert springs from the poet's tune. Sometimes the suggestion is to be traced to the contour of a striking phrase, at other times to the general swing of a metre. A bold lilt with plenty of trisyllables and double or triple rhymes caught his ear and awakened tunes in his head. His romantic poets revelled in such a movement (to give an English equivalent) as ' Bird of the Wilderness, blithesome and cumberless ! ' In many of Schubert's songs we can imagine him as having hummed over some such verbal tune until it grew into a full-fledged melody. His ear was unsophisticated. Experiments in classic metres, dear to several of the German poets,[1] meant nothing much to him. He could set the asclepiads of Hölty's ' Wann der silberne Mond durch die Gesträuche blinkt,' like Brahms after him, without a suspicion of their form. (Observe, by way of comparison, Wolf's scrupulousness towards Goethe's elegiacs in ' Anakreons Grab.') But Schubert, given a simple ripple of rhymes, was off like a bird. This sort of thing was the delight of his easier hours :

> Herze, das sehnende,
> Auge, das thränende,
> Sehnsucht nie endende,
> Heimwärts sich wendende
> Busen, der wallende
> Klage verhallende,
> Abendstern blinkender,
> Hoffnungslos sinkender !

[1] He set Pyrker's hexameters, Matthisson's sapphics, Salis's distichs, and Hölty's asclepiads and alcaics.

If Schubert's melody was suggested by the poet's phrases or metre, what of his lapses into false accentuation ? Well, when these occur, Schubert has, we shall find, just seized, or is about to seize, on a point in the text which has appeared to him of superior importance. His susceptibility to the tune of words is proved somewhere or other in nearly every song he wrote. But when he had hold of the heart of the matter it was enough. He fitted music insurpassably well to the text at the crucial points, and was apt to leave a certain looseness elsewhere. This was not only because he often worked in too debonair a mood and with strokes too broad and rapid for such perfected attentiveness to the verbal stresses as is found in Hugo Wolf's style ; it was also because musical form as he knew it had claims of its own to which it was only proper that a text, no matter how august, should make allowance. Here was the traditionalist in Schubert, the Schubert who was too deep in music to abandon it by an eccentric leap ; who moved, indeed, but in a way which he made sure did not lose him the element that was his breath. Wolf was similarly a traditionalist, whose later art was to ripen in the light of Schubert's, Schumann's, and Wagner's examples.

Aufenthalt shows us Schubert's method typically. The melody is dictated by the force of the stresses in ' Rauschender Strom, brausender Wald, starrender Fels.' The musical translation is magnificent :

Let us call these feet choriambi. In the poet's fourth line the stress is shifted. ' Aufenthalt ' is a dactyl. But Schubert must have a final heavy syllable to set off against ' Strom,' ' Wald,' and ' Fels.' For the sake of musical symmetry he brings ' halt ' in on a down-beat. Wolf can better be imagined writing something like :

Auf - ent-halt.

We are not for a moment deploring Schubert's practice, while sensible to Wolf's delicate pains. The generations of men lose here to gain there. The careless rapture of song which came in with Schubert went out with him. Even the positive negligences here and there discerned in his accentuation are an insignificant charge on a music so swift and joyous and untrammelled.   Here is one in   Prometheus ' which is noticeable if we are comparing Wolf's setting of the poem :

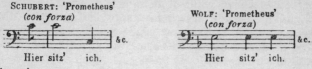

and again :

where the point of the hero's boast is, as Wolf has made plain, that he will found a race of freemen ' like unto *Me*.'

 However, arbitrariness in Schubert is casual, and rare at that.   In principle he was all against such high-handedness as is found in Brahms, who can hardly have had an ear for prosody, and who in some of his supremely fine songs seems to have fitted verses to an existing melody (e.g. ' WIE *bist du* MEIN*e König*GIN ').

Wolf would not have set the first phrase of Heine's *Atlas* with Schubert's disregard for just emphasis :

But passing to the very next words, we observe that for ' Eine Welt, die ganze Welt ' Schubert has found the perfect match.   That, then, is what has struck his fancy—' a world, the whole world of woe, is my burden.'   For that key-phrase he devised a finely adequate motive.   It formed the musical cell from which the rest grew.   In this phrase ' Eine Welt,' the ' eine ' has suggested the strongly marked ' anacrusis ' or up-beat by which the musician conveys a gathering of forces for the uplifting of the burdensome ' Welt ' :

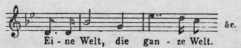

By an extension of the idea, all his exordium must, he feels, be a preparation for that rising minor sixth and weighty minim. Working back, then, he sets the opening words twice over to a motive which, while it does not, as we have seen, fit ' Ich, unglücksel'ge,' serves to assure his principal stroke by minor attacks at the same spot (anacrusis of semiquaver instead of dotted quaver and semiquaver, interval of fourth instead of minor sixth).

Working further back still, he sets the bass of the pianoforte prophesying with a fragment, likewise anacrusic, of the ' Atlas ' motive. In a word, ' I ' is nothing and the intolerable world everything. The whole theme (to which the double striking of the tonic is preliminary) is now one of symphonic grandeur.

Those familiar with Wolf's vocal writing may feel that Schubert's practice of placing prepositions and conjunctions on an important beat needs excusing. The apparent stressing of ' in,' ' auf,' ' wenn,' and so on, is frequent ; as, for example :

In des See's— Wo - gen-spie - le.

Wolf's inclination was to make his writing foolproof by lifting the weight from such an ' in ' ; but that is not enough reason for wishing for anything in Schubert's music that would be detrimental to the breadth and ease of its periods and their natural songfulness. There is to be prized in Schubert an overflowing spirit, care-free and irresponsible almost, whose like is not to be met with in music. The lines just quoted would not, as a matter of fact, have been set otherwise by Wolf—simply because he, with his acute and searching mind, would not have condescended to touch Bruchmann's trifling barcarolle, or any other of a hundred such texts of Schubert's, whose words were in themselves idle, not worth a significant style of declamation, and yet served well enough to release in Schubert the spirit of the burgeoning May morning, and song in a kind of natural, wild state.

But we have also said that the stressing of the prepositions is apparent. It is actual only to the literal-minded singer who has not got beyond counting beats and bars to a feeling of rhythm. Schubert did not reckon on an interpreter to whom words would be meaningless. Thought for the words formed part of his general charge to the singer : without which thought the actual musical effect of the songs is impoverished. There is a rhythmical impoverishment if the

singer considers nothing but note-values, and sings his part
as a clarinettist would play it. The voice is rare that can
match the purity of the clarinet's tone, but the singer has
another means of interest, and that is the accent which is
dictated by the verbal interest. In the first bar from *Am See*,
quoted above, the singer will not give the usual down-beat
accent to the first note, for the word ' See's ' claims a special
stress. In the next bar the first beat is strong and the second
exceptionally weak. The metre is indicated by the note-
values, the rhythm by the words ; and due observance of the
latter, which often results in the effect of a cross-rhythm
against the pianoforte, makes one of the charms and subtleties
of Schubert's song-music.

The opening of *Am Grabe Anselmos* is an example of the
sort of phrase that is often spoilt by being sung metrically
and not rhythmically :

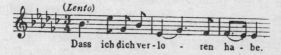

Dass ich dich ver - lo - ren ha - be.

It is not one of the great melodies which can survive almost
any rough treatment. It is modest, and begs for a little sympathy. The phrase quoted, taken without words or harmony,
is not very significant. It is enriched on the one hand by
pathetic harmonies, and on the other by the moving cry in
the text. ' Verloren ' is, of course, the heart of the phrase.
' Dass ' is hardly anything, and ' habe ' is not much, compared
with that inconsolable word, which should appear written in
fire before the singer. The only accent worth mentioning,
then, falls on the first beat in the second bar ; and the singer
has no other for some time until he comes to the word ' Grabe.'
But observe how Schubert was at pains, even in this youthful
and quite secondary song of his, in which pianoforte and voice
keep very much to the same theme, to distribute the interest.
For while the voice throughout the first bar is leaning forward,
as it were, towards the second the pianoforte has a heavy
dominant seventh upon the word ' dass,' which it at once
resolves. It is, in fact, concluding its prelude while the voice
begins. Then in the next bar Schubert has strongly accented
the second beat in the pianoforte part, while it is quite out
of the question for the voice to stress its corresponding note.
In effect, while the metre of the two parts is the same, the
composer has indicated different rhythms—but indicated
them insufficiently, if the singer is one for whom a peremptory-

looking down-beat can obliterate the thought of the loss of
Anselmo, his dearest friend. In short, the question of the
prepositions in Schubert is simply solved by the singer's
sense.

*   *

*

If a word is to be given to Schubert's rhythm, a premise
must be allowed on a point of diction ; namely, that metre
is a matter of numerable things, bars and beats, and that
rhythm lies in the usage of metres and accents. Thus,
Schubert's fondness for Siciliano and Piffero metres is to be
noted, and also his particular expression in the use of them—
that is to say, the Schubertian rhythm. A poet or musician
will habitually use metres in common with others ; his
rhythm is the purely personal factor. A great vehemence
of accentuation may be one man's rhythm, and another's a
virtual obliteration of metre.

Schubert used a great abundance of metrical forms. The
variety of them in the songbooks catches the eye, and gives
the pages their individualistic, nineteenth-century look. He
took up almost any form that came, for he, with his ninety
poets to set, could not have too many ; but, as with his poets,
we feel that he did not go far out of his way to search for
them. They were there, close at hand, only waiting to be
thoroughly Schubertianized—the ländler to be merrily mated
with Shakespeare, if it so chanced, and the polonaise and
quick-march with Scott. His assimilation of all he put his
hand on was the proof of his sense of rhythm. No song is
more Schubertian than the last of them all, *Die Taubenpost*,
but there is nothing elsewhere really like its syncopated
dancing measure.

Not, of course, that there was a new measure every time.
The oldest ones served again and again. That Schubert was
consciously exquisite we cannot believe. His charm resembles
that of certain poets who have written entrancingly on lines
suggested by the first-opened hymn-book :

> Well, let them fight for honour's breath,
>   Or pleasure's shade pursue—
> The dweller in the land of death
>   Is changed and careless too.

In a good poet there is nothing deterrent in finding a familiar
metre or stanza used again and again. So with Schubert's

most usual movements—for instance, his favourite pastoral measure in 6-8 time with the predominating metrical foot of quaver-crochet, quaver-crotchet. Matter and treatment can be counted on to be fresh. This Siciliano movement is found in his early, as in his latest, music, and we never tire of finding it, knowing that there will every time be a peculiar interest. In effect, these pastoral songs, which range from *Schäfers Klagelied* (1814) to *Das Fischermädchen* (1828), are full of charming Schubertisms, both modulatory and rhythmical, and they are rarely quite as innocent as they look at a first glance. *Schäfers Klagelied*, indeed, brings off a happy but too audacious stroke which, if it had become habitual with Schubert, would be with difficulty defensible.

A musical period has sections corresponding to the lines of a poetic stanza. The four-bar section is the standard unit. Schubert adhered to it on principle, and departed from it on countless occasions. His general adherence is the sign of the reasonableness and normality of his art ; the departures are its waywardness, playfulness, fancy. His flexibility and enterprise of rhythm have much to do with the charm that is first felt in his music by those who have never looked far into it, for rhythm makes the first call on attention. Looked into for a moment, it is seen to be for ever varying the prosaic way, while keeping to the direction ; and we think of Schubert as the country child whose paths are free, and who delightfully takes a short cut or a long one more or less at his own sweet will—comparing him with a composer like Mendelssohn, the town child, whom we see as vivacious and yet prim, conscious of his gravelled walks and fenced-in grass plots.

A perfectly square period of eight bars is exceptional in Schubert, and is characteristic of his expression of studious simplicity or else of deep seriousness. *Wohin?* is built up of precisely symmetrical sections, for the wanderer's tune is dictated by the regular babble of the unvarying brook to whose course he has confided his future. The unbroken rhythm of the C major melody in *Am Meer* is in keeping with the poet's fatal vision of the desolate sea and the irresistible oncoming of night. Schubert's first and most obvious variation is the extension of the last section of his period by two bars, frequently a virtual repetition :

'Taubenpost.'

bis   zu der lieb-ster Haus,   bis   zu der lieb-ster Haus.

To prolong the period by an echoing of the cadence in the pianoforte part is almost a mannerism :

The device has a lingering and haunting effect, and Schubert's tenderness of heart and fond regretfulness come out in its uncounted recurrences.

He was almost as fond of varying his rhythm by extending the second half of a period by a foot or a bar. The prelude to *Frühlingsglaube* is an example. A charming instinct bade the composer repeat the second foot of the third bar at the beginning of the fourth :

We were half expecting the third and fourth bars to repeat the pattern of the first two, and the insertion causes a mild surprise, one that is matched in the delicate harmony. There is also a languorous little extension of the first period of the vocal part. The whole song, so transparently simple, is wonderfully written to express the rather tremulous welcome offered to the joyful season by a mind debilitated by sorrow.

For special purposes Schubert freely builds with melodious sections other than two or multiples of two. *Täuschung* in the ' Winterreise ' offers an example of the persistent use of three-bar sections. Its irregularity conveys a sense of oddity and unrest which is that of the illusory gleam described by the song ; and the pianoforte's cæsural bars faintly mock the singer's words at the end of each line. The whole song is a remarkable work of the rhythmical imagination.

Quite as characteristic is Schubert's expressive play with the cæsura—by which, in music, is to be understood a much more variable quantity than in verbal prosody, the range of rhythmical expression in music being so much greater. We

count as cæsuras, for instance, the pauses in the vocal part of
the Rellstab *Ständchen*, while the serenader seems to hold
his breath to listen for a sign from the balcony and hears
only the echo of his own cadence, taken up, as it were, by the
nocturnal breeze and the rustling foliage. The singer of
Schubert should scrutinize curiously the disposition of his
rests. It is very artful, and is in fact one of Schubert's great
devices for making vivid the emotional situation. Almost
every other page offers an example. Observe in *Die Post*
the irregularity in the breaks—a bar, three bars, half a bar—
all indicating the agitation of the cast-off lover, and the last
gasping of his fond hopes, while the post-horn sounds in the
street.

Schubert already played in masterly fashion with this device
when quite young. It gives a special charm to *Schäfers
Klagelied*. The love-lorn shepherd's plaint begins in the
most homely strain ; but Schubert has a surprise for us in
the fourth bar by his omission of the normal cæsura :

It is an example of the way in which Schubert was seized
by the sense of a poem. Goethe has here led him to press
on from ' On yon hillside often and often do I stand . . .'
to ' . . . leaning on my crook and staring down into the
valley.' The average youthful composer of the time would
assuredly have pulled up on a dotted crotchet at the end of
the poet's second line. Schubert gets another foot into his
melody in place of the conventional cæsural pause. His
eight-bar period is built up not of 4 + 4, but of 2 + 4 + 2
sections. The rhythmical carrying-on between the fourth
and fifth bars may be compared with the overriding of the
cæsura by the French symbolists of the eighties in their
alexandrines. The effect here makes for a dreamy melancholy. There is, however, a sequel, an immediate sequel,
to Schubert's interesting little stroke. With his extra foot
he has used up a word of the third line before its due time.
Goethe's lines have each three stresses, and so has each of
Schubert's two-bar sections. But the melody has left the

beaten track. It needs another word to help it back into the
measure. What does Schubert do but adapt Goethe ! He
calmly adds a word and a fourth stress to the line (' hinge-
bogen ' for Goethe's ' gebogen '). It is safe to say that no
one, hearing the song casually, would notice that the altered
line limps. In the setting of the second quatrain the variation
from the normal lies in the bar-long cæsura between lines
3 and 4, where the sorry shepherd pauses to reflect how vain
is his errand. And so on. Only the fifth quatrain of the
little song is rhythmically quite regular. The opening melody
returns in the sixth quatrain, and again it is necessary to
amend Goethe in the interests of the musician's rhythmical
variation. The word ' nur ' is therefore interpolated into
the last line but one. This licence is exceptional in Schubert,
but not unique. In the last period of *Erster Verlust* :

he feels the need of an ' anacrusis ' for the sake of expressive
variation at the end of a song in which the principal phrases
have begun on a down-beat, and he calmly inserts the last
' wer ' into Goethe's verse. Ordinarily, however, Schubert
was able to make reiteration of the poet's words serve such
purposes. An example of this, of the same early period as
the *Schäfers Klagelied*, is in the refrain of the admirable
Gretchen am Spinnrade. The song is a long one, and with
the sustained whirring of the wheel in the pianoforte part it
would in another man's hands easily have become monotonous.
As Schubert composed it, it is one of the lasting wonders of
music. Calculated monotony is, indeed, its primary rhythmical characteristic ; but against that is the beautiful variation
in the second section of the refrain (' Ich finde sie nimmer ').
This consists of an extension of a bar's length, on a repetition
of the words, ' Ich finde,' giving us an irregular period of
4 + 5.

A glance at *Das Fischermädchen* of 1828 shows with what
refinement Schubert, at the end of his career, treated a
simple 6-8 movement. The prelude of eight bars is quite
unpunctuated, and this, taken at the ' rathe1 quick ' tempo

indicated, gives a vague kind of flowing impression, a suitable background to the waterside courtship. The first two lines are set to four normal bars. The voice pauses, to allow the greeting and invitation to make their effect, while the pianoforte echoes the last two bars. The next two lines are set similarly, then repeated with a virtual repetition of the melody, and then there is a further extension—for, just when the close was expected, Schubert, with the effect of a nonchalant turn on his heel, takes the voice up a minor seventh from the tonic (with a diminished seventh in the accompaniment), and repeats the last line yet again. The settings of the three quatrains are alike, except that from A♭ the middle one is taken into C♭. There is something about the brusqueness of this modulation, as also about the repetitions of the words, that is elegantly idle and even a trifle impertinent. In short, Schubert, starting with a motive that looked the most familiar possible, made a song that is as individual as any   It is clear enough how the ground he broke by his rhythmical enterprise bore fruit in the general instrumental music, notably Brahms's, of the following generations.

*   *

*

It is not suggested that there is anything finicking about Schubert's refinements. Between the extremes of his most easygoing moods and his deepest earnestness the man is felt to be undeviatingly natural and unassuming. If there is an extravagance in Schubert it is nothing far-fetched, but a wild looseness of animal movement, a throwing of the reins to Nature. There is no perversity in the course, and no forcing of the pace. This ' pace ' is what some would call Schubert's rhythm by a generalized use of the term, to which one may prefer the word ' tempo.' It can, perhaps, be roughly defined. It is a healthy and regular pulse, buoyant but not remarkably quick. As Schubert in actual time came between Mozart and Wagner, so his tempo is midway between Mozart's springy vivaciousness and Wagner's superb deliberation. Schubert's music does not care to race, for all its activity. It does not trouble to ponder, for all its sensibility. This music has the leisureliness of Nature.

It is more mistaken to sing Schubert too fast than too slowly. Slow singing may, if due regard is not paid to the rhythmical incidents, sound nerveless and dull ; but excessive speed means the trampling down of all Schubert's characteristics. The richness of his texture, the full harmonies, and in parti-

cular the fine, sturdy basses, act as a brake. Music that
would be speedy must strip. Look at ' Largo al factotum '
and ' Numero quindici ' in Rossini's ' Barber ' ; at Sullivan's
' Heavy Dragoon ' song ; at ' Fin ch' han del vino.'   Schubert never wanted to spring so lightly. He gave his basses
weighty work to do, and they put on muscle. Their handsome sturdiness it is, in good part, that has led one's fancy
into seeing in Schubert a countryman, and in his music a
similitude of the growths of the earth, sappy and ramifying.
They behave with doggedness and native dignity ; they
disdain to pretend to be dapper and urbane. Almost every
song might provide an example. One or two may be quoted
as much as anything for the sake of pointing to a song or two
that is rarely or never sung. *Am Flusse* (1822) is one of the
simplest of the songs of Schubert's maturity. Nothing
could be more bare, more transparent. Under the watery
flow of the even quavers in the right hand there is a steadying
value, an embanking, so to say, in this bass figure, which
becomes slightly more pronounced in the course of the song :

Such a bass as that of *Totengräbers Heimweh* is the making
of a song :

Schubert nearly always used German for his speed directions.
They are curt, and do not convey much. Very rarely a
quicker pace is indicated than a look at the music without
reference to the text would have suggested. *Geheimes*—
marked ' etwas geschwind,' rather fast—is an example.
But Schubert's ' geschwind ' is not to be taken too excitedly.
Invariably if ' geschwind ' or ' schnell ' is read as though
the song were an instrumental piece it will be too fast, and
the words will be more or less a gabble. *Frühlingssehnsucht*
is marked ' geschwind,' and a glance at the notes suggests
a winged movement. But that is to reckon without such
verbal obstacles in the path as ' Grünend umkränzet Wälder
und Höh' ! schimmernd erglänzet Blüthenschnee ! ' which
are bound to reduce the haste if not the warmth of the rap-

turous expresssion.   Similarly with *Der Jäger*, in the Müllerlieder, which is commonly rushed into nonsense by English
singers when they use the original text.   Renouncing a
little speed, the singer is more than compensated by the
contribution made towards the expression of the young miller's
excitement and anger by the hurtling of full-sized words that
are like brickbats.

*   *
*

German has a heavy gait.   Great energy, surprising to us,
is generally applied to the articulation of everyday sentences.
It is habitual to dwell on consonants and consonantal groups.
The genius of the language naturally pervaded Schubert's
style, when he, virtually the first to do so, set himself to write
music for German poetry ; and it unmistakably influenced
his tempo.   The German language strikes the stranger as
uncouth and repellent ; but the very ruggedness and asperity
of its forms and sound are a value in the sum of Schubert's
music, which is very little inclined to be mordant on its own
account.   This is one of several arguments for singing the
original text of the songs—arguments which are, in the most
favourable circumstances of performance, irresistible,[1] but
not always and everywhere.
It is common to hear Schubert sung in German, some sort
of German, when German is understood neither by singer
nor audience.   This is pedantry, which has done untold
harm to music in England.   It accounts for much tepid and
accentless singing of Schubert's songs, in which, if the music
is to give up its full sense, the images evoked by the words
should all the time be felt by the singer and his listeners—
should be seen passing before their very eyes.   Perhaps (so
it may occur to one when those images cannot well be focussed)
it is necessary to be at least half-Germanized to apprehend
Schubert in his true vividness ; and the rest of us may be,
as it were, merely peering through railings at the intangible
garden.   An upbringing amid a special lore alone can, so it
is said, serve to discriminate all the poetical flavours of such a
piece as *Ueber allen Gipfeln*.   It would have been better if
from the first a really delicate attempt had been made to

---

[1] Cf. Dante's dictum—' And yet everyone should know that nothing har-
monized by music's bond can be translated from its own tongue without
breaking all its harmony and sweetness. And it is for this reason that, unlike
other Greek writings, those of Homer have never been translated into Latin.
(Convivio, I. 7.)

supply Schubert with a new poetry for the English world—if
Victorians of the first order, like Tennyson, Fitzgerald, and
Rossetti, had felt disposed to make free and exquisite translations. This would have meant a rather different Schubert,
for poetry is not translatable, and what is called a translation
can only be a new poem ; but it would have given Schubert-
singing in England a vitality denied by the pallor and flatness
of the versions that occupied the field for nearly a hundred
years, and equally by what may be called St. John's Wood
German—a German which, even if correct on the singer's
part, is not really vividly impressive to the listening circle, for
it is useless to pretend that more than a meagre and reluctantly
acquired knowledge of German is possessed by ordinarily
literate English people.

A special training is needed to become disinterested in the
text of the vocal music one hears. On this particular ground
the English musical public, long accustomed to performances
in more or less unknown languages and to ensuing licensed
inarticulateness of singers, is no doubt as cultivated as any.
There is no general principle to lay down. Performances of
music are bound to become more and more adaptations, the
farther they are removed from the music's time and circumstances of origin. We had best be pragmatists. It would be
a practical mistake to translate *Ombra mai fu*, for the text
amounts to nothing, and the song translated would simply lose
the open Italian vowels which are a good part of its music.
The sensible singer similarly will not think of singing Brahms's
Four Biblical Songs, Op. 121, to an English audience except
in translation, since there exists a perfectly fitting English
version (Paul England's), and since the strength of these
songs lies so largely in the majestic words. The singer might
indeed trust to his sense more often than he does ; but the
vogue to-day, in London at all events, is all for the imitation,
as near as may be, of foreign tongues, a vogue which only
exceptions like the St. Matthew Passion, ' Elijah,' and the
Brahms songs named can withstand.

Applying pragmatism to Schubert's songs, we find some
that any singer who is, as well as the owner of a voice, a lively,
communicative artist can hardly bear to sing in a language
foreign to the audience : songs whose dramatic or evocative
words are to such a singer no less than the notes a vehicle of
his art. Thus *Erlkönig*—unless the singer is certain that
every listener has Goethe by heart—had surely better be
translated, although so nearly untranslatable, and culture be
speared on the point of the great story. The B.B.C's broadcast-

ing of *Erlkönig* in German is surely the crowning of pedantry.
There are also songs whose words are either about nothing
in particular (*Auf dem Wasser zu singen*), or else (e.g. *Litanei*)
are much less fine than the theme and music have a right to.
These are well enough left in the obscurity of German in
circles where German is more or less obscure but still not
unheard of. But pedantry has actually been known to introduce songs in German at village concerts and competition
festivals, before audiences who are so naïve as to expect as
the first thing when a person opens his mouth that intelligible
words shall issue. In such surroundings any and every
song must be translated, even the untranslatable ones.

The difficulties of translation are always formidable—a
scope for the most ingenious pens. Sometimes they are
insuperable ; an example in Schubert is *Sei mir gegrüsst*,
for which no one has yet been able or is likely to find an
English equivalent for the characteristic and repeated phrase
with its essential rhyme, so perfectly matched in Schubert's
music. The difficulties are increased by the general familiarity
with the songs in their original form. This almost forbids
alteration of note-values for the convenience of a new text,
even alterations that would be of no real musical significance.
The subtraction of a quaver from such a purely declamatory
phrase as the last line of the *Erlkönig* is at once noticed and
censured. The pity is that the great composers, Schubert
and Wagner in chief, had not foresight of our present needs.
Then they would surely have called in skilled translators,
and would have lent a helping and modifying hand at awkward
corners. But Schubert actually lacked presage to the point
of setting poems by Pope and Scott to music that does not
serve the original text. Regard for a composer's least notes,
even when their raison d'être has disappeared, amounts
to superstition. In England it sometimes touches the height
of absurdity, as, for instance, when Rossetti's ' Blessed
Damozel ' has to be rewritten from the French version when
our choirs sing Debussy's setting, all for the sake of the
composer's ipsissimæ notæ !

' Schubert's Songs Translated,' by A. H. Fox Strangways
and Steuart Wilson,[1] addressed the problem with a literary
conscience not known before in this connexion. Not one
of the solutions in the book is without skill. Nothing could
be more elegant than the best of them. Given this chance
a generation or two ago, such pieces as *Wohin?*, *Der Musensohn*,
and *Geheimes* (translated to perfection) would by now have

——— [1] Oxford University Press, 1924.

become truly English songs. As for the version of *Das Lied im Grünen* in this book, no English singer should be able to resist it :

> . . . Fair sights beckon all men and sundry to follow ;
> The song of the lark and the flight of the swallow,
> The carpet of bluebells that fills every nook
> Lead on by the meadow and down to the brook
> In spring-time.

The versions that are less finished often have brilliant points. *Aufenthalt* is rather spoilt by the flat-vowelled ' spate ' for ' Strom ' in the first line ; but what could be better than ' Wind-circled tor, storm-riven trees ' ? The adagio songs are obviously hardest to translate. The curious thing to notice is how in the course of englishing Schubert's songs not only the atmosphere and imaginative associations are changed but also the pace. The quick songs, as soon as fitted with the new words, go quicker still. The Oxford translators have pricked *Der Musensohn* and *Im Grünen* with spurs, and they race as no German song ever did. On the other hand, the slowest of Schubert's songs can never be provided with enough broad, dilatory vowels. These are, as well as crunched mouthfuls of consonants, a great character-istic of German. ' Heil'ge Nacht ! ' they say ; it is as though the wheels of the busy day were indeed slackening speed, and under that round weight of speech Schubert's semiquavers naturally flag nearly to immobility.[1]

This dilatory force of ponderous words helped to the making of the richest of Schubert's purely vocal effects. His long-drawn-out melodic line in such songs as *Nacht und Träume*, *Im Abendrot*, *Du bist die Ruh'*, *Litanei*, *Freiwilliges Versinken*, and *Am Meer*, when well executed, affords the ear the finest pleasure as sheer sound ; and in this music Schubert has, almost certainly without premeditation, presented the singer with one of the most delicate technical problems in vocal art. He who can perform *Litanei* extremely adagio, with soft and yet full tone, giving just value to the different vowels, all with unexceptionable serenity of effect, knows most things about the technics of singing. The slow crescendo ascent from B^b to A^b towards the end of *Du bist die Ruh'* calls for a more difficult and more valuable mastery than the kind of clarinet-cadenza exercises one finds in books of instructions

---

[1] No English Schubertian will be ignorant of Richard Capell's own excellent translations. See Preface. M. C.

for singers. And similarly this beautiful spreading phrase—

Schubert sang well as a boy, but as a man not otherwise, one gathers, than composers usually do. His vocal writing was not based on any splendid school of singing. It originated, as did his instrumental style, in a circle of more or less domestic music-making where no doubt the will had often to be taken for the deed. The grand singing of the day was (as in the main it continued for long) Italian. Schubert's friend the barytone Vogl, whom he had much admired some years before he knew him, was distinguished by his culture, his intelligence, his interpretative gifts, and the literary and dramatic sense in his declamation. He deplores in his memoirs that there was no German school of singing able to do justice to Schubert's vocal writings. Schubert composed, whether instrumentally or vocally, for the sake of the thing done and not with his eye on the effective doing of it. Nine times out of ten his intentions are intimate. In all his characteristic pieces his thought is set not at all on singing as such, but on the musical expression of the poetry in his mind, and out of that poetry arise his vocal style and the particular demands it makes. There are fairly frequent remains of grand formal styles in his work—imperious recitatives (e.g. *Dem Unendlichen*), and cantilenas that derive ultimately from Italian music. But the origin of the vocal style in the great mass of typically Schubertian songs is not so far to seek. It is simply folksong, which Schubert enriched by all the treasures of his quick, sympathetic nature and his musical genius.

There is, then, hardly any call on the Schubertian singer for virtuosity. This music is not, like Handel's, Mozart's, or Rossini's, a school for singers. Can it then be taken up simply by the light of nature? No. The call it makes is rather for what may be termed post-virtuosity. The composer's preoccupation with other than technically vocal concerns is only a reason why the executant (who, after all, is not a whistling miller, and must go round the long way of art to suggest that which is not) should first form himself so safely on the vocal writings of consciously stylistic

composers that he can, when he comes to Schubert, afford to
be, with him, technically unpreoccupied too.

To suggest anything unvocal in Schubert's style would be
absurd. Nor was his circle without good singing. As well
as Vogl there were Anna Fröhlich, who taught singing at the
newly founded Vienna Conservatorium, and her sister ; and
then Baron Carl von Schönstein, whom Schubert met through
the Esterházys and to whom he dedicated ' Die schöne
Müllerin.' Schönstein was an amateur tenor who had until
he came upon Schubert sung only Italian music. He must
have been a fine singer and good artist. Liszt heard him in
later years and left an account of the moving effect of his
Schubert singing. Our point is that Schubert's composition
was not, like Handel's or Verdi's, inspired by the imposing
presence of a vocal school of great prestige and magnificence.
His flowers were grown of his own cultivation, in a comparatively modest corner. It is the exception for a song of
his to require (as does *Die Allmacht*) a voice of rare power.
Now and then one of the more extended songs falls into
monotony by reason of its narrow vocal range, for instance
the first *Suleika*, where several long periods are contained
within the interval of a fourth. The big songs are often
magnificent ; but a longer experience of opera and of what is
and is not telling on a large scale would, it is sometimes felt,
have been to Schubert's advantage. *Der zürnenden Diana*
may be cited. Despite a splendid movement and any number
f bold, energetic phrases it remains an ineffective song.

Schubert's musical instinct led him again and again to write
perfectly for various types of voices. The mere look on paper
of *Die Rose* conjures up the sound of a delicate lyric soprano,
and *Grenzen der Menschheit* of a rich bass. The triumphant
Allmacht demands an exceptionally brilliant dramatic soprano.
The composer's practice was, however, not infallible. Transposition is at times defensible. The tessitura of some of
Schubert's tenor songs in the earlier years is tiresomely high.
One example is *Die Entzückung an Laura* (1816). There are
also extravagances in the other direction. In *Auf der Donau*
Schubert, taking the gloomy text rather too literally, half hides
the music in the darkness of the tones, and finally he descends
on the word ' Untergang ' to F , a note that is out of place in so
small a lyric. The exceptional low notes in *Das Abendrot*
(Schreiber, 1818) must have been written with a view to a
particular singer—almost certainly Count Johann von Esterházy. The song is a chance for the contralto or bass proud of

sonorous low E's ; but the vowel in ' sil ' is not an attractive
one for the adventure. The song might be transposed ;
but at any pitch the voice is exceptional that commands at
the extremities of two octaves such handsome notes as
Schubert here demands. In a few songs there is a touch of
freakishness in the immense intervals over which Schubert
requires the voice to leap, a German freakishness one must
call it, remembering farther exaggerations of the sort in
Wagner and Strauss and utterly preposterous ones in
Schönberg. In *Memnon* there is an interval of an octave
plus a major sixth ; in *Freiwilliges Versinken* there are ninths
and sevenths.

 Is the transposition of Schubert's songs defensible ? Again,
it is a question for pragmatism. The answer depends on the
song and on the transposition. To judge from the numbers
of versions of the songs that exist in different keys Schubert
was not always attached to the key of his first conception. The
first three versions of *Geistesgruss* are in E♭, the fourth in
E ; and the first *Auf dem See* is in E, the second in E♭.
Unlike many composers, notably Beethoven, Schubert does
not seem to have attributed peculiar characteristics to the
different keys. (' B minor is black-coloured,' said Beethoven ;
and again, ' D♭, always maestoso ! ') The difference in key
that is frequent between Schubert's MSS. and the original
publications may sometimes be put down to the prejudice
of a cautious publisher against extreme keys. Hence, no
doubt, the appearance in A minor of *Du liebst mich nicht*,
whereas the MS. is in G♯ minor. We find the publisher
Schott of Mainz making a request for ' something in an easier
key,' and again, once at least, Schubert declining to transpose :
' I cannot write it otherwise, and anyone who cannot play
my work as it is had better leave it alone. Anyone who finds
some keys unmanageable is simply no musician at all ' (letter
to Spaun). Five of the ' Winterreise ' songs were transposed
down a tone, or in one instance (*Einsamkeit*) a minor third,
in the original publication, not on account of the pianist, but
obviously for the sake of a consistent vocal tessitura in the
cycle. It is not known whether this was Schubert's or the
publisher's doing ; but the only MS. is in the higher keys.
Die Rose, on the other hand, was published twice in Schubert's
lifetime in G, while the surviving MSS. are in F. *Sternennächte* was composed in D♭, but was published a minor
third lower.

 For the benefit of those who do not know Mandyczewski's
edition, be it said that the different versions he prints (as

distinguished from the different compositions of certain
poems) rarely offer any interest in their divergences.
Schubert hardly ever gave a glimpse into his workshop.
Thus *Erlkönig* from the first was, except for minutiæ, what
it was at the last. The impression nearly always is not of
deliberate revision, but of casual alterations made by Schubert
in the course of writing out a fresh copy for a friend. His
habit was not to work over a composition, but, if dissatisfied
with his music (or feeling that there was more to be said about
his delight in a poem), to write an entirely fresh setting.

Vogl, we know, used to transpose the songs. It is possible
to be fastidious beyond reason. Some listeners who cannot
help conjuring up the printed look of the music they hear,
dislike the transposition of *Erlkönig* to F minor, which quarrels
with their familiar mental picture. The objectionable transpositions are those that really alter the character of the music.
Erlkönig in E minor becomes a bass song. A minor third is
a serious difference in pitch, but not so serious as the exchange
of bass darkness and weightiness for the brilliance of the
tenor or high barytone. On this score Chaliapin did not
sing *Erlkönig*. Similarly *Die Allmacht*, transposed for contralto, is no longer the music that Schubert meant. He
obviously meant the high A in the last line, and nothing
else. It is a rather rare note in Schubert's song-writing ; he
did not ask for it without cause. It comes again at the
ringing climax of *Auflösung*, so emphatically in the design
that it would be improper to modify it by a single semitone.
There are, all the same, songs in which transposition can be
a positive advantage. *Aufenthalt* is more often well sung by
barytone in D minor than by tenor in E minor, the original
key, for the former voice has generally the wider effective
compass ; the tessitura of the song is unusual ; and the tenor
who is at home on the high G's rarely gives due weight to
the low B's on which at the beginning the music so much
depends. Schubert in composing the ' Winterreise ' thought
generally of a lower and darker voice than for ' Die schöne
Müllerin ' ; a good part of the music is in the normal high-
barytone compass. But, carried away by the spirit of certain
songs, the composer cast his mind back to the lighter and more
ringing voice ; and in *Wasserflut*, *Auf dem Flusse*, and *Mut*
he did not spare high A's. Already in the first edition, as
we have seen, some of the songs were transposed for the
sake of the cycle as a whole. In Peters's edition for medium
barytone only two songs are put down by as much as a minor
third below the 1828–9 edition ; and five are in the keys of

Schubert's MS. In the same edition of ' Die schöne Müllerin ' only two songs (*Mein !* and *Der Jäger*) are in the original keys ; three songs are down a minor third and three as much as a major third. Now, transposition by more than a tone is to be looked at askance. We draw the conclusion that Schubert's miller must be a tenor or a very light, high barytone, for the sake of brightness in the earlier scenes of the song-cycle and the general effect of youthfulness evidently designed by the composer. The adjustment needed to bring the ' Winterreise ' into the ordinary barytone range is excused by being less as well as by the more sombre spirit of the music. These considerations only regard the public presentation of the songs, when there are listeners to be convinced and won over. The domestic singer will naturally employ the most convenient means of approaching and exploring the music.[1]

Transposition of the songs affects the pianoforte only a degree less than the voice. Against drastic transposition there is the consideration that Schubert was reluctant to use the upper treble of the instrument in his song-writing. Even in the original keys the rippling that is characteristic of his pianoforte style is often rather surprisingly low on the keyboard. This rippling is the ' real ' music in Schubert's pianoforte writing as distinguished from what may be considered its allusions and reflections. Instances of these last are the noble progressions of semibreves in *Meeresstille* and *Grenzen der Menschheit*, in which Schubert was obviously referring the listener's mind to sounds beyond the actual sounds heard—to the thought of trombones, bassoons, and bass strings. The suggestion of sustained music is there conveyed also as much by the notation as by the too rapidly evaporating tone of the pianoforte. Schubert freely availed himself of both the oblique and the direct music of the instrument. The latter was not enough for all his purposes, but he delighted in it. How many of the favourite songs are about rivers and lakes, fishermen, millers, and mermaids ! To the Viennese the Danube is what to us is the sea. The great yellow river and the lakes and streams that feed it had for Schubert the pleasing associations of

[1] The first three volumes of Peters's popular edition are issued in three keys. There is an equal demand by high, middle, and low singers for Vol. I. Vols. II and III are in equal demand by middle and low, but the sale of the high-voice volume is 50 per cent. less. Vols. IV–VII are published in one key only and there is a steady if small demand for these. The information is given by Messrs. Hinrichsen.

holiday-land, and romance in the suggestion of a perpetual
journeying towards the unknown. As a duck to water his
fancy took to watery themes. A certain part of their attraction may be supposed to have lain in the ready expression
the pianoforte could give to thoughts of wavelike and eddying
motion. It was not a question of reproducing natural sounds.
These hardly serve the art of music. Schubert made a
number of pretty effects from birdcalls—lark, nightingale,
quail. But, for the rest, when there is a relationship between
a musical expression and a natural phenomenon the link is
simply the abstract idea they have in common. Schubert
was always drawing on his other senses to vivify his feeling
for sound ; and when a song of his is a comparative failure,
the reason, more often than not, is the failure of the poet
to create a clear visual impression. From time to time we
find the composer fumbling among confused images ; but
not when the poem describes coherently the things that he
knew. And given in particular a word about running water,
the plash of an oar, the glimpse of a trout, the possibility
of a nixie, he is quite happy. It is hard to count Schubert's
barcarolles. Sometimes the notes of the pianoforte seem to
drip from dabbling fingers :

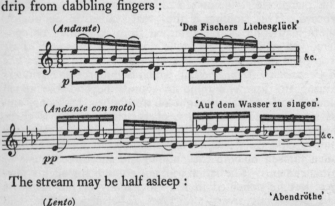

The stream may be half asleep :

Sometimes there is a leaping waterfall :

Tne brook haunts ' Die schöne Müllerin ' in a succession of moods. All these water motives are true pianoforte music and sound delightful, like the nearly related motives suggested by the waving of boughs (*Abendbilder* and *Lindenbaum*) and the spinning-wheel, and furthermore a great many figures of arpeggios and broken chords with rather less definite associations. The sweeping arpeggios of *Auflösung* make a fountain of music. The ' dripping ' figure of *Auf dem Wasser* must have remained in Schubert's mind with associations of happiness. In the late *Lebensmut* (1828) it developed no longer indolently but with exuberant spirit. *Das Lied im Grünen* is, as the pianoforte makes clear, really a brook song. The simple reiteration of chords is common in Schubert. It is a true pianoforte effect, one that offered the early composers for the instrument a dynamic variety and different degrees of staccato new in domestic keyboard music.[1] The

[1] Early pianofortes date from the beginning of the eighteenth century. In about 1770 the instrument began to appear as a serious rival of the harpsichord, which was ousted before the end of the century.

sonority obtained when the dampers were raised was an interest in itself, independent of figuration. Schubert resorted to this reiteration in *An die Musik*, his hymn to the art, in which he seems to have sought to reduce his utterance to the plainest and most essential state. The repeated chords simply add fullness to the sound and an emotional throbbing, and nothing in the way of extra argument.

It is a piece of fortune for us that Schubert's lifetime fell within the age of the pianoforte. The instrument was essentially what it is to-day. Only its compass was not so extended. Beethoven's Broadwood (1817) had only six octaves. Its tone was thinner, and the upper treble notes were no more than a tinkle. This Schubert found to have its value in instrumental works. In the B*b* pianoforte trio he used f''''. But in ' Die schöne Müllerin ' it is quite rare for the music to move within even two octaves of that note. The brook's purling is kept to the middle of the keyboard and is more often than not written in the bass clef. This brings us back to the thought of the intimate surroundings for which Schubert composed most of his songs. No doubt he wrote the almost symphonic trio with a view to an audience. In the ensemble, heard at a fair distance, the high notes would make a glitter. But in his song-writing Schubert must have feared the hardness of the highest octave, heard at close quarters. Judged by the sonorousness of the modern instrument he is felt to have been over-discreet.

*   *

*

Schubert's forms of song are two : the strophic, and the ' durchkomponiert ' or, as we might say, continuous, cyclic, onrunning. The origin of the former is folksong ; of the latter the operatic scena. The difference is, roughly, that between the stanza and blank verse. From one end of his career to the other Schubert composed in both forms, and he was never at the end of his resources in adapting them to his various purposes, either by stanzaic variations or by introducing into his ' blank verse ' different degrees of lyrical expression. *Die Erwartung* (1815) is a succession of declamatory verses alternating with lyrics. *Prometheus* (1819) is worked on a similar plan, but the texture is more closely knit and more artful ; the ' blank verse ' (recitative) tends towards songfulness and the lyric movements maintain the dramatic expression. *Grenzen der Menschheit* (1821) and *Der Zwerg* (1823) are astonishingly original compositions in

the onrunning style. Recitative and song merge here and
make a new unity. Such pieces, better than his operas, show
Schubert to have had within his grasp a lyrico-dramatic
style that might, in a few more years, and with the luck of
good poetic instigation, have carried all before it in the
operatic field. Here was the foundation of something very
like Wagner's melodious declamation.

The strophic songs do not call for the might-have-been
tense. They are the heart of Schubert. They vary in form
a good deal among themselves. There are a great many
examples of 'simple strophic form' (e.g. *Heidenröslein,
Who is Silvia?*), in which a set of stanzas is sung to identical
repetitions of a tune. Then Schubert writes a song like
Greisengesang which is in two parts, the second being a
repetition of the first with small but significant modifications.
This is the first stage of 'modified strophic form.' In
Greisengesang the sense of the text has suggested the modification ; in *Das Fischermädchen* the risk of monotony. The
three stanzas have the same tune only with the difference
that the middle repetition is modulated a minor third higher.
In many songs of three stanzas the first and third are set
alike and the middle one is given a contrasting setting (e.g.
Ihr Bild, Hölty's *An den Mond*). Or the first and second are
alike and a departure is made in the third (e.g. *Du bist die
Ruh'*). Or the first, third, and fifth are alike, and the second,
fourth, and sixth (*Fischerweise*). And so on, with any number
of variations and, according to the character of the poem,
additions of new material ; until in such a song as *Heiss mich
nicht reden* (the 1826 setting in E minor) Schubert is seen on
the point of departure from strophic form, for while the music
here is mainly lyrical and the poet's lines and stanzas are
clearly demarcated, not only is the second stanza set differently
from the first, but the music of the third makes no more than
allusions to the first, and is at moments definitely declamatory
in style.

'On the point of departure' is not meant to suggest a
progress. Schubert's song-writing in the simplest form was
not rudimentary. Works of art are not appraised according
to the degree of their elaboration, and there is no analogy
between artistic creation and natural evolution. Some of
Schubert's simplest strophic songs are negligible ; others
are miracles of art. It was not a form that he discarded as
he grew up. The form served a particular purpose, that is,
particular poems ; and so Schubert is found as late as 1827
using it at its barest for Herder's translation of *Edward*. It

was the most natural music for a narrative ballad. The
tune is in this case given over almost as raw material to the
singer ; or let us say a framework which the recital fills in,
rather on the analogy of plainsong psalm-tones. Repetition
does not stale a tune that is well composed for this purpose,
but can—as everyone knows in the case of plainsong—
strengthen it to the point of an incantatory effect. These
songs are only for the singer who is also something else—
an interesting narrator. The type has been styled ' the
simplest ' on grounds of musical texture ; but no one will
consider it a simple matter to compose tunes that defy repetition and are only strengthened by wear. They came as a
gift to Schubert. The wandering minstrels whose art has
survived only in folklore must have composed like this. Yes,
in Schubert we have a specimen of an elusive race, a folksong
composer, pinned down for once and documented ! It
happened, however, that few of his poets wrote narrative
ballads quite as naturally as he wrote tunes. Goethe could,
of course, do it better than anyone ; but *Der Gott und die
Bajadere*, to take an example, is really anything but the folk-
tale which Schubert, to judge by his simple minstrel-like
setting, took it for. This narrative is the poet's excuse for
displaying his art and pointing a more or less moral significance. Schiller's ballads were still less like the real thing ;
but for these Schubert had a different form and style. He
had an elaborate, illustrative style with nothing of folksong
in it ; and this, we may be sure, he would have developed
to dramatic purpose if he had lived into the 1840's and 1850's.
But our point at the moment is that Schubert had it in him
to be more primitive than the age into which he was born.
Some men are artists by a gift of expressing the particular
outlook of their contemporaries. Schubert was one of those
who would have been a singer, and simply a singer, in any
time or clime.

*   *

*

There is an idea of tune common to music and verse. Either
artist may draw on the other's work for tune ; the composer
finds it in the poet's verses, which in their turn may have
been started by music. And either may go for it to sources
behind words and tones—to the original pre-artistic tune in
things, the rhythm of a cantering horse, the beating heart.

> When that I was and a little tiny boy,
> With hey, ho, the wind and the rain.

That is the poetry of tune ; and when the musician who has a singing mind hears it, nothing else matters much, not scenery or psychology, but he is up with his answer to the challenge like the pugnacious nightingale that will wake at any hour to outsing the fellow in the neighbouring copse.

The instinctive bird in the young Schubert trilled delightfully at these provocations. The pages and pages of simple strophic songs in the 1815 volumes show how often the tune was the first and all-important thing to be made out of any set of lyrics he came upon. On one day (October 19, 1815), having composed a long and stately dramatic scene—the farewells of Hector and Andromache, from Schiller—he turned to song-writing and set seven of Kosegarten's poems. All these are in strophic form, and in fact anything more elaborate would have been almost impossible in a day's work, seeing that *Idens Schwanenlied*, for instance, consists of seventeen stanzas, *Schwanengesang* of seven, and *Luisens Antwort* of nineteen. In such pieces Schubert was often unsupported by the poet. What he had taken to be a song would turn out in the course of a stanza or two to be a piece of argument or reflection, and would go on far too long. It happens now and then with Schubert's strophic songs that one strophe is enough. *Sprache der Liebe* (A. W. Schlegel, 1816) is certainly spoilt by being sung four times. This beautiful serenade works up to a passionate effusion in the last eight bars. To repeat it da capo would make an effect like an Albert Hall encore. In *Lebensmut* (Rellstab, 1828) Schubert in the highest spirits has on the strength of the first stanza set out to write a dashing, captivating strophic song. His tune, however, is impossibly jaunty for the last stanza. Either he found it intractable or had not time to prolong and modify the music ; the song remains a fragment.

It is easy to use the word ' instinct ' too lightly. There is plenty of evidence of deliberation in Schubert's song-writing. When two ways of approach presented themselves, the lyrical and the dramatic, he hesitated, he experimented, he fumbled at times. An odd example is his setting of Goethe's *Sehnsucht* (1814). Caprice or obtuseness led him to break up a flowing lyric into little sections of recitatives and airs. There are a number of poems that he composed more than once, in different styles. The first of the three settings of *Des Mädchens Klage* (Schiller, 1814) is an onrunning composition, a more or less dramatic recital. Schubert returned to the poem in 1815 and again in 1816, and each time gave it a strophic setting, the 1815 song being the familiar one. Similarly

there are settings in different styles of Schiller's *Thekla*
(onrunning in 1813, strophic—the well-known song—in
1817).

There are others, but this is enough to show that Schubert
did not look upon the strophic song as an inferior or un-
developed form. There are hasty and trifling examples to
be found, but also, among the very slightest of his songs, a
profusion of little pieces so exquisitely wrought that while
another musical treatment might have been richer, nothing
could be more beautiful. Schubert knew better than anyone
how to let well alone. Consider the bareness of *Heidenröslein*,
and the absence of anything that could take from the plain
rustic impression of the song, once it had been safely provided
with its beautifully articulated melody. Brahms composed
settings of Hölty's *Mainacht* and *An die Nachtigall* magnificently, but he did not invalidate Schubert's settings,
which are tiny songs, but as precious as gems. One of the
simplest and least of all the songs in the ten volumes is the
Schweizerlied (Goethe, 1815), a sturdy little peasant tune.
Within eight bars Schubert writes something quite characteristic and memorable. The ease and accomplishment of
his movements in the smallest room are really incomparable.
Schubert may have been a rustic, but in such a song as *Die
Spinnerin* he exhibits a native aplomb in which no one has
ever surpassed him. He enters the scene, salutes, says something apt, and departs—all in a call of the briefest duration,
and with a simple grace so winning that all would like to
bring the pastoral melodist back. Which is the effect intended
—there are repeat-marks and more stanzas ready to gratify
us. In *Die Spinnerin* he does it airily ; in *Wehmut* (Salis,
1816) pensively, with a memorable modulation into the key
a minor third above his tonic in the course of his period of
sixteen bars. This is the gift of musical epigram ; possessing
it, Schubert (who has sometimes been held up as a meandering
and unpurposeful character) was ready to set Heine's poems
when they came his way, without a drop of dilution.

The small strophic songs are, however, not fully typical of
Schubert. They were only one side of the activities of his
youth. The other—less engaging in itself—was the production of dramatic and descriptive pieces, immensely long and
ambitious. Compositions like *Hagars Klage* and its successors
are derived through Zumsteeg from grand opera ; the little
songs so characteristic of 1815 from the ' Singspiel ' or ballad
opera. The mass of Schubert's representative songs belong
to the latter family ; which became in his hands so immensely

enriched and almost transformed by the characteristics of varying expression and illustrative detail taken over from the former. Typical Schubert is the simple strophic song with scenic accompaniment or (principally) the strophic song with modifications. Occasionally in his young days the composer, uplifted by the finest inspiration, wrote with all the richness of his maturity. But the style that became his to command was not all at once acquired. When at last he possessed it, we find that the descriptive narratives and scenas had contributed picturesque effects and dramatic accents, but that the foundation of the great lyrics was generally the ballad-opera ditty.

There are, after all, degrees of richness in beauty. Nothing could be better in its way than Schubert's *Schweizerlied*; and Wagner's music is no doubt not more beautiful than Morley's ' Lover and his Lass.' But practically these are after all small and rustic songs. There are degrees in the adequacy of equally beautiful musics to the contemporary need. There is Schubert's *Mainacht*, which is ousted, while Brahms's setting is sung every day : it is ideally beautiful, but it does not quite occupy the contemporary singer and it does not half occupy the pianist. The poetry of sheer tune is as precious as anything, and Feste's songs will outlive many philosophies ; but it is not the only poetry—was not, in Schubert's day, the only kind ; and Schubert, though he would have done no less well as an earlier or as a later man, belonged, after all, as the best artists do, to his time. We are fortunate in what was then surviving of the spirit of vagrant carolling ; and fortunate in that Schubert could in the very last of his songs still take down the homely zither and thrum for Nell and Fan so delightfully, with no more than a champion of village minstrelsy's awareness of the burden of art. But we are grateful too for the earnestness and pathos in the various new attempts made on the realities of feeling in the lyrics of the time ; for they induced Schubert to disclose more of himself and to expatiate (the more the better, since he was he)—notably by conveying much of the scene and the sense through the pianoforte, which could help immensely when sense and scene were serious and illustratable, and not divinely jingling nothings like Feste's wind and rain.

The romantic poets allowed nature and the weather a moral and not merely a tuneful importance ; and Schubert was at one with them. And they idolized the heart. They did not try to protect their sensibility ; they exposed it. All things were considered in relation to the heart. Nature's storm and

shine and the cycle of the seasons were looked on as the
reflections of a love affair. ' Mein Herz sieht an dem Himmel
gemalt sein eig'nes Bild.' They made a morality of living
passionately. If, as was more than likely, the worst happened, the consolation lay in the victim's pride in seeing all
the ruder sites of the world and nature's fiercer moods as
extensions of his unhappiness. ' Wie des Felsen uraltes
Erz, ewig derselbe bleibet mein Schmerz.' It was an ingenuous
outlook, but the typical poets of the time were extraordinarily
ingenuous in their expectations from life, in the importance
they attached to their feelings, and in their wounded
outcries, like disappointed children. ' Ich bin von aller
Ruh' geschieden, ich treib' umher auf wilder Fluth.' It was
not a witty literature. All this had something to do with
the genius of the German language. Even Goethe's love
poetry is not, like Dante's and Shakespeare's, intellectual.
He is close to nature (' Frühling, Geliebter ! ')—ready to
sink upon her bosom (' Balde ruhest du auch ! '). To the
last of his mistresses he writes with something of a boy's
candour. Petrarch showed his century one way of poetic
sentiment ; and Goethe another to Schubert's generation.
It did not trouble about intellectual subtleties, but claimed
attention by a spirited sincerity that rendered a declaration
important by the force of the relation between its words and
the facts. The romantic poets felt, or at least did their best
to feel, with terrible intensity, and to mean what they said.
A serenade would end with a threat of suicide ; and that
was not to be taken simply as a convention, since a crop of
actual suicides had been produced by Werther's example.
It seems to us that Schubert felt the intense and moving
modern poetry to demand an especially rich and novel music.
His sympathy with the new schools of German verse was in
part the cause of his embellishing and development of the
strophic form which had been used at its simplest for a good
proportion of his 1815-17 settings of the minor eighteenth-
century poets, Claudius, Hölty, Matthisson, Jacobi, Kosegarten, Salis, whom he presumably felt to be as a rule more
formal and old-fashioned in sentiment. He was capable of
treating their pathos nonchalantly. Thus *Daphne am Bach*
(Stolberg, 1816) is, in spite of Daphne's tears, merely a ditty,
not a declaration or a lament. The pianoforte's semiquavers
do indifferently for the brook and for the poplars in the
second stanza. The brook has, in fact, not taken Schubert's
fancy. Nor has the maiden's plaint made any particular
impression. He evidently considers it quite perfunctory.

Perhaps the name ' Daphne ' seemed to his simple taste pretentious and make-believe. The song, the dullest of Schubert's brook songs, has however the interest, rare in our composer, of hinting at a later song, no other than *Wohin?* Daphne's first words are ' Ich hab' ein Bächlein funden,' and when in 1823 Schubert came upon the miller's ' Ich hört' ein Bächlein rauschen,' the similarity of the line must have called up the 1816 song :

But the brook is all-important in the miller's song. He has taken it for his guide. Where are those triplets off to ? From G into D, and then with a twist to E minor—then with an artful return to what looks like the beginning of the song ; but nothing is quite the same again, for the miller is off on his travels and every stage of the journey is different.

But if *Wohin?* is a masterpiece and *Daphne* only a trifling song, it does not follow that stationariness is less interesting in Schubert than development. A strophic song that he enriched by his scenic art to a degree as interesting as dramatic development is *Auf dem Wasser zu singen*. It is a song of idleness that says nothing and goes nowhere, but swings delightfully at its mooring in the summer twilight ; and Schubert makes us content with idleness. The composer sometimes chose the stationary scene as the better part even when the poet had indicated a development. *Auf dem Wasser* calls to mind *Des Fischers Liebesglück* with its similar barcarolle figure. A whole series of events between the lover's first anticipation and the gratification of his desires are in this song of 1827 merged by Schubert into one impression of indolent serenade and purling river. He saw that there was nothing of much dramatic interest in the boatman's natural satisfaction, and that the charm lay in the romantic surroundings of the assignation. The lover is an oarsman, not a self-analyst, and Schubert is right in sweeping all his words, such as they are, along to the one tune of the dark river.

With this general treatment, let us compare the composer's delicate touch in *Greisengesang*, which was mentioned a

moment ago as a song in which the second half is a repetition
of the first with very small modifications. The key is B minor,
and a characteristic of the first melodic period is the full close
in D major in the fourth bar and again in the twelfth. The
effect is of well-pondered statement. ' Frost has berimed my
house-roof ; age has whitened the thatch of my head.' But
in the second part questions are asked where statements had
before been made ; and now in the D major cadence the
composer raises the voice at the end of the enquiring phrases
from tonic to mediant. ' Are the streams of happiness dried ?
Have the nightingales all taken wing ? ' This delicacy
was not a lately acquired characteristic of Schubert's. As
early as 1814 he wrote an unmodified strophic song when
a poem struck him as rather a synopsis than a developing
statement (e.g. Goethe's *Nachtgesang*) ; but into his setting
of Goethe's *Schäfers Klagelied* he introduced several variations
of treatment, charmingly attentive to the details of the shepherd's predicament. The poem is in six quatrains. Schubert
uses four different melodies, all in pastoral 6-8 rhythms, in
the order *a b c d b a*. ' How often have I stood staring down
towards the valley ! ' The plaintive melody is in C minor.
' Following my browsing sheep, I have to-day come down—
but truly I know not why.' The melancholy of the opening
lifts a little. The flock and the friendly dog distract the
shepherd's thoughts for a moment ; and, besides, he nurses
a secret hope. The new melody in E♭ is placid. As the
shepherd pauses to sigh there is a break of a bar, and then a
modulation to G minor. ' The grass down here is full of
flowers. I gather them—but for whom ? ' The springing
flowers set up a dance of semiquavers, and the melody *c*, in
A♭, is a particularly graceful one. ' And now it thunders
and down comes the rain ; and no shelter for me but a tree.'
The storm breaks in A♭ minor. ' For the house-door is
bolted and barred. Ah, it was all a dream ! ' These are the
last two lines of the fourth quatrain. The storm music has
ceased, and the words are uttered above a subdued accompaniment with the effect of recitative. ' Now a rainbow stands
out clear above the house. But she, she has left the country,
has gone far away.' The rainbow brings back the placid E♭
melody. ' Gone away, and where and how far, who knows ?
Perhaps beyond the sea. Come, sheep, move up ! Ah,
how heavy your shepherd's heart is ! ' G minor leads this
time back into C minor ; and to the sad strain of the opening
the pastoral group moves out of sight.

Such is an early example of Schubert's ' modified strophic ' song-writing. In this form or rather style he was in the next fourteen years to compose a marvellous music ; a music which, while retaining the prized ' idleness ' of lyrical quality, enriched itself through its author's delight in landscape and atmospheric influences and his fund of sympathy with all the vicissitudes of the heart. The variations in Schubert's free strophic songs are not to be classified. They are his appropriate response to endless different appeals. At this point, then, generalization had better give place to another manner of approach. Let us take the songbooks in their order, and glance at the individual pieces.

IV

THE SONGS OF 1811–1814

SCHUBERT was born a schoolmaster's son on January 31, 1797, at Lichtenthal, a suburb of Vienna. Music was cultivated at home, and the boy's ability was further developed by lessons from the parish organist in whose choir he sang. In the autumn of 1808 there was an examination of candidates for the imperial court chapel choir. Schubert's voice and his ready sight-reading easily won him a place. The choristers were foundationers at the ' Konvikt,' an institution established by Francis II in 1802. It was the principal boarding-school in Vienna, attended by the sons of officials and the upper burgessy. At the imperial chapel Antonio Salieri (Mozart's and Beethoven's Salieri) was the first choirmaster. Not only the choristers received musical instruction at the Konvikt. Music was an important subject. Violin and pianoforte were taught by Wenzel Ruziczka, a Moravian, who also conducted the school orchestra. Detailed accounts of Schubert the schoolboy have come down to us from some of his schoolfellows, notably Spaun and Holzapfel. The boys were ill-fed, but we hear nothing of bullying, although Schubert was a small and shy boy. The musical instruction was not very methodical, but then the Konvikt was not primarily a school of music. Schubert might have been more conscientiously taught ; but at least he was by no means starved for music. As a violinist in the school orchestra he learnt to know the works of Haydn, Mozart, and Cherubini.

The earliest known compositions date from 1810. A set of pianoforte variations of that year is lost, but there exists a long duet fantasia, ' begun April 8, finished May 1.' To the year 1811 belong the first of the songs and a number of instrumental works—a pianoforte fantasia, a string quartet, a quintet. Spaun speaks also of a short opera. This was the period when (according to a myth, first propagated but later denied by Walter Dahms) Schubert's father, exasperated by the boy's neglect of general studies in his preoccupation with music, forbade him the house. During the proscription his mother died (on May 28, 1812, of typhus), and father and son are said to have been reconciled at her grave.

A great number of compositions belong to 1812, including four string quartets, a Kyrie in D. minor for choir and small orchestra, an overture in D written for the school orchestra, a trio for pianoforte, violin, and viola, and a number of minuets for strings, with which (says Spaun) Schubert himself felt pleased. Salieri began to show interest in the boy and gave him lessons, which were continued after Schubert's Konvikt days.

The 1813 compositions include five string quartets, a birth-day ode for his father (written for two tenors, bass, and guitar), a fantasia in C minor for pianoforte duet, funeral music for wind instruments, and the opening movements of two masses. At the end of the school year, in August 1813, Schubert left the Konvikt and went back home. His father had already re-married. Too short to be conscripted into the army, Schubert decided to take to his father's profession, and in the autumn of 1813 he began a course of ten months at a teachers' training college. He completed in this October his first symphony in D.

Schubert was not entirely absorbed by his studies at the St. Anna College, as the copious compositions of 1814 prove. He wrote his first mass in F between May 17 and July 22. The first performance, on October 16 at the Lichtenthal church, was a great family event. There were also two string quartets written in 1814, in D and B♭, Schubert's Nos. 7 and 8. The latter was first performed publicly in 1862 and published a year later. To 1814 belongs the opera ' Des Teufels Lustschloss,' which Schubert wrote under Salieri's guidance. Meanwhile, in August, he passed the leaving examination of the training college reasonably well. The examiner's report gives him ' good ' in most subjects, ' moderate ' in a few, and ' bad ' only in divinity. He is industrious. He is passed as an assistant master. In the autumn of 1814 Schubert entered his father's school, where he taught for the best part of three years. Schubert was seventeen ; and on October 19 he wrote the first of his Goethe songs, *Gretchen am Spinnrade.*

* *

*

Mandyczewski's first volume opens with *Hagars Klage* (poem by Schücking of Münster), which Schubert dated March 30, 1811. Subject and manner were directly derived

from Zumsteeg, whom Schubert had adopted as his tutor.
The poor victim of Abraham's and Sarah's ruthlessness
sustains her lament throughout thirteen movements, occupy-
ing fifteen pages. Such compositions, of which the youthful
Schubert left several examples, are not songs ; and they call
for no more than a passing reference. The vogue of this
kind of cantata has so far disappeared that it is difficult to
imagine what was its practical function in musical life. Vocal
compositions on the scale of Schubert's *Hagar* and his settings
of enormous extracts from Schiller and Ossian require some
other interest—of form, of technical display, or of orchestral
colour—which Zumsteeg and Schiller did not provide.
Imagine Wotan's tale in ' Die Walküre ' with nothing before
it or after, no stage picture to distract the eye, and no orchestra
to relieve the ear. The music of the Zumsteegian cantata is
loose and rambling. It forgoes form on its own account.
It does not grip the poem, but hangs to its skirts. Yet
Zumsteeg had a vogue, which must be put down to the
extraordinary admiration general at that time for the poetry
he illustrated, and to a lingering primitive feeling that all
verse was naturally meant to be chanted. He charmed the
schoolboy Schubert, and that has its interest for us. He
encouraged him in diffuseness, he set before him poems that
were little suited for music. But he also opened to him
vistas of the romantic world. Technically, his changes of
key and time signatures gave Schubert the hint to shift his
ground in quick obedience to his poet. It has been suggested with cogency[1] that Schubert's early exercises in
Zumsteegian recitative and arioso helped to form his ability
later on to draw out the melody implicit in any verse. Not
that there is anything Schubertian about Zumsteeg. He is
mediocre and dull. His declamation in *Hagar* is perhaps
more consistent than Schubert's ; but Schubert, who stumbles
now and then, shows already an imaginative eagerness and
a will to soar (for instance, in the phrase in the first page
when the Egyptian wails that her son is in the throes of death,
and especially in the broad phrases of the final adagio, ' Open
your parched lips, Ishmael, cry out upon injustice to just
God ! ') which overwhelm Zumsteeg.

Schubert, who has begun his *Hagar* in C minor and has
wandered through many keys, finds himself at the end in A♭.
Salieri might disapprove, but sanction was to be found in
Zumsteeg. For although the latter does manage to end his
Hagar as he began, in C minor, he has a setting of Schiller's

[1] By A. H. Fox Strangways.

Ritter Toggenburg which begins in G, spends some time in F, and ends in A♭, an unconventional not to say vagrant scheme. There are half a dozen examples among Schubert's 1811-14 songs of such meanderings, for which even later he now and then showed a weakness, for instance in *Berthas Lied in der Nacht* of 1819, which begins in E♭ minor and ends in F♯ ; and in *Orest auf Tauris* of 1820, which begins in C minor and ends in D.

Schubert's first attempt at setting *Des Mädchens Klage* (Thekla's song from Schiller's ' Piccolomini ') is a curious juvenile piece. The odd thing is that he refused to see Schiller's lyric as a song. ' Thekla takes her lute and sings,' says the dramatist's direction ; but Schubert insists on staging the maiden's plaint as a scena or cantata. There are three main movements and a piece of recitative. Words and phrases are helplessly repeated. Schubert tells us four times in ten bars that the oak-wood roars. The syncopated misaccentuation of the first words, ' Der Eichwald,' is like nothing else in Schubert. Perhaps it was meant to suggest the dislocation caused by the storm ; but it was not a happy device and seems less so than ever now that the musicians of the cotton plantations have made it their own. The one interest of the song resides in the dashing D minor strokes by which Schubert has indicated the storm. Of his three settings of this poem, the celebrated one is the second, dated 1815.

We come to *Eine Leichenphantasie*, a prodigy of application and copiousness, running to eighteen pages. It was like a schoolboy to be interested by this schoolboyish set of verses. Schiller attempts to freeze our marrow by describing an unconventional funeral. The deceased is a young man of promise, and the sole mourner his aged father. The humanity of the case is, however, not the poet's subject. It is an exercise in the macabre. Therefore the funeral is at night, the wind is a ghost and the attendants at the ceremony are ghostlike. The thud of the coffin is made much of, and the creaking of the gates of the vault. The imagery and the ideas are alike in poor taste ; but the verses served the boy Schubert to practise his pen. At Christmas that year Schubert's amusement took the form of working on a similar large and grisly composition, *Der Vatermörder* (Pfeffel). This is a ballad of a parricide, his remorse, madness, confession, and doom, with an envoy addressed to conscience. It is dated December 26, 1811.

The peculiar interest attaches to *Der Jüngling am Bach*

(Schiller) of being Schubert's first true song. It is moreover
a piece of real beauty. Schubert dated it September 24, 1812.
The verses, a set of four stanzas, are to be found in a comedy,
' Der Parasit,' translated by Schiller from the French of
L. B. Picard. The attraction they had for Schubert is shown
by his returning to them twice again in later years. The poor
soul who sits sighing by the stream and weaving a wreath
of flowers is a youth whose fair is above him in station. He
says nothing that characterizes him very distinctly ; but the
young Schubert had compassion to spare, and he found for the
trochaic verses an engaging melody. This he effectively
varied from stanza to stanza, notably by a passionate descent
to D minor (the main key being F) when the complaint is
that cheerful nature's thousand voices cannot find an echo in
the love-lorn breast. The vocal part of the song is genuinely
Schubertian ; only the pianoforte part is a mere accompaniment, and frequently wooden at that. The composition
had a sequel, one of an uncommon sort in Schubert's practice.
In 1815 he took up this 1812 song again and much revised
and simplified it. He changed the key from F to F minor,
brought the melody (which had ranged over an octave and a
fourth) within an octave, and set all four stanzas to it without
modification. The result is a little song, more smooth and
neat than the first, but not distinguished. The uncouthness
was gone, but something of value too. Better known than
either the 1812 song or its revision is the entirely new setting
of the poem composed in 1819.

Klaglied (Rochlitz), also of 1812, was Schubert's first song
in simple strophic form. It is a maiden's lament, full of
tenderness and pathos ; and coming so early it does something
to prepare us for *Gretchen am Spinnrade* of 1814 :

'Klaglied.'

(*Lento.*)

Mei-ne Ruh' ist da-hin,   mei-ne Freud' ist ent-floh'n

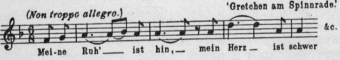

'Gretchen am Spinnrade.'

(*Non troppo allegro.*)

Mei-ne Ruh'___ ist hin,___ mein Herz___ ist schwer

Hölty's name first appears on a song of 1813, *Totengräberlied*.
A gravedigger sings thanks to his spade in a spirit of mock
merriment. The voice starts off ' Dig, spade, dig ! ' in
declamatory manner, in E minor, and then breaks into a

jovial G major ditty. Schubert gives the song a forced, irregular, and sardonic character by starting the stanzas in different keys (G, C, A minor), inventing for them varying but similarly shaped tunes as he goes along. It is a curious little piece.

Schubert's first setting of Schiller's *Sehnsucht* is dated April 15–17, 1813. The poet here describes the world of the ideal—an air filled with harmony, incessant sunshine, gardens productive of golden fruit and flowers all the year round. He has had glimpses of it all through the clouds of normal existence, but a torrent rolls between this land and that. There is a boat by which to cross, but no pilot. Never mind! Trust to Faith as pilot. Trust to a miracle, for only by a miracle can the miraculous world be entered! This poem is high-minded but rather vague in a truly Schillerian way. The young Schubert starts off without a qualm to describe the aspiration and the vision in a swinging D minor movement. The obstacle of the torrent brings in a figure of solemn dotted semiquavers, the rocking boat also gets a descriptive page. This leads to a victorious finale in F, in which Schubert shows every confidence in the easy triumph of faith over reality. The last section is all that was retained in the more familiar setting of the poem composed in 1819. Schiller, reproached with having in his celebrated ' Wallenstein ' trilogy left uncertain the fate of the gentle Thekla, Wallenstein's daughter, replied with the stanzas *Thekla, eine Geisterstimme* which Schubert first set in 1813 and again (the familiar song) in 1817. Thekla, says the spirit voice, is reunited with him she lost on earth, and her father too is there, washed clean of all the blood he had shed. The 1813 setting, in which recitative alternates with small stretches of melody, hardly detains us.

Der Taucher (Schiller), begun in the same year, and finished in 1814, imposes itself by sheer bulk : it is a matter of thirty pages. It is moreover the earliest of these enormous ballad-cantatas to be well known through being included in Peters's edition. Schiller tells of a medieval king who casts a precious goblet into a whirlpool, offering it as a free gift to anyone of his courtiers who will retrieve it. His entourage are unresponsive, but at last a youth volunteers to make the attempt. He dives into Charybdis, and presently emerges with the goblet. It is, however, his misfortune to be so eloquent in his description of submarine monsters (dragons and sea-serpents were, he avers, among the horrors he encountered) that the king induces him to explore once more

the deeps, promising him this time his daughter's hand in
marriage. The bold youth plunges again into the whirlpool
and is seen no more.

The tale (said to have originated in an episode at the court
of a fourteenth-century Sicilian prince) somehow leaves us
cold. It is no surprise to learn that Schiller admitted to
Goethe he had never seen even a waterfall, let alone Charybdis.
Boccaccio could have told the story; but Schiller was
lacking in fantasy, and his expositions of exaggerated chivalry
seem in consequence to verge on the fatuous. There was
nothing to be done musically with his *Taucher*, but the attempt
served Schubert at sixteen as an exercise. He had by this
time a good deal at his finger-tips. And what activity and
self-confidence ! *Der Taucher* shows him covering yards and
yards of surface, like a scene-painter. The result is not
intrinsically interesting. It could not have been said on the
strength of this music that the composer had genius; but
it proved him extraordinarily enterprising and competent.
His ballad could hardly have been bettered; it was the very
thing for an audience that liked to hear Schiller's works
arranged for musical declamation.

In the song *Verklärung* of 1813 Schubert has set Herder's
translation of Pope's *Vital spark of heavenly flame*. Many
grown composers might have been proud to acknowledge
this song. The recitatives are telling; the short cantabile
sections have upward-striving phrases and a serious pulsing
accompaniment. Oddly enough, Pope's last words, ' O death,
where is thy sting ? ' fit Schubert's notes better than does
the German. Although not like mature Schubert, it is not
immature music. The association of Pope and Schubert is
curious enough to make the song memorable. The first
of the Italian songs which Schubert wrote for Salieri's eye
also belong to 1813. The best is *Pensa, che questo istante*
(text from Metastasio's ' Alcide '), for bass : a piece of music
of grave and perhaps rather consciously noble character.
The accompaniment is very repressed. It is noticeable in
all Schubert's Italian songs, beautiful though they often are,
how little there is of his picturesque fancy in the detail.
The stately vocal line in this song makes it grateful to a
sonorous bass. *Don Gayseros* is a set of three songs (text
from a novel by La Motte Fouqué), of minor interest. The
swinging melody of the second is more characteristic than
the rest.

In 1814 Schubert set thirteen poems by Matthisson. These
songs are small and do not assert themselves much, but they

have no little sweetness and tenderness. Take *Andenken*.
The poet tells when and how he thinks of his fair ; and asks
how and when she thinks of him. Beethoven set this poem
in a peculiarly unsympathetic way. Schubert has by force
of simple, affectionate feeling got nearer the mark. This
Andenken foretells many of the lesser German love songs
of the century. Schubert's *Adelaïde*, on the other hand,
cannot vie with Beethoven's classic song. It is altogether
more modest and more intimate. The melody is rich at the
beginning, but is not well sustained. The song rewards the
sympathetic eye with pretty and sensitive details ; but
Schubert's inexperience is seen in the trying tessitura.
It is almost impracticably high, at least if the song is to be
sung in an intimate style. There are little jets of pure melody
in the Matthisson songs, for instance in *Lied aus der Ferne*.
In two of them, *Die Betende* and *An Laura*, Schubert drew
on rich and unctuous hymn-tune harmonies as suitable to
accompany a maiden's devotions. It is not a very far cry
to Elizabeth's prayer in 'Tannhäuser.' *Der Geistertanz*,
a puerile poem about midnight spectres in a church,
was not worth setting ; but Schubert after all was still a
boy. He found a pointed and straddling C minor theme
for this trivial dance of the dead. Another ghost story is
Romanze, which tells of an heiress who perishes, the victim of
a miserly uncle ; and who haunts a tower, the place of her
death. *Trost an Elisa* is interesting. It is a delicately written
piece of accompanied recitative, which the pianoforte enriches
at the cadences with expressive part-writing. Interventions
of recitative are frequent in this set of songs, even when purely
lyrical treatment was to be expected. Usually they are formal,
making a distinct break in the movement ; but in the middle
of *Totenopfer*, an affecting little composition, there is a
deviation, quite slight, from song to declamation, such as
we often find in the later Schubert. A variety of small
devices (for instance, the different accompaniments to the
repetitions of the melody in *Andenken* and *Lied der Liebe*)
makes these little Matthisson songs attractive to the
Schubertian.

There are two Schiller songs of the same period. *An
Emma* is an address to a lost mistress—lost but not (this is
the poet's last drop of grief) not dead. He could, he says,
have borne her death better than his rejection. The sentiment, which Schiller expresses apparently without a suspicion
of irony, was a difficult one to make a song of. The youthful
Schubert observes that something serious is in the air (' lost

happiness, stars, death, life, dead love '), and composes sad, deferential harmonies, which might have recaptured the lost Emma if she was sentimentally disposed, but would not have overcome a sense of humour. There are three versions with smallish divergencies The song was the earliest of Schubert's songs to be published in his lifetime except as supplements to periodicals. It appeared as Op. 58 together with two other Schiller settings in 1826. *Das Mädchen aus der Fremde* is again a rather vague allegorical poem. A mysterious maiden brings rare gifts for mankind, the best being reserved for loving couples ; she goes, and leaves no trace of her passage. The setting is a simple pastoral 6–8 movement.

Gretchen am Spinnrade was Schubert's first song on a poem of Goethe's. It was composed on October 19, 1814. Was it suggested that an earlier song had prepared us for it ? That must be retracted. Nothing explains such things. In the thirty songs that came before it Schubert had toiled, tested himself, had had his charming moments, and now and again had fumbled. This time he was transported by his genius.

Faust has wooed, he has won. The poor girl sits at her spinning-wheel bewildered in the throes of first love :

> ' My heart is lead. I shall never, never again know peace of mind. My crazy head thinks of nothing but him. How handsome and noble he was ! Then his laugh, his way of speaking, the touch of his hand, the touch of his lips ! Something in me cries out for this—to kiss him once more and then to die.'

The verses of her song are beautifully simple, touching, and true. It was not only that. Schubert had not merely picked out the song ; he had been reading ' Faust,' so much we know from the setting he composed a few weeks later of the Church Scene (for two soloists and chorus). Let everyone think of his first reading of ' Faust.' The thought is irresistible of Schubert's quivering over Gretchen and her troubles. She was real, a suffering human. That must have seemed wonderful after the allegorical virgins with accessories in the other poets. The ensnared girl, the lovely verses, and the spinning-wheel—these all seized hold of Schubert, they extorted a song out of him. He saw, he heard, he understood in a marvellous moment. His everyday songs are before us, they are likeable. But in the light of this *Gretchen* they are seen to have only the attraction of the relations of a beloved person. Traits that were dimly Gretchen-like have been noticed in earlier pages; but returning to the song again we admire it with a renewed emotion and wonder.

The wheel whirrs, the foot mechanically works the treadle; that is the picture in the music, that and the distressed singer who begins her soft monotonous wail that is to rise to an outcry. Peace of mind is all, so far, that is lost. The heart is heavy only with longing. The sorrier stages are to come later in *Ach, neige, du Schmerzenreiche* and *Wie anders, Gretchen*. The poem consists of ten little stanzas, the first of which is twice repeated in the way of a burden. Schubert brings in the first lines yet again at the end. Gretchen has cried her longing for death—death in the lover's arms—but she has to live yet, oppressed and bewildered. Unrest, let it be observed, and not despair is the mood of the song; but the singer may also remember that Gretchen is to despair before long. The wheel and the treadle make a music that is at once monotonous and agitated. Then the girl's heart beats faster the more she thinks over her torment; and unconsciously her foot works faster too, sending the wheel up in pitch from D minor to E minor and to F. The recurrence of the burden always brings back D minor. She pictures her lover's look, his laugh, his words, the pressure of his hand; and the pitch rises excitedly to B*b*. His kiss! The wheel is still. Entranced, she has without noticing it stopped her foot. She pauses; but must return to the task and the sad refrain, and the wheel takes up again its semiquavers in D minor. In the latter part of the song comes the cry for love and death: an unanswered cry, and at the end the whirring slows down in the overcast key of the beginning.

It was Schubert's first masterpiece. There had been nothing at all like it in music before. The plan of the song—an extended plaint, freely varied from stanza to stanza, but held together by persistent rhythmical figures of poetic origin and picturesque value—was as original as everything in the working-out was faultless. Yet this was no long-elaborated achievement. Every probability is that Schubert composed the song in a kind of transport, and did not himself appreciate all its implications; for we find him a few weeks later setting another poem of Goethe's, *Sehnsucht*, in a way that is no more than quaint and juvenile, with short alternating recitatives and airs essentially inappropriate to a headstrong lyric of passion. *Sehnsucht* is a Zumsteegian cantata on a small scale. That December 7 was then for Schubert a rather dull day ; and yet *Sehnsucht* contains details so pretty that it would have made a red-letter day for another man.

Gretchen am Spinnrade was published as Op. 2 on April 30, 1821, dedicated to Moritz Count von Fries, the banker, Anselm Hüttenbrenner's patron, to whom Beethoven had dedicated some of his early chamber music. Fries gratified Schubert with 20 ducats. Other settings of ' Meine Ruh' ist hin ' are by Zelter, Loewe, and Spohr.

Schubert's second Goethe song was *Nachtgesang* (November 30, 1814). The poem is one of the most delicate of serenades. The lover does not ask more of his fair than to listen to his rhymes in her sleep. These rhymes are only two. On them Goethe prettily rings the changes through five little quatrains. Schubert's setting is one of the tiniest of his strophic songs. In the space of fourteen bars he has written a perfect little piece of music, a trifle playful, a trifle appealing, a trifle sleepy. *Trost in Thränen* (Goethe) was composed on the same day. The poem is an exhortation to a sentimentalist in the form of a dialogue. The sentimentalist has the last word : his reason for moping is that he enjoys moping. Schubert sets the questions simply in F major, the answers in F minor with a characteristic turn towards the major at the end.

There comes an exquisite song, *Schäfers Klagelied*. Goethe wrote the poem at Jena in 1801. His shepherd says :

> ' I could not help driving my flock down the valley to-day. Why ? There was no reason. And why have I gathered these flowers ? There is no one to give them to. The house is shut, the door bolted. And she—she is gone, she is so far away that I cannot think how far. Come, sheep, come up ! Ah, if you only knew how heavy your shepherd's heart was ! '

The song looks ordinary enough at a passing glance. Schubert had already used all these means before : the pastoral 6-8 movement, the different figures of broken chords. The piece is crystal clear. Yet it is packed with artfulness in workmanship. A glance has already been cast at a few of the points of its workmanship. It is a sweet song ; it is dainty, amusingly dainty. Is that unfair to the sorrowing swain ? We are perhaps not quite sure about him. He is rather too

charming for the shepherd he pretends to be. Goethe began
his poem in the manner of German folksong, but some graces
belonging to another clime found their way into the piece.
Schubert has perhaps not been able quite to picture to himself
this tender shepherd ; and hence his song sets us exclaiming
rather at its prettiness than its sorrow. But what a prettiness
—in the chain of melodies, in the modulations, in the picturesque illustration of the flowers, the shower, the shut
door ! The *Schäfers Klagelied* crowned the career of the
marvellous boy who on the strength of this song, and the
Matthisson series which led to it, might at this moment have
been judged almost too clever and delicate and certain of
stroke to possess the passion and adventurousness of genius.
It happened, however, that on a recent and precise date the
man of genius had been disclosed. The *Schäfers Klagelied*,
so charming in its melancholy, so trained in expression, in
design so intricate and balanced, appears to us like a priceless
little object of virtù. It is therefore surprising to read of
its composer :

   ‘ Schubert is conspicuous among great composers for
   the insufficiency of his musical education. His extraordinary gifts and his passion for composing were from the
   first allowed to luxuriate untrained. He had no great talent
   for self-criticism, and the least possible feeling for abstract
   design, and balance and order. . . .’ (C. H. H. Parry’s
   ‘ Art of Music.’)

Mandyczewski prints two versions of *Schäfers Klagelied*,
the first in E minor, the second in C minor. Virtually the
only difference between them is the prelude of four bars
which is deleted from the second version. We hear of public
performances of the song in 1819, and it was published with
three other short Goethe songs as Op. 3 in the summer of
1821, dedicated to Ignaz von Mosel. He was vice-director
of the court theatres, a composer of a sort (his perversions
of Handel earned him Beethoven’s ridicule), and also, it is
said, the first conductor to use a stick.
   At the end of the year 1814 there came Schubert’s first
Mayrhofer song, *Am See*, composed (on the same day as
Goethe’s *Sehnsucht*), before the musician had made the
poet’s acquaintance. What attracted Schubert was evidently
the description of the pleasing scene of the lake where the
poet sat musing. This is set to an easy barcarolle movement
in G minor. The musings become less tractable, and

Schubert resorts to recitative and two or three different movements. Singers have no doubt been puzzled by Mayrhofer's praise here of the heroic Leopold whose deeds dimmed Thermopylæ and Marathon. The reference is to Leopold Duke of Brunswick, soldier and philanthropist, who lost his life in rescuing victims of a flood at Frankfort-on-Oder in 1785.

V

SONGS OF 1815

SCHUBERT is eighteen, an assistant master in his father's school at a yearly salary of 40 gulden or about 32s. It is the year of an immense number of compositions. Schubert had begun his second symphony in B♭ in the previous December. The work was finished in March. His first pianoforte sonata in E♭ (unfinished) was written in February. In the first week of March he composed his second mass in G, and later in the month (also within a week) his ninth string quartet in G minor. Another symphony, the third in D, was composed in the summer, and in the late autumn another mass, No. 3 in B♭. There were a number of lesser church compositions, secular choruses, and pianoforte pieces, as well as four operatic works—' Der vierjährige Posten ' (libretto by Körner), ' Fernando ' (Stadler), ' Claudine von Villa Bella ' (Goethe), and ' Die Freunde von Salamanca ' (Mayrhofer). It was also the year of 144 songs.

About twenty of these are of the very finest quality. A good many more are songs the Schubertian finds interesting. Beyond these are a number that are more or less negligible. That word will become harder and harder to use in our progress. Here it is used only reluctantly, on mere practical grounds. For hardly one of the light and slight little songs would, in point of fact, fail to repay an adequate singer. Thus a tenor with John MacCormack's persuasiveness would make an irresistible thing of the high-lying melody of *Als ich sie erröten sah* (Ehrlich). It is a simple-looking song; but only a tiro or a virtuoso would essay it. Then there are the numerous extended compositions in various movements. They are usually less inviting than the little strophic songs; yet hardly one is without a beautiful page, whatever the inequalities of the whole. The first of the 1815 songs, *Auf einen Kirchhof* (Schlechta), is one of these. It opens with beautiful, serene expression; but Schubert has adopted a quasi-dramatic form and the song fails through excess of exertion. The poem, moreover, is rather trying, like so many German churchyard soliloquies.

Some of the longest pieces ' are settings of Schiller's poems.
Die Erwartung is a cantata of eleven pages. In five long
stanzas the poet's fancies play about the expected coming of
his mistress. Five times he believes her to be approaching,
and is mistaken. In the envoy she steals upon him unawares.
It is one of the Charlotte von Lengefeld poems. To compose
music for it was an impossible enterprise ; but Zumsteeg
had attempted it and therefore Schubert did. He followed
Zumsteeg's plan of alternate recitative and arioso and far
outmatched him. He did everything that was possible.
The piece contains numbers of good things, if nothing that
is pre-eminently Schubertian. It is thoroughly well-written
music, and yet as the piece goes on circling and we find there
is to be no advance, it has to be admitted dull. A still longer
composition, *Die Bürgschaft* (Schiller), a matter of nineteen
pages, is markedly inferior. This ballad tells the story of
Damon, Pythias, and the tyrant Dionysius, with much im-
probable detail. In *Die Erwartung* Schubert exerted himself
to enrich a stationary subject. In *Die Bürgschaft* his music
is the merest accompaniment to the moral and panoramic
narrative, with hardly one characteristic touch. *Klage der
Ceres* is but another of the youthful exercises in Zumsteeg's
manner. It is a setting, sixteen pages long, of all Schiller's
eleven stanzas of lament for Proserpine. Schubert began
the composition in November 1815, and finished it in the
next year. The date could never have been guessed. It
might have been thought that years separated such music from
the masterpieces of the period. These compositions show
Schubert in the act of practising his pen in the intervals
between the visits of his genius.

Hektors Abschied (Schiller) is a dialogue between Hector
and Andromache, for two voices. The writing is formal
and stately. The piece was published with two other early
Schiller songs as Op. 56 in 1826. *An die Freude* (Schiller)
—the ' Ode to Joy ' of Beethoven's Choral Symphony—
was set by Schubert as a strophic song with chorus. It
looks as though it was thrown off extempore for some sociable
occasion. A more economical composer would have saved
up the brilliant melody for some extended instrumental
use. The song was published as Op. 111, No. 1, in 1829.
The second and most celebrated of Schubert's three settings
of *Des Mädchens Klage* is dated May 15, 1815. This time the
setting is strophic ; a pathetic melody hovers above pulsating

---

¹ The longest of all is the setting of Bertrand's ballad *Adelwold und Emma*
(26 pages).

triplets in C minor. The third setting of the poem, likewise
a strophic song in C minor, was composed in March 1816.
It is inferior to this 1815 song, which is the most charming
of all Schubert's settings of Schiller's lyrics. Curiously
enough, in *Amalia* (the heroine's song in Schiller's ' Räuber '),
which was composed a few days later, Schubert reverted to
the quasi-dramatic style.

Das Geheimnis is a small love song of rare delicacy and
tenderness, curiously suggestive of Schumann. Later on
Schubert wrote another and more elaborate setting, feeling
perhaps that this dreamy melody did not support all four of
Schiller's heavy stanzas ; but the important 1823 song by no
means eclipses the first, which most beautifully expresses
the shyness of young love. The song is not in Peters's edition
and is generally overlooked. The Schubertian who has
missed it will be grateful for this indication. *Hoffnung*
(Schiller) is a bluff little piece in folksong vein. *An den
Frühling* (Schiller) is again a mere trifle, but in the prelude
Schubert has thrown off a most charming ländler-like tune.
Later in the year a second setting of the poem was written,
also in an innocent 6–8 rhythm.

All Schubert's thirteen Körner songs date from 1815 except
one (*Auf der Riesenkoppe*, 1818). The long ballad, *Amphiaraos*,
telling of the visionary hero's death in the Theban war,
was composed by Schubert in five hours, so he has stated
on the manuscript. This fine, bold, slashing music would
reward study by a bass-barytone with exceptional power
and range. Within a very few days Schubert wrote two
different settings of *Sängers Morgenlied* ; the first pretty
and jaunty, a song for light soprano, the second more pensive.
There are also some slight love songs, a cradle song, and a
piece of rustic humour, *Das gestörte Glück*, about a youth
whose fate it was to be always interrupted when on the point
of kissing. The songs of war are a reminder that Körner
heard the national call and fell fighting in the anti-Napoleonic
campaign of 1813. There is *Gebet während der Schlacht* :

' Father, I call on thy name ! Lightnings are round about
me. God of battles, lead me on ! The sword in my hand
is the sword of righteousness. Sustain me ! In my
agony, when the body is shattered, be thine my spirit.
Father, I call.'

The soldier's prayer failed to move Schubert to great purpose.
The song is pathetic but monotonous. The *Schwertlied*

plucks the heroic chord in a great number of stanzas.
Schubert has given his tune a truculent turn by switching
between C major and D minor. This song and the *Trinklied
vor der Schlacht* belong to the male-voice choir rather than
the solo singer.

Nine of Schubert's twenty-three settings of Hölty were
composed in this year. They include some exquisite pieces.
The first is *An den Mond* (' Geuss, lieber Mond ') :

> ' Show me, moon, the trysting-place of old. Ah, enough,
> enough ! Now draw your veil of clouds. The place is
> deserted, and your suppliant is solitary and forsaken.'

The deep bass theme of the prelude is heavy with the sense
of night. The undulating F minor arpeggios suggest the
clouds that are about the moon. The voice enters with a
tender melody so beautifully poised that it seems to hover
on wings. Time and key change for the two middle stanzas
(2–2 Ab). But the unveiled beams have revealed too much
and too little. The obliging moon withdraws, and the cloud
of minor arpeggios comes down again upon the scene. This
lovely song is the most celebrated of Schubert's settings of
Hölty. It was published in 1826 as Op. 57, No. 3. The
pianoforte part of *Die Mainacht* (Hölty) is less characteristic ;
and lovers of Brahms's noble composition will hardly allow
an equal rank to Schubert's, especially since the notes of
the first bar do not fit the words very truly in any stanza.
But the song should certainly not be ignored ; its sorrowful,
purling melody is pure Schubert. It was composed on the
same day as *An den Mond*. Brahms's setting of *An die
Nachtigall* (Hölty) has likewise eclipsed Schubert's. The
latter is a delicate little strophic song with much finesse in
its few bars. This and two other Hölty songs, *An die
Apfelbäume* and *Seufzer*, were composed on the same day
(May 22). The setting of the alcaics *An die Apfelbäume*
spreads a little beyond the tiny dimensions of most of the
group, to which also belong *Der Liebende* (a merry song),
Der Traum (a gem), and *Die Laube*. These are not concert
songs. They are only for music-making in the smallest
and most intimate circle. The exception is the rather un-
interesting ballad *Die Nonne*, which tells a typical romantic
story of abduction, treachery, revenge, and a ghost.

Five of the nine Ossian songs were composed in 1815.
For all but two of these—*Ossians Lied nach dem Falle Nathos'*
and *Das Mädchen von Inistore*—' song ' is hardly the right

word. Such outpourings as *Der Tod Oscars* (1816), which
fills fourteen pages, belong to no category. What all these
compositions pointed to was Schubert's readiness, fired as
he was by the mysterious Caledonian poesy, to compose an
opera about Ossian's heroes, if only a man of letters in his
circle had thought of casting one of the campaigns or disasters
into dramatic form for him. Schubert had not Wagner's
strength to grapple with that part of the task himself. But
the fine landscape descriptions in these Ossian pieces, the
pathetic declamation and the free purling of melody, hint at
the masterpieces which with the collaboration perhaps of
Grillparzer might have enriched German opera. As they
stand, the characterization is vague and there is a depressing
preponderance of dirges ; and for all the beauties they
contain, most of them must be relegated to the lumber-room
of music.

Ossians Lied nach dem Falle Nathos' (a lament, from ' Dar-
thula,' for the young hero Nathos, Dar-thula's lover, who
was slain in the fighting with Cairbar, the usurper of the
throne after Cuthullin's death) is, by exception, compact ;
a piece of simple and majestic music in E major. *Das
Mädchen von Inistore* [1] (from ' Fingal ') is a dirge for Trenar,
killed on the first day of the epic battle between Cuthullin
and Swaran.

> ' Trenar, graceful Trenar died, O maid of Inistore !
> His grey dogs are howling at home, they see his passing
> ghost. His bow is in the hall unstrung, no sound is in
> the hill of his hinds.'

It is a true song of no small interest. *Kolmas Klage* is
more extended, but not unmanageably. It is one of the finest
of the Ossian pieces. The text comes from ' The Songs of
Selma.' Colma, who loves Salgar, son of a hostile family,
finds one night at the secret trysting-place her lover and her
brother both dead, each having slain the other. *Lodas
Gespenst* is long and inferior ; but it has a curious interest
in that it deals with a situation very similar to the scene
between Siegfried and Wotan in ' The Ring.' The spirit
Loda (Odin) appears by night before the Hebridean King
Fingal to dissuade him from his enterprise in raising the siege
of Carric-thura. Fingal scouts the god's behest ; and,
wearying of argument, he at length strikes at Loda's spear
with his sword, whereupon the god with a shriek vanishes into

[1] Inistore = Orkneys.

smoke. But the hour of 'The Ring' had not sounded.
Schubert makes little of the hero's defiance. The twelve
pages of *Lodas Gespenst* are singularly barren.

Shilrik und Vinvela is an episode from the same poem
('Carric-thura'). It is a dialogue, twelve pages long, of
farewell between lovers. Shilric is off to the wars. Both
anticipate the worst, and Shilric's last words are a behest
for the erection of his funeral monument. The sequel is
in the beautiful song *Cronnan* (1816), which is distinguished
by its musical descriptions of the mountain stream and the
wind on the moor. Shilric has returned sound and whole,
only to find that his mistress has died of grief. Her ghost
appears and speaks with him lamentably, in a voice 'weak as
the breeze in the reeds of the lake.' Here we may glance at
the later Ossian pieces. *Der Tod Oscars* tells of the romantic
friendship of Oscar and Dermid, whose tragedy it was to
love the same woman, King Dargo's daughter. The tale
is one stream of blood. There are some good things in
the music, but it is loose and improvisatory ; and the self-
conscious heroism of all concerned is hard to believe in.
Lorma (1816), on a text from 'The Battle of Lora,' is a fragment. *Die Nacht* (1817) is a piece of fifteen pages, including
a finale which was added by the publishers after Schubert's
death and which consists of a *Jagdlied* (text by Werner),
composed by Schubert also in 1817.

Schubert in 1815 set twenty-one of Kosegarten's poems,
all in simple strophic form. Eight of these were composed
in one day (October 19). It is unlikely that Schubert expected
the singer always to make his way through the whole poem,
seeing that *Idens Schwanenlied*, for instance, has seventeen
stanzas and *Luisens Antwort* nineteen. Some of the Kosegarten songs are negligible, the best are small and secondary.
The delicate three-part writing in the little song *Von Ida*
will please the Schubertian. *Die Erscheinung* has an amiable
melody rather like that of *Die Forelle*. *Das Sehnen*, an agitated
little song in A minor, should not be overlooked ; its thirteen
bars are genuine Schubert. *Die Mondnacht* sets us, by its
title, thinking of Schumann. It is a beautiful little song,
and one of the best of the group, even if not a match for
Schumann's *Mondnacht*. The song begins in B, though its
main key is F . *Alles um Liebe* is a pretty trifle. *Die Sterne*
moves in the hymntune-like manner which Schubert may
have derived from the male-voice choirs of the time; but
who save Schubert in writing a placid hymntune of sixteen
bars in B♭ would have thought of modulating so far as A♭ ?

Nachtgesang, the eleventh of the Kosegarten songs, is, like *Das Sehnen*, a tiny piece, but Schubertian in every trait. Solemn harmonies express the watcher's quiet wondering at inscrutable nature. The Schubert of *Wanderers Nachtlied* is announced.

In September and October 1815 Schubert turned to Klopstock. Nine of his thirteen Klopstock songs date from those months. They vary a good deal. There is *Vaterlandslied*, a little comic-opera ditty in which ' ein deutsches Mädchen ' calls attention to her blue eyes and patriotic heart. There is *Hermann und Thusnelda*, a large and pompous scena, in which a proud wife welcomes her hero home from the wars in the Zumsteeg style. The piece is hardly interesting ; but it is curious to find in the pianoforte part of the movement ' Erzählt's in allen Hainen ' the characteristic accompaniment (note for note, for some bars) of Schubert's ' Lady of the Lake ' song, *Soldier, rest ! thy warfare o'er*, of ten years later. The key even is the same (D*b*). The Klopstock songs include one masterpiece on the grand scale, *Dem Unendlichen*, and among the smaller songs one, *Das Rosenband*, of much sweetness and charm. That this *Rosenband* should be ignored is symptomatic of the world's light appreciation of the Schubertian heritage. It has every right to be a favourite song, so tender is its feeling and suave the expression. *Dem Unendlichen* sounds the sackbut and psaltery in religious exaltation. Powerful chords, plentifully double-dotted, lead in the recitative, which is one of Schubert's finest pages of pure declamation. Then the poet calls on the leaves of the tree of life to rustle harp-tones in consort with the universal magnificat. The harmonies soften, the right hand has harp-like arpeggios, but the bass maintains a majestic tread, while the cantilena soars. *Dem Unendlichen* is, like *Die Allmacht* of ten years later, to which in spirit, if not in form, it is akin, a song for a powerful and noble voice. Mandyczewski prints three versions. In Nos. 1 and 2 the introduction begins in F, in No. 3 in G. The cantilena is in all three in E*b*.

Belonging to 1815 are also a few songs which are of no great moment but which are settings of poets who were to play a large part in Schubert's work in the next few years. Thus there are two Mayrhofer songs, *Liane* and *Augenlied*, both graceful. Two Stolberg songs, *Morgenlied* and *Abendlied*, are very small and almost trifling. We meet with Friedrich Schlegel for the first time in *Der Schmetterling*, in which the butterfly's ramblings take rather a square form. It is a chirruping songlet which might be paired with the setting of the same poet's *Die Vögel* of 1820. Then we find the first setting of friend Schober's verses, *Genügsamkeit*, which makes the impression of a jaunty sociable song, lightly thrown off.

VI

SONGS OF 1815 (*continued*): GOETHE SONGS

SCHUBERT composed thirty settings of Goethe in 1815. About half of these are among his famous songs ; and some of them (*Erlkönig, Rastlose Liebe, Heidenröslein, Meeresstille, Erster Verlust, Wanderers Nachtlied*) are universally celebrated. Goethe is again, as in 1814, found to lift Schubert above his everyday level ; and one after another of these Goethe songs stands out from the rest of 1815 by such force of character and individuality that if we had to guess at dates by intrinsic evidence, no one would dream of ascribing the best of them, any more than *Gretchen am Spinnrade*, to this early period. Not all are so intensely characteristic ; but even when Schubert set a poem of Goethe's, like *Der Sänger*, with what was then his conventional treatment of narrative verse (frequent change of movement, mixed recitative and arioso), and without anything like the astonishing novelty and unity of the *Erlkönig* music, there was nearly always a particular warmth of tone and vividness of detail.

Der Sänger was the first of the 1815 Goethe songs. In the second book of ' Wilhelm Meisters Lehrjahre ' there is introduced into a breakfast party of disgruntled actors the mysterious Harper, whose songs shed a ray of poetry into the squalid company. A few of the Harper's songs are cited in ' Wilhelm Meister,' but all too few ; for if that fantastic rigmarole is beyond question the work of a man of genius, the incidental songs are more—they are the genius's consummated art. Schubert did not set Philine's song, but he set all the Harper's and Mignon's songs, most of them more than once.

Mignon in the novel is the fairylike Italian child whom Wilhelm rescues from a troupe of rope-dancers. She and the crazy Harper join for a time the actors' party, under Wilhelm's protection. She lives, she loves, she dies of home-sickness and a broken heart ; and not till afterwards do her well-guarded secrets come out—hers and the Harper's, for they are linked, and without his knowing it she is the child of the incestuous love the memory of which has driven him to wander out of his wits up and down the earth. In 1816, and again in 1821 and 1826, we shall come upon groups of further settings of ' Wilhelm Meister ' songs.

Der Sänger is a ballad of idealized medievalism. A king
and his court pay unbounded homage to poetic art, represented by a wandering minstrel ; while the latter is equally
ideal in attitude, refusing a material reward and saying that
a poet, like a bird on a bough, has reward enough in the
pleasure his songs bring him. Such a pretty fancy was
natural enough in Goethe, who never in all his life had to
think of ways and means ; it is more curious that Schubert,
who could so well have done with a ' golden chain ' or two
as a reward for his songs, should have taken up *Der Sänger*
without irony. The setting, we have said, is in the old-
fashioned style ; but there are several engaging passages
and the piece is more interesting than most of the sort.
Loewe, Schumann, and Wolf also set the poem. What
attraction it had for them all is a little hard to understand.
All these songs sound indeterminate, simply because Goethe's
poem leaves out the ' thrilling strain ' with which the minstrel
charmed the court and which seems to be needed to form the
core, not indeed of the lyric but of a musical composition on
the subject.

The famous settings of the Harper's three other songs belong
to 1816 ; but in 1815 there was a first one, in A minor, of *Wer
sich der Einsamkeit ergibt*. This is the second of the two
poignant songs (the other being *Wer nie sein Brod*) sung by
the Harper on the occasion of Wilhelm's first visit to his garret.
The plaintive music moves gracefully in 6-8 measure. It
is eclipsed by the 1816 setting. We also find in 1815 the
first of Schubert's six different settings of *Nur wer die Sehnsucht kennt*. Two more were composed a year later ; then
a setting for five-part male-voice choir in 1819 ; then the
well-known song in A minor, Op. 62, No. 4, in 1826, and
at the same period a duet setting. This last is in a way the
most Goethean ; for *Nur wer die Sehnsucht kennt* is not, as
the publishers of Op. 62 in 1827 called it, ' Mignon's Song.'
It is in the fourth book of ' Wilhelm Meister ' sung ' as an
irregular duet ' by Mignon and the Harper by the bed where
Wilhelm lies recovering from the wounds of the affray with
the freebooters, and sickening with a new love for the mysterious Amazon. The history of Schubert's treatment of the
immortal lyric is further complicated by the existence of two
versions of the 1815 setting between which there are rather
considerable differences. Both versions are dated October
18. One is in A*b*, the other in F. In this very beautiful piece
of music Schubert has sought to express unrestful and
frustrated longing by persistent variation of key. The one

commonplace passage is the chromatic modulation after
the recitative, leading back to the A♭ variant of the opening
melody. The compass of the song is extensive (very nearly
two octaves), but if that is an objection, the A♭ version (compass, a minor thirteenth) might be sung. Although the
popular 1826 song has a more lyrical flow, this first and
little-known setting is perhaps the finest and most expressive.
Innumerable composers have attempted *Nur wer die Sehnsucht kennt*, including Beethoven (four times), Loewe,
Schumann, Tchaikovsky, and Wolf.

The most admired lyrical poem in German literature is
Mignon's song, *Kennst du das Land?* which stands at the
head of the third book of ' Wilhelm Meister.' It was Mignon's
aubade to her protector ; and when he mentioned Italy,
' If you go to Italy,' said the poor child, ' take me with you,
for I am too cold here.' But we never think of it as a child's
poem. The haunting verses express more than the sun-
stinted northerner's longing for the south. They seem to
spring from a deeper nostalgia, they tell of man's age-long
dream of a world that the world's not. The first stanza
describes the benign Hesperian land, the second the marble
halls of Mignon's infant days, the third the terrors of the
Alpine pass across which the kidnappers dragged her north-
wards. In the three stanzas she addresses Wilhelm pro-
gressively as ' beloved—protector—father.' ' Beethoven's
setting apart,' said Schumann, ' I know of none that renders
anything like the effect made by the poem itself, without
music.' For all that, he himself wrote a setting, and a very
beautiful one. Beethoven's Op. 75 is stately ; Hugo Wolf's
setting is extremely rich and passionate. Schubert composed
his *Kennst du das Land?* on October 23, 1815, and it was not
the only song he wrote that day. He faced fully the technical
difficulty of the enterprise, which lies in the length of the
lines (iambic pentameters) and the great spread of the six-
line stanzas. His melody, beginning in A, has strong wings
and strikes off on a brave course, reaching C in the poet's
second line and F in the fourth. The mention of the balmy
winds of the south sets up an accompaniment in waving
triplets. Another triplet figure of thirds moving chromatically, which accompanies the refrain, ' Thither, thither ! '
makes one of the beauties of the song. The music is simply
repeated for the second stanza ; and there is a move into the
minor for the third. The sentiment in us that ever desires
the impossible—the sentiment so well expressed in the poem
—has made all the attempts of the musicians seem a little

less than adequate; and none of them are great favourites.
Wolf's is too elaborate and grown-up for Mignon. We come
back to Schubert's, and feel that if his *Kennst du das Land?*
has not all his most thrilling magic, no one has done it better.
The time is, of course, past for the poem ever to be set again.
Schubert, we make so bold as to think, might have given a
more appropriate and unappeased expression to the refrain
by stopping the voice on the dominant, instead of carrying it
up to the high A on the last 'dahin.' His accentuation in
this song is not impeccable. The singer must beware of
making too much of the down-beat on ' die ' in the third bar,
and on ' seinen ' in the corresponding place in the third
stanza.

To be mentioned here, although it does not actually belong
to ' Wilhelm Meister,' is the little song *An Mignon*, written
in 1796 and composed by Schubert on February 27, 1815.
The music is plaintive and sweet. Goethe's verses are less
obvious. After singing pathetically to the chimes of ' heart '
and ' smart ' (' Herzen ' and ' Schmerzen '), he ends with
a shrug—' I shed my tears freely in private, but in company
I can be cheerful and I look healthy ; for the heart's smart is
not fatal, or I should have been dead long ago.' Schubert
made his song out of the ' Schmerzen ' and left out the shrug.
It was composed in G♯ minor, and published in G minor
as Op. 19, No. 2, in 1823, dedicated to the poet. But now we
find ourselves in the midst of numbers of gem-like songs,
some extremely familiar and others, for no reason, comparatively unknown. One of the latter is *Am Flusse*, composed
on the same day as *An Mignon* :

' Dissolve and drown and vanish, songs of mine ; and
may you never haunt the lips of lovers, since she for whom
alone you were scorns love. O written in water, flow
down into Oblivion's tide ! '

The poet's musical plaint is perfectly matched by Schubert's
page of thirty short bars. The piece brims with sweet and
juvenile pathos. There are few notes, but they are exquisitely
disposed. To the interest of the touching and highly
articulated D minor melody there is that of four different
accompaniment forms : equal semiquavers ; left-hand octaves
on and right-hand chords off the beat ; a ripple of demisemiquavers ; and (in one bar) a dotted semiquaver figure. The
poem was composed again by Schubert in 1822, in D major.
The love song *Nähe des Geliebten* (1795) strikes chords of

deep and almost solemn feeling. The lover finds everywhere in nature associations with his absent mistress, and stands in awe before the beauty that his passion reveals to him in the sunlight and the moonlight, in the sound of welling waters, in the dustcloud raised by a horseman on the road. Schubert set the verses in strophic form. His melody is only six bars long, but it has an appropriately noble sweep ; and the composer had the art to suggest in it the necessity of the repetitions ;—sung only once, it would sound incomplete. It is characteristic of Schubert that even in this very brief melodic period he momentarily glances away from his main key, G*b*, into E*b*. The pulsing triplets of the pianoforte part add to the nobility of the expression. The two versions in Mandyczewski are nearly alike. The first is in 6–8 time with semiquavers for the pianoforte. Across the manuscript Schubert wrote ' won't do ' (' gilt nicht '). The second version, composed on the same day (February 27), is in 12–8 time with a quaver accompaniment. Schubert first of all modified his melody to suit Goethe's words ' Im stillen Haine geh' ich ' in the third stanza ; then decided that the anacrusis was essential to the musical phrase and inserted a ' da ' into Goethe's line. A like audacity was remarked in *Schäfers Klagelied*. *Nähe des Geliebten* was published as Op. 5, No. 2, with other Goethe songs, in 1821.

Die Liebe is a setting of Clärchen's song ' Freudvoll und leidvoll ' from ' Egmont.' Love, declares the brave and charming heroine, Egmont's sweetheart and Alva's victim— love is worth the cost of any tribulation, and who knows it not knows not life's blessing. The famous lines are short and few for the musician's purpose, but both Beethoven and Schubert have composed them admirably. Beethoven resorted to more repetitions of words than Schubert, but he was writing for the stage. It was a feat to entice a music so broad and strong-winged into the space of twenty short bars. No less fine is the almost immobile music of *Meeresstille* :

> ' A breathless world ! There is no ripple in the waste
> of waters ; and the becalmed sailor stares with dread at
> silence, at death made visible.'

The poem is from Goethe's epigrams and has a pendant in the animated ' Glückliche Fahrt.' Schubert has admirably depicted the awful calm with a slow succession of thirty-two semibreve chords—an evocation of nature as serene as implacable. In such a page Schubert's musical sense seems positively to approach the visual. The song requires fine singing, substantial and unfaltering, and nothing will do short of perfect vowel-values. It was published with other Goethe songs in 1821 as Op. 3, No .2. Another, similar version of the song, composed on the previous day, was published in the *Schweizerische Musikzeitung* for November, 1952.

Similarly, with the distribution of a few chords in a dozen bars, Schubert composed a page of ever-living beauty in *Wanderers Nachtlied* (I) (' Der du von dem Himmel bist '). The poem, one of singular harmoniousness and limpid depth, is a sigh for peace, and almost a prayer, uttered in a moment of world-weariness. Goethe wrote the lines on the Ettersberg in 1776, and addressed them to his Egeria, Charlotte von Stein. Schubert also composed on the day of this song (July 5) *Erster Verlust*. Infinitely tender and pathetic are the F minor harmonies and sighing melody of this short but celebrated page. There is a certain innocence in such expressions of grief in Schubert. He is, as it were, taken by surprise by unkindness and wounds ; there is an appeal in his reproaches, and not anger or hopelessness. *Erster Verlust* is not more sad than sweet ; and the singing of it, to be right, must be sweeter than words can say, and also youthful, not to say naïve, in character. Mention has been made of Schubert's interpolation of ' wer ' in the last line for the sake of an anacrusis. The song is related in style to *Nur wer die Sehnsucht kennt* (first setting) and to a much later song, *Wehmuth* (Collin, 1823). It was first published as Op. 5, No. 4, in 1821.

Goethe's celebrated and beautiful poem *An den Mond* (' Füllest wider Busch und Thal ') was set twice by Schubert in 1815, the first time on August 19, a day of several other songs. He was justified in returning to the charge, for the first setting, a strophic song in Eb, was nearly insignificant and far from adequate to the meandering but exquisitely harmonious verses. The poet, wandering alone by moonlight in a mood of rich melancholy, is invaded by memories both gentle and sorrowful. He is grateful for the moon's bland and peaceful influence, but the sigh of the passing stream reminds him of the days that have gone to return no more. What possible happiness is left ?—one, and that would be communion with a sympathetic friend who would understand the mingled memories and emotions evoked by a night like this. Schubert's second setting, in Ab, is in modified strophic form. Something no doubt has still eluded him ;

and indeed to catch the various shades of the poet's feelings, in which exalted serenity exists side by side with wild regret, was a hopeless task. Schubert has found a very beautiful, tranquil melody, which embraces two of Goethe's quatrains in each repetition. There are an effective variation and crescendo in the invocation to the river. The song is unduly neglected.

Wonne der Wehmuth is hardly attractive. Beethoven set the six short lines of this poem once for all in a superb and classic song. Schubert found little to say about it. But he was obviously enthralled by the idea of *Geistesgruss*, which is indeed something singularly sensible among romantic ghost-poems. The spirit of an antique hero observes the endeavours of the living and bids them godspeed —'Once were my sinews tough, my heart bold, my beaker brimming ; I knew the storms of life and the haven ; now may you, vessel of the living, fare as well ! ' There are four versions of Schubert's setting in Mandyczewski. In the first three the recitative is in E♭ and the Maestoso (the ghost's utterance) in G♭. The final version (published as Op. 92, No. 3, in 1828) is a semitone higher and the recitative is accompanied by a tremolando.

A light group of a dozen little strophic Goethe songs, in which the pianoforte is usually the merest accompaniment and which look as though meant for performance in sociable circles or in ballad operas, also belongs to this year. The most familiar is *Heidenröslein* :

'The rose on the spray seemed to ask to be plucked. "You are mine," said the boy. "Take my thorn too," said the rose. The boy grasps the flower, the thorn stabs deep. Long and long will it rankle.'

Like the verses, the tune might be taken to be pure folksong. In a collection of rustic lore it would certainly appear a gem, but no suspicion would be excited. Goethe wrote the lines in about 1771. A German poet could, like Burns, pipe without affectation on the pastoral flute in a way impossible in the England of the period. Schubert's success comes of his having seen in a flash the one appropriate musical treatment. The bucolic air might be thought to have been born of one mind with the poem. It fits the six-line stanza to a nicety, with its four bars in the tonic, six in the dominant, and four again in the tonic to balance. The song, which was

published as Op. 3, No. 3, is a singularly popular example of
a generally neglected type of Schubertian song.   It is perhaps
the best of our little group, but is by no means incomparably
the best.   It might have been outrivalled by that tripping
little ditty *Die Spinnerin* if the rueful spinster's misadventure,
described so racily by Goethe, had not been an anecdote
inadmissible   in   the   nineteenth-century   drawing-room.
Schweizerlied[1] is the jolliest of ländlers.   Its twelve bars
cry out to be encored.   *Der Goldschmiedsgesell* is another in
the series.   The goldsmith's prentice sighs for a pretty
neighbour.   Ah ! when will the ring he is at work on be
hers ?   It is not as easy as it looks to write fetching little
tunes like this.   *Wer kauft Liebesgötter ?* is a saucy one.
' Love-gods for sale !   Who'll buy ? ' it calls.   In *Liebhaber
in aller Gestalten* the swain retails a catalogue of disguises
that might improve his chances with the fair.   The tune this
time is quite naïve.

Tischlied is convivial—a farewell toast to a friend departing
for the French wars.   Schubert has written one of those
hearty tunes that German students love to sing in chorus.
Bundeslied is in much the same vein, but the tune is not so
racy.   Rather more serious is *Hoffnung*, a short page, Goethe's
poem being one of six lines.   The square, marching music
belongs to the sociable and not the lyric order.   The tunes
of the pieces in this group already named are enough to have
made the fortune of a ballad opera.   There remain a few
narrative songs, for instance *Der Fischer* :

> ' The fisher-lad sat whistling and thinking of nothing,
> when what should come out of the water that lapped at his
> feet but a mermaid, green-eyed and dripping, with river-
> weeds in her hair.   And she to him, "Instead of luring
> my fishy folk away, O man, come down among us and see
> a world prettier than a dream."   Her eyes promised more
> than her words, and whether he plunged or was dragged
> in, from that day he was no more seen.'

It is a simple strophic song.   To suggest the gurgling of
the stream there is a pretty figure worked in the pianoforte
part with a little more elaboration than anything in the other
small songs.   The story is not told in the music, and quite
properly not ; for the poem, although it affects narrative

---

[1] There is an excellent translation in Devonshire dialect by Fox Strangways,
See *Music and Letters*, July 1921.

form, is a fancy—clearly, since there was no witness of the
seduction and no word came back from the lost young man.
It is a fancy crooned to a folksong-like tune ; with its quiet
ripple of semiquavers in the accompaniment it might be a
lullaby. The song is better known than some of its fellows
through having been published in Op. 5.

Schubert judged equally well in setting the nine long stanzas
of the Indian legend *Der Gott und die Bajadere* in strophic
form. The poem tells of one of Mahadeva's incarnations.
The god bestows himself upon an outcast girl. After a night
of pleasure she finds the mysterious lover dead in her arms.
At the funeral the bayadere, broken-hearted, is about to
immolate herself on the pyre when the god revives and carries
the humble harlot with him gloriously to heaven ; and the
moral is, ' God delights in sinners' rue, and the fiery-armed
immortals uplift the lost children of earth to the holy heights.'
The poem, a fine one, makes no call at all for music ; but if
music there was to be, Schubert's unobtrusive hymnlike
tune was better than an elaborate setting which would for a
certainty have been tiresome.

Der Gott und die Bajadere was composed on August 18.
On the next day Schubert wrote five little Goethe songs. One
of them was *Der Rattenfänger*, the song of the Pied Piper of
Hamelin. It is a cheerful ditty, but Schubert might have
been expected to find more in it than that. The rat-catcher
with his magic fiddle—Goethe gives him strings, not a pipe—
who avers himself a child-catcher and on occasion a girl-
catcher too, is an eerier character than Schubert seemed to
see. The wizard's song had to wait for Wolf to give it music
odd and grotesque enough. In Wolf we can really believe
that—

> ' his lips he wrinkled,
> And green and blue his sharp eyes twinkled
> Like a candle-flame where salt is sprinkled.'

Der Schatzgräber, composed on the same day, is a simple
setting of a celebrated poem which treats a rather Faust-
like theme. The treasure-seeker, cursing his poverty,
summons aid by witchcraft. A beauteous youth appears in
answer to the spell, bearing a chalice. ' Drink,' says he,
' the potion of Strength-of-Mind-to-lead-a-Decent-Existence.
Give up these absurd incantations. *Honest work* is the most
effective of magic formulas.' It is pure Goethe, this mixture
of fantasy and sane sense ; but what composer could have

made an apt music for it ? Most likely the poem does best
without music. Schubert's song is strophic. The first
two stanzas (the complaint against poverty, the evocation)
are in the minor, the last three (the apparition) in the major.
The two last Goethe songs of the year are both surprising
masterpieces. The poem of *Rastlose Liebe* dates from the
early days of Goethe's love for Charlotte von Stein. It may
be explained that Goethe's career is rather like Henry VIII's,
in that it is chronicled according to the brief reigns of a
succession of queens. The fine passionate poem was written
during a Mayday snowstorm in 1776. It is a whirl of feeling,
not a logical statement. ' On, on, without respite, through
snow and wind ! ' cries the poet. ' It were easier to die of
sorrow than to live bearing life's burden of burning bliss.
On, on ! But what forest shall hide me ? ' But for Goethe
there was no escaping love, and he comes back to it—' the
crown of life.' The lines, so it is recorded, transported
Schubert into a kind of ecstasy ; he read, and he instantly
wrote down his music with passion. It was not the only
song he composed in some such hyperphysical state ; but
this time the seizure was particularly intense, it remained vivid
in Schubert's memory and he referred to it wonderingly.
When in the next year *Rastlose Liebe* and *Amalia* were somewhere sung, he mentions in his diary that the former was
the more applauded ; then characteristically, ' and while I
agree that it is the better song there is no denying that a
great deal of the success was due to Goethe's genius.' The
song has a tempestuous dynamic new in Schubert, but which
we are on the point of finding again in *Erlkönig*. The
melody rides a whirlwind of semiquavers, while the bass
beats its way upwards. The veering between major and
minor, the chromatic harmonies and the modulations all
help to suggest wild weather in this astonishing piece of
musical imaginativeness. The wind slackens a little in the
G major section, but in a moment it is up again, blowing
protests aside and driving the protester precisely there whence
will and activity were to have rescued him, back into the thick
of love. It is not too much to say that Schubert has here
explained Goethe. The poem threw out hints of a mixed
mood, turbulent and triumphant, that wanted music to give
it coherence ; and this is done by the waves of sounds that
waft the song from E major to victorious E major again.
Rastlose Liebe was a strange offspring to come of Salieri's
teaching ; nevertheless, to the old master it was dedicated
as No. 1 of Op. 5 when it was published in 1821.

Erlkönig was one of the last of Schubert's 1815 songs. It is not exactly dated. Spaun in his memoirs tells how he and Mayrhofer called one afternoon on Schubert, who was then living at his father's, and found him reading Goethe's great ballad aloud. Glowing with excitement, he paced to and fro, then sat down and wrote, and within the least possible time the song was on paper. Schubert not being in possession of a pianoforte, the three friends hurried off to the Konvikt, and there that same evening the *Erlkönig* was first sung and admiringly received. Schubert's old teacher, Ruziczka, played it through carefully and approvingly. The piercing minor ninths on the words, ' Mein Vater ! ' seem to have caused questioning in the audience. Ruziczka defended the clash and the progression on both theoretical and artistic grounds. Randhartinger, then a boy of fourteen, was chosen to sing the ballad, and was twice encored. In the second performance Schubert tired of the triplets,[1] and played eight quavers to a bar, with the remark, ' The triplets are too difficult for me : it needs a virtuoso to play them.' Randhartinger received a copy of the song as a reward for his singing. This copy came into the possession of Clara Schumann, and is reproduced in Mandyczewski's second version.

In the Schubertian circle, *Erlkönig* had the success that can be imagined. The strange thing, according to modern ideas, is that it should have remained for years unknown outside that circle. A copy was sent (with the simplified pianoforte part) in 1817 to Goethe at Weimar, with a number of other Goethe songs of Schubert's, accompanied by a letter from Spaun. It was not acknowledged ; and Goethe seems not to have heard the song until after Schubert's death. Vogl took up the song ; but the first to sing it in public was August von Gymnich, on January 28, 1821. Vogl followed him with it at a concert in the Vienna Opera House on March 7. Anselm Hüttenbrenner played for Vogl, Schubert being in too great nervousness. In the next month, six and a half years after its composition, the song was published as Schubert's Op. 1. Surely the most remarkable Op. 1 that ever was !

The Viennese publishers had all in turn rejected Schubert's

---

[1] Cf. D. F. Tovey : ' . . . an " accompaniment," the adequate perform-ance of which is one of the rarest *tours de force* in pianoforte playing. Liszt's transcription of *Erlkönig* as a concert-solo is far easier, for the added fireworks give relief to the player's wrists ' (' The Heritage of Music ' (Oxford University Press), p. 90). This essay of Mr. Tovey's is the finest piece of criticism in Schubertian literature.

songs, on the ground that the composer was unknown and the
pianoforte parts too difficult. Now an admirer of his, Ignaz
Sonnleithner, a prominent lawyer, thought out a scheme for
publishing the songs on commission. *Erlkönig*, in 1820,
had been sung by Gymnich at Sonnleithner's house, where
considerable concerts were regularly given. The firm of
Cappi & Diabelli fell in with the scheme, which might have
been the saving of Schubert if later on he had not wrecked it
by his thoughtlessness and inexperience in affairs. *Erlkönig*
came out dedicated to a patron of Schubert's, the ' court
music count,' Moritz von Dietrichstein, an amiable and
influential personage and in a modest way a musician. It
was an immediate success, a sign of which was the appearance
of ' Erlkönig ' marches, galops, and waltzes. Anselm Hüttenbrenner actually perpetrated a set of these waltzes, which
drew down on him a snub from Schubert ; but it is only fair,
at the same time, to mention that there are records of Schubert's performing the masterpiece, in congenial company, on
a comb.

Goethe's ballad is, like Schubert's setting, far and away
the finest piece of writing of its kind : not an affected imitation
of distant folklore, but a genuine poem in its own right.
It occurs in a ballad opera of Goethe's, ' Die Fischerin,' which
was produced in 1782 : an incidental song, with no more to
do with the play than in ' Faust ' has Gretchen's ' König in
Thule.' There is no Erlkönig in German folklore, but
Goethe found in Herder a ballad of the Elf-king's daughters,
from the Danish. A new demon had emerged in the process
of translation, the Danish elf-king (*ellekonge*) somehow becoming not Elfkönig but Erlkönig, a warlock of the alders. Here
is the gist of Goethe's ballad :

' Midnight ; and the man gallops hard through the storm,
hugging close his small son. " Son, what ails you ? "
" Father, can't you see the Erl King ? " " There's only
a streak of mist there, laddie." " Pretty boy, won't you
come along with me ? Come, and I'll show you all fairy-
land." " Father, can't you hear what Erl King is saying ? "
" Don't talk so, my sonnie. It's the wind in the dead
branches." " Come, pretty one, and fairy princesses shall
play with you, dance with you, sing to you." " Father,
father, there are Erl King's daughters ! " " My boy, there
is nothing there but the old grey willows." " I want you,
pretty one, and come with me you shall, willy nilly."
" Father, he has me ! Save me ! " The child shudders.

The father spurs his horse. Gasping and sweating, he pulls up at the gate of home. But the child in his arms is dead.'

How is it that a piece of rustic scaremongering has power in it yet to chill the blood ? It is, of course, that the artful poet has told not so much of a mere quaint superstition as of the terrors of a child. The alders' twigs have for us no grisly fingers, the osiers no peril of nymphs ; and a direct spectral tale about such things would not hold water. But fears are born in the sensitive child, who must painfully learn to banish the visions of the dark and to cease in defiance of nature to quake. Meanwhile, at the representation of his dread, we cannot but shudder in sympathy. For the father in the ballad, there are simply the gnarled and shaking willows, but that is no more than his own reality, and others have theirs ; so he quakes, and we with him, at the horror of the unreal which to the creature near and dear is inexorcizably real, visible, audible, and grasping. Who shall know a child's realities ? What is for us real enough and agitating is that he can, on the strength of them, frighten himself to death. That is the unfailing point of this irresistible *Erlkönig*, in comparison with which the typical imitative folklore and spectral claptrap of the romantic period are pointless.

There are said to be over fifty different musical settings of Goethe's ballad. The first of these was composed by the actress,[1] who sang it in the original production of ' Die Fischerin.' Beethoven sketched a setting in his early days.[2] He used the material in Nos. 2 and 4 of the Bagatelles for Pianoforte, Op. 119. Like Schubert's, Reichardt's setting is in G minor, but there is no other resemblance. It is a simple piece, in the manner of a folksong. One setting has not been wholly eclipsed by Schubert's Op. 1, and that is Carl Loewe's, which was written in 1818, when the composer was twenty-two. This, by the most curious of coincidences, was also his Op. 1, appearing (with two other ballads) in 1824. The Germans overrate Loewe's music, but his *Erlkönig* is a good song. Sir George Henschel, who familiarized it in England, even showed a preference for it over Schubert's, no doubt because it is more manageable by a singer who is

[1] The remarkable Corona Schröter, who played the siren on the Weimar scene in Goethe's young days.

[2] Beethoven's sketch is in D minor. There are about 40 bars of the vocal part and a suggestion of the pianoforte part in seven bars, on the strength of which Reinhold Becker ventured to complete the song. (Schuberth, Leipzig, 1897.)

his own pianist. Loewe's key, by another curious coincidence, is G minor. Both composers have set the last words as recitative : otherwise, they are very different. Loewe's music is an accompaniment to the narrative, on which it wholly depends. He was himself a singer ; and he obviously thought of the music of a song as a means of effect for the singer and the unfolding of his tale—rather as an actor regards his costumes. The actor-singer may well prefer Loewe. The story is all left for him to tell ; and if he has the glittering eye with which to hold us, he may fairly call the triumph at the end, of a thrilled and penetrated audience, his own.

Schubert's care, his passion rather, was to evoke the scene. The great stretch of the pianoforte's first fifteen bars is awful, not only in movement but also in spaciousness. We are not so much auditors to a tale as witnesses of the event. We too plunge through the moving landscape to the rhythm of beating hoofs and beating hearts, are brushed by the boughs, and catch glimpses of uncertain passing things, while the clouds race abnormally across the moon. The pace and pulse are feverish, and tell so well of hallucination that when, after the momentary subsidence into D major, the voice enters—an entry admirably suggestive, by the prevalence of the dominant harmony, of questioning—it has no informatory function, but rather answers to the overwrought state in which one mechanically tries to shape in speech some evidence that the senses have difficulty in accepting. The excitement of the vision has made the Schubertian movement, which does not derive from Goethe's anapæsts ; and on this account, and because after the rush and roar of the exordium we have no need to be told anything in so many words, it is irrelevant to object that Schubert's stresses do not closely correspond to those of the verse. The engrossed voice falls into the wild prevailing rhythm, and in a properly poetic rendering Schubert's accentuation of the first syllable in ' seinem ' is not too heavy. Similarly with the ' an ' in the Erl King's first invitation. For all that, the translator of the song (which has so far baffled all who have essayed it), will do well to bear the unimaginative singer in mind and to take every precaution he can.

The *Erlkönig* commonly suffers from the singer's self-importance. The music tells so much that it is impertinent to be too explanatory. Ventriloquism is out of place. Schubert has set the father's phrases low, the boy's high, the Erl King's are pianissimo. The singer had best use his normal voice for all three, avoiding fancy tricks. The song is, of course, exacting to the last degree. The Erl King's pianissimo cannot be too soft, but it must be a tense, distinct and full-throated softness. The fortissimos in the last page cannot be too powerful, but to shout here, instead of singing, is an outrage. The singer who commands a pure tone at these extremes has the technical foundations, and the less he thinks of 'word painting' the better. It remains for him to sub-jugate himself to the movement of the music, and to blot out from his mind all things except the horrifying vision. While *Erlkönig* has sometimes been impressively sung by dramatic mezzo-sopranos of the quasi-virile type (e.g. Schumann-Heink), it is properly a man's song.

The earliest critics of the *Erlkönig* made a point which has often been repeated and which is worth answering. Reichardt had set the Erl King's inveiglements as a murmured monotone (dominant pedal). It was objected in 1821 that Schubert, in the third and fifth stanzas, had given the ogre melodies altogether too charming, considering that the child, through whose senses we witness the apparition, is from the first moment terrified and utterly heedless of the lures. But after all, the lures are there in Goethe's poem, and expatiated upon—the promise of gay games, of flowers, cloth of gold, and fairy playmates. The fact is that the objection would never have occurred to anyone who did not know other and less richly coloured settings of the ballad. The minor com-posers had a more precarious hold on effects of fearfulness. Their 'Erlkönig' songs could not have well supported the introduction of anything that was not simply sinister. But Schubert started with such a motive power that his Erl King could entice delightfully in major keys—B♭ first, then up to C, then (in the seventh stanza) up again to E♭—without a check to the grim ride or to the heart's wild palpitations. The glitter of the tempter's trinkets enriches the scene without being a distraction.

The primary impulse of the music, which is not relaxed until the very end of the song, successfully carries also an extraordinary enrichment in the way of modulations. For a piece in G minor it is curious how little in G minor there actually is ; but Schubert knows that we cannot forget the key he has laid down so formidably in the first page. The father's question leads into C minor, and his reassuring answer into B♭. In the middle part of the song, G minor is merely brushed in the first of the child's three despairing appeals. These, like the Erl King's addresses, rise in pitch one above the other. The second is in A minor and the third in B♭ minor, whence at last a turn is made to the fearful home-coming in the original key.   Even so, before the stern ending of the song there are passionate lunges towards other keys—towards C minor with a sentiment of desperate grief, and then towards A♭ major with an admirable penultimate effect of hoping against hope.   The whole is an unsurpassed example of Schubert's expressive use of modulation—bold and new and instinctive, yet perfectly balanced.

Modulations are in music the equivalent of the painter's chiaroscuro.   Loewe, too, is of course alive to this, notably in his last stanza.   But the comparative flatness of his setting is accountable by the general prevalence of G minor and major.   The Erl King's invitation is each time expressed on the notes of the G major common chord ; the child's appeals to his father are each time in G minor ; the pause before the fatal announcement is simply on the 6–4 chord of G minor, while in Schubert it is as far away as A♭.

The scrupulous Mandyczewski prints four versions of the *Erlkönig*.   No. 3 is the simplified one.   The differences between the others are small and not significant.   No. 4 is the best.   Its principal advantage is that at the G minor ' homecoming,' the pianist's left hand is brought in to reinforce the octave triplets, while in Nos. 1 and 2 the disposition at this point is similar to the opening page.

Another coincidence remains to be mentioned in connexion with the *Erlkönig*.   There were at Dresden two other Franz Schuberts living at the time—father (1768–1824) and son 1808–1878), both violinists of note in their day.   Spaun, seeking a publisher for Schubert, in 1817 sent a copy of *Erlkönig* to Breitkopf & Härtel at Leipzig.   The publishers suspected a misuse of the name of Franz Schubert the elder, the violinist, and submitted the manuscript to him.   His answer [1] sounds almost too good to be true :

' The cantata *Erlkönig* is not my composition, but I shall make a point of getting in touch with whoever forwarded that claptrap to you, so as to find out what fellow it is that is thus misusing my name.'

The publishers therefore did not even reply to Spaun. When a little later they rejected Loewe's *Erlkönig*, they did at least send him back his manuscript.

[1] First published by Max Friedländer in 1893 and quoted, without acknowledgement, in Walter Dahms's ' Schubert ' (Berlin : 1912).

VII

THE SONGS OF 1816

EARLY in 1816 Schubert attempted to improve his position by applying for the vacant place of music teacher at a teachers' training college at Laibach (Ljubljana). He was not successful, but remained at his father's school and composed as copiously as in 1815. Salieri gave him somewhat meagre recommendation to the Laibach authorities, but Schubert bore no grudge, and composed a cantata for the celebration of his old master's jubilee. There were two 1816 symphonies, the C minor (' Tragic '), Schubert's fourth, composed in the spring, and the fifth in B♭, in the autumn. There was also a mass in C, No. 4, and a number of other church compositions. The chamber music of 1816 included the first three violin sonatinas. It was also the year of 104 songs.

The Schiller songs of 1816 number six and are not very considerable. The most curious thing to notice is that Schubert for all the achievements of his originality, now numerous, returned in his setting of the ballad of *Ritter Toggenburg* to an almost slavish imitation of Zumsteeg. Schiller tells of a maiden who rejects an enamoured knight and vows herself to the religious life. The knight flees the scene of his disappointment and goes crusading. After a year he returns home hoping against hope ; but the girl is now irrevocably a nun. Thereupon he builds him a hut so situated as to command a view of the convent, and there lives and dies. Nothing survives in the ballad to explain the charm exercised round about 1800 by such wan interpretations of the middle ages. Schubert was obviously not much interested. He copied his exemplar movement by movement, and just as at the end of the fifth stanza Zumsteeg tires of the onrunning style, and sets the remaining five stanzas to a repeated tune, so too does Schubert.

In *Laura am Clavier* Schiller pays many a compliment— drawing on both pagan and sacred lore—to a young woman's pianoforte-playing. In Schubert's setting the instrumental interludes depict not the poet's hyperbole but the girlishness of the admired executant. Singers (if there are singers of *Laura am Clavier*) may be puzzled by the ' Philadelphia,' with whose magic powers Schiller compares the pianist's command over life and death. This was the name of a conjuror whose feats entertained Frederick the Great. *Die Entzückung an Laura* is more attractive. The poet's infatuation is expressed by one streaming melody more than forty bars long, above a gentle movement of arpeggios. Schubert did not here discriminate between the various emotions aroused by Laura's singing, her dancing, her glance and her smile, but fused them all in one dreamy rapture. Returning to the poem in 1817, he set out to illustrate the four stanzas with more particularity, but threw up the task unfinished. Two fragments are published in Mandyczewski's tenth volume.

Schubert might in a less judicious mood have set the twelve stanzas of Schiller's poetical history of literature, *Die vier Weltalter*, as an onrunning song of many movements and pages ; but as luck would have it he gave the first stanza a jolly tune (G major, 6–8) in the style of a drinking song, and left it to the singer and the company, presumably convivial, to choose how far the progress of poesy should be followed in its course as described by Schiller from the Saturnian to the heroic age, and thence to the art of the Christian troubadours.

The intractable poem of *Der Flüchtling* could only have been attempted by a composer who was bemused by Schiller's prestige. Here Schubert was again following Zumsteeg. The ode consists of an enthusiastic appreciation of a spring morning, of Aurora and of Zephyr. It seems to be only by force of romantic obligation that the poet after many agreeable reflections lapses into misery—' the smiling earth is for me nothing but a grave.' Schubert's music contains a good march theme in the opening movement. To feel oneself an exile upon earth, wandering in perpetual dissatisfaction because dreams do not come true, was an extremely fashionable sentiment ; and *Der Flüchtling* might, if the subject had been grasped more decisively, have had some of the success that fell in abundance to another song of 1816, *Der Wanderer* (Schmidt of Lübeck)—

' Homeless, I, in the wide world and a stranger everywhere, for I have wandered far and have known many lands but not the land of heart's desire. Ah, where is that country green as hope, where the secret language of the heart will be spoken by all and my dead will walk clothed again in life,—where is the happy land ? Happiness ! A ghostly voice murmurs, 'Tis there, ever there where thou art not ! '

Next to *Erlkönig*, *Der Wanderer* was Schubert's most popular
song during his lifetime and for many years afterwards. The
poem first appeared in an almanac in 1808, under the title
' Des Fremdlings Abendlied,' and then as ' Der Unglückliche '
in 1815 in an anthology, where the poet's name was given as
Werner. Schubert's setting (October 1816) became the
delight of Viennese drawing-rooms some time ·before it was
published. At length it appeared as Op. 4, No. 1, in 1821,
dedicated to the Patriarch Pyrker, who gratified the composer
with 20 ducats and a letter of charming compliments. *Der
Wanderer* is said to have brought in 27,000 florins within
forty years to Diabelli, the publisher. It remains the most
familiar, if not the finest, of Schubert's songs in scena form.
The music begins superbly with a movement of tragically
palpitating triplets worthy of the composer of *Erlkönig*.
Nothing in the song quite equals this opening page ; there is
indeed nothing in the weakly keepsake poem to sustain such
grandeur. The C♯ minor Adagio melody (' Die Sonne dünkt
mich ') has expressive charm, but the song unmistakably
weakens here, and the quick movement verges on the trivial.
And small wonder ; for Schmidt's melancholy is too vague,
too self-indulgent, it lacks ' fundamental brainwork.' But
there was at least this luck, that Schubert was able to round
off the composition with a return to rich poetic gloom. The
compactness of the song is one reason for its success over
most of the others of its kind ; and another reason is the
grateful character of the writing for a fine basso-cantante
voice. There is every chance here—free declamation and
broad cantabile, minor sorrow and major animation, a
number of top E's and a well-justified bottom E to end on.
That is its compensation, even though the song that began
by looking like one of Schubert's finest masterpieces turns
out to have something of the mere ' period piece ' about it.
The ' Die Sonne ' melody was to form the basis of the
celebrated ' Wanderer-Phantasie ' for pianoforte of 1822.
The first version of the song printed by Mandyczewski
(called *Der Unglückliche*) carries the voice up to F♯ at one
point.
Schubert's settings of the poet Uz, five in number, were
all composed in 1816. All are neglected. Not very much
is to be claimed for them ; but certainly the spritely little
strophic song *Die Liebesgötter* deserves to be remembered
among Schubert's lesser gems. *An den Schlaf* is a modest
relation of *Wanderers Nachtlied* (I). *Gott im Frühlinge* has
a pretty semiquaver figure maintained from end to end,

derived from the 'spring's shimmering robe' of the poet's
first line. *Der gute Hirt*, a paraphrase of the 23rd psalm,
is set in a strain of homely piety, not without expressive
harmonies. *Die Nacht* is sweet and tender in its very modest
way, but four repetitions are too much for its slightness and
it becomes monotonous.

Thirteen Hölty songs were composed in 1816. The 1815
settings of this gentle poet have prepared us to welcome the
reappearance of his name. The new group is again all of
little pieces of much simplicity of facture ; all, whether gay
or sorrowful, of modest and not intense feeling ; and all
written with minute delicacy. What in practice is the purpose of a music so unassuming ? One can imagine that
there are retired corners far from the ordinary and strenuous
ways of music-making where the Hölty songs are cherished.
Schubert was no doubt well satisfied by simply finding with
his magical faculty the just musical equivalent of a handful
of lyrics that had taken his fancy. Hölty's strains were
more often than not pathetic. Two different songs are named
Klage (*Trauer umfliesst* and *Dein Silber schien*). We need
not smile if in the latter the poet tells the moon how all
too soon its ray will fall no more on his pale cheek but on
an untimely tombstone ; remembering that this time it was
not a conventional melancholy but a plaint wrung from one
cruelly doomed in youth. *Auf den Tod einer Nachtigall*,
a type of these sad little songs, shows how true was Schubert's
sense of proportion. The dead nightingale moves him to a
pitying thought, but to no flood of woe. Still on the same
small scale there are songs of the seasons, spring (*Frühlingslied*), harvest (*Erntelied*), winter (*Winterlied*) ; and innocent
love-songs—*Die Knabenzeit*, *Minnelied*,[1] *Die frühe Liebe*, the
dainty *Blumenlied*, the merry *Seligkeit* in ländler rhythm.
There are two versions of the pathetic little song *Der Leidende*
with the curious difference that where one moves up the other
moves down. Schubert used (*a*) as the basis of the 'Rosamunde' Entr'acte in B flat.

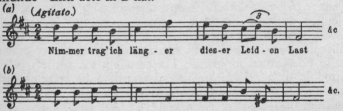

¹ Brahms's famous song, Op. 71, No. 5, is a setting of the same text.

There is also a second song *An den Mond* ('Was schauest du so hell') but, like the whole group, it is not comparable with the other song of that name ('Geuss, lieber Mond') of 1815; nor has any one of the group the melodic strength of the 1815 *Mainacht*.

Most of Schubert's Salis songs belong to 1816. They are secondary, but they possess modest charms, for instance, the genuine rustic flavour of *Pflügerlied* and *Fischerlied*, the bubbling of spring water in the triplet accompaniment to the contented melody of *Die Einsiedelei*, the sudden enrichment by the modulation from F to Ab in *Die Wehmuth*. One of these Salis poems is celebrated, the *Lied : In's stille Land*. It expresses with fine pensiveness and dignity thoughts on man's transition to the 'silent land.' Schubert has felt at once the poet's seriousness and reserve. He enlarges on none of the scenic phrases, (the gathering clouds, nightfall, the wreck-strewn coasts of life), and sets all three stanzas to the same gravely flowing music. The song deserves to be better known.

Schubert returned for the last time to his old friend Matthisson in 1816. There are seven of these songs, some of them planned on rather ambitious lines—for instance, *Entzückung*, a taxing song meant for a splendid tenor voice. *Klage* ('Die Sonne steigt') and *Julius an Theone* might also be made effective by fine singing, although for Schubert they are but indifferent. The little pieces are preferable; thus the innocent and folksong-like *Geist der Liebe*, the placid evening love-song *Stimme der Liebe* (Schubert's second setting), the light *Skolie*, a toast to all things young and fair, and, last of the series, *Lebenslied*. There are, all told, twenty-five Matthisson songs and two fragments, but not one is near being first-rate Schubert. We thought much the same of the Kosegarten songs of 1815; but there comes in 1816 a last setting of that poet, *An die untergehende Sonne*, of distinguished beauty. Such a song indicates Schubert's increasing mastery in the hours when his inspiration was not at its most intense. This address to the setting sun is in form a kind of rondo, with two returns of the apostrophe in Eb and two considerable episodes. The sentiment is rich and noble; the piece extensive but not to excess. Schubert was critical enough to omit half the poem. The song was published as Op. 44 in 1826.

Jacobi's name is first met with in 1816. There were eight settings of his verses written then, including the song by which Schubert perpetuated his memory—the *Litanei*—falsely ascribed to August 1818.

' Surely they rest well, the souls of the departed, there
where all wounds are stanched and the mourner is comforted.
They have passed from the world's mercilessness to the
everlasting mercy.'

There was never a truer or more touching expression of
simple devotion and of grief consoled and yet still near
weeping. Jacobi's poem consists of nine stanzas—far too
many, of course. It is usual to sing the first, third, and sixth.
The poet's six-line stanza has prescribed the shape of Schubert's melody. The first line, a kind of refrain, is set to a
strain of ideal sweetness and calm in plain E♭ major. The
four middle lines admit a pang, an unabsolved sorrow. The
music starts from C minor on the thought, and makes a
troublous way over a chromatically descending bass. This
is a matter of only two or three bars. The return to E♭ is
attained, and with the sixth line the peace of the refrain.
Orpheus is a large dramatic piece. Schubert's more intimate
songs are too frequently sung on inappropriately formal
occasions. Such a piece as this pompous and not very
characteristic *Orpheus* might well be remembered for those
purposes. Schubert was this time writing with an exceptional
operatic voice in mind—so exceptional that beginning as a
bass in the address to the shades it is called on to work upwards
into lyric ecstasy as a tenor. This is in the first version of the
song. The more manageable second version is written down
a fifth from C minor to F minor in the middle part, and a
third, to B♭, in the finale, thus avoiding high A's. The other
Jacobi songs are all small and sometimes negligible. *In der
Mitternacht* records with a few hushed notes an impression of
nature in a solemn hour. *Trauer der Liebe* is an amiable little
love-song. The D minor song *Die Perle*, another trifle, has
a characteristic little hopping accompaniment descriptive
of the agitated search for the lost pearl.

Two little settings of C. F. D. Schubart belong to this year.
The poet was also a musician ; but the verses set by Schubert
as *An mein Clavier* were at first put into a musical maiden's
mouth, and called *Serafina an ihr Clavier*. Schubert leaves
the unregrettable Serafina out, and also two stanzas, one
of them with too much in it about angels, the other with
feminine inflexions. He makes of his song a personal expression, giving thanks for the consolation afforded by music
in a troubled life. From the date of his career, C. F. D.
Schubart's instrument may perhaps not have been a pianoforte,
and from the repeated epithet ' sanft ' not a harpsichord, but

rather a clavichord, the gentlest and most confidential member of the keyboard family. *An mein Clavier* is a modest song, but it will always be affectionately regarded for the intimate expression that is in it of Schubert's feeling for the art that was for him the whole of life. *Grablied auf einen Soldat* sounds funereal C minor harmonies ; but the strain is short and we tire of the repetitions before coming to the eighth stanza.

The last of the Klopstock songs were composed in this year. *Das grosse Halleluja* is written on two staves only. It was first published (after Schubert's death) for three-part women's choir with pianoforte accompaniment. *Schlachtgesang* may similarly have been meant as a choral piece. *Die Gestirne* is a litany sung by nature to its Creator, in fifteen stanzas. The song is unsatisfactory. Schubert has set the first stanzas to a good, bold F major melody above throbbing triplets ; this music he does not develop but leaves to be repeated. The effect is either incomplete if only one or two stanzas are sung, or else monotonous. *Edone* is by far the most likeable song of the group. It utters a fond sigh for an absent or lost mistress, whose image the poet sees in everything. Schubert's gentle melody begins in E*b* and turns plaintively into C minor. The middle part of the song is freshly composed, and then there is a return to the first strain.

The greater Schubert appears in one of the Stolberg songs of this year, viz. *Stimme der Liebe* (' Meine Selinde '). How it came that these few and ordinary lines warmed the musician to such a pitch of passion there is no knowing. The musing lover murmurs his mistress's name to a softly throbbing accompaniment ; the thought inflames him, and all the music blazes up, tearing its way from D to D*b*. ' Thine ! '—he comes out with the word rapturously ; and then in a new hush, ' mine ! ' Almost extravagant modulations (the key shifts about ten times in the short song) and dynamic variations depict his exaltation and desire. The middle part of the song is quiet but tense. Then towards the end comes another superb crescendo, and the return is made to D major with a triumphant ' thine ! ' on the high A. The song is one for an exceptional voice. The tone, whether loud or soft, is to be kept streaming abundantly at a very slow pace.

The nine little Claudius songs are by turns merry, pathetic and idyllic, and all are likeable. Strephon in *An eine Quelle* sweetly deplores his Daphne's absence from the fern-fringed spring. The music is gracefully slender and charming. *Phidile* is the tale of a nymph's first glimpse of Cupid, told perhaps in rather too many stanzas, but with a little music as dainty as it is limpid. There is in the two settings of *Ich bin vergnügt* as much jollity of movement as suits a small room, there is the most placid and mild of meditations in *Abendlied*. *Am Grabe Anselmos*, is a singularly delicate expression of youthful sorrow. ' Never, never,' sighs the bereaved friend, ' shall I be able to be happy again.' It is touching ; but a certain sweetness in the music and a slenderness depict an adolescent mourner whose life is probably not in peril, however sharp the momentary pain. There remain in this group two jewels of song. *An die Nachtigall* (' Er liegt und schläft ') is not much sung. It is no doubt too small and brief to carry weight outside an intimate circle ; but there is exquisite writing in its two-score bars. ' Love lies sleeping,' say the verses, ' and this is my hour of freedom. Nay, nightingale, I beg you, do not awaken love ! ' The melody has the peculiarity of beginning in C, although it is mainly in G. The song was published in 1829 as Op. 98 together with the Claudius *Wiegenlied*, which was composed in the same month (November 1816). This ' Schlafe, schlafe, holder, süsser Knabe,' is the very paragon of cradle songs. The melody springs among the A♭ harmonies as naturally as a daisy in the grass. Except perhaps *Der Tod und das Mädchen*, it is the best known of the Claudius songs. Richard Strauss borrowed the melody for his own purposes in the opera ' Ariadne auf Naxos.'

The Goethe songs of 1816 belong to the latter part of the year. Schubert went back to ' Wilhelm Meister,' and composed the three celebrated settings of the Harper's songs (published in 1822 as Op. 12), as well as two other settings of *Wer nie sein Brod*, (both virtually unknown),[1] and two more of *Nur wer die Sehnsucht kennt*. In Book II of ' Wilhelm Meister ' the hero seeks out the Harper in his wretched lodging. Waiting outside the door, he hears the harp and catches the words of *Wer nie sein Brod* :

> ' Whose bread was never salt with tears, who never suffered nightlong on the rack of despair, he has yet to know the heavenly powers for what they are. By them are we unasked, brought into life. By them is our path beset with pitfalls. They do not care ; and stand aside when fate exacts the penalty.'

The stanzas, so Goethe says, were now sung, now recited, and they were repeated more than once, while Wilhelm stood

---

[1] Professor O. G. Deutsch assigns *Wer nie* (IV., 258) to 1822.

listening on the landing.   Schubert was then formally justified
when in the Op. 12 song he set each quatrain twice over.
In the first repetition the A minor melody begins in the major
with softened and resigned effect, and it is further modified
to end on an F major cadence.   This cadence is strangely
marked with a diminuendo so difficult as to be almost
impracticable :

ihr   himm - li-schen Mäch   -   te

The second stanza begins in Bb major and the repetition,
with an effect of reinforced reproaches, in the minor.   There
is a wrenching return to A minor, a subsidence, and a final
and helpless repetition of the last two lines—a despairing
wail.   At the end of his four wonderful pages Schubert has
ranged over the whole gamut of grief.   So much music
could not have been packed into one statement of the words,
and Schubert would in all probability have repeated the lines
even without Goethe's authority.   The song well supports
comparison with Schumann's and Wolf's compositions.
Schubert's two other settings of the words are both in A
minor.   The first is a simple plaint in 6–8 time, in the vein
of the 1815 *Wer sich der Einsamkeit*.   The second
(Mandyczewski, No. 257) is a fine song in a novel, stormy
movement, with powerful modulations.   It would be well-
known but for the grander conception of the Op. 12 song.
Wilhelm, pushing open the door, found the minstrel alone
on his straw bed.   Sitting by his side, he praised the old
man's art as a consolation in solitude and compensation for
all society.   The minstrel took his harp and on the word
' solitude ' he improvised the song *Wer sich der Einsamkeit
ergibt* :

' Some live for life's sake, some for love ; but for me,
grief in solitude, the grief that leaves me never alone but
creeps in as a lover to his mistress.   Grief, I hug thee to
me.   But better were the utter solitude of the grave.'

Schubert's setting in A minor, Op. 12, No. 1, is a worthy
companion to *Wer nie sein Brod*.   The music is broadly

planned, it is filled with passionate feeling, it is adequate to
the poet's wonderful .expression of heart-breaking sorrow,
simple though the texture looks in comparison with Schumann's and in particular with Wolf's highly chromatic setting.
All three composers have given of their best to the tragic
Harper, each seems to have unsealed his private grief in
sympathy. Wolf's *Wer sich der Einsamkeit* is especially fine,
as is Schumann's *An die Thüren.* The lines of the latter
occur in Book V of ' Wilhelm Meister.' After the mysterious
conflagration and the rescue of the child Felix from the crazed
Harper's strange assault, the old man is lost to sight for a
time. One night, however, Wilhelm hears him near the
garden-house singing a song of which only the last stanza is
recorded. *An die Thüren* is then a fragment, but the musicians
have found the gentle melancholy of the lines irresistible.
Schubert's setting in A minor, Op. 12, No. 3, depicts in the
melody the broken Harper's new mood of resignation and
in the bass [1] his dragging footsteps—' I shall wander from
door to door, kindly folk will give me bread and kindly eyes
perhaps drop a tear, and I shall wonder why they are so
moved.' The music of the second stanza is essentially a
repetition of the first, but is scrupulously modified to accord
with the words. The 1816 settings of *Nur wer die Sehnsucht
kennt* are in A minor and D minor. Both have a more
simply lyrical character than the beautiful arioso of 1815,
but again in both there are sharp modulatory twists, as
though Schubert's musical sense were shuddering under the
poignancy of the lyrics. The A minor song, in 2-4 time, is
good music, but the three-fold repetition of the first two
lines at the end of the song is here felt as a weakness. The
D minor song is, in general design and movement, rather
like the celebrated setting of ten years later, Op. 62, No. 4.
  Schubert composed *Der König in Thule* from ' Faust ' in
this year. It is not one of the great songs. The tune is

---

[1] Cf. the bass of Beethoven's ' Bitten,' Op. 48 :

BEETHOVEN: Op. 48

&c.

SCHUBERT: Op. 12. Nº 3.

&c.

particularly square, and the music draws much on the primary pathos of D minor harmonies, with the effect of some monotony by the time the end of the third stanza is reached. The simple ballad style shows that Schubert had in mind the scene of Gretchen's idle carolling of the old tale with her thoughts not at all in Thule. The song was published in 1821 as Op. 5, No. 5. *Jägers Abendlied* is a forester's or gamekeeper's love-song :

> ' Out on the moors with my gun, I am haunted by the thought of that pale, lovely girl. And she, has she ever noticed me when I cross her path and slip again into the thickets ? '

Schubert left out the third of Goethe's four quatrains, no doubt because it introduced a more unrestful sentiment than the others, which were well served by the one small and sweet melody. The poem is musical but obscure. The eye fails to focus this romantical rustic lover. ' Reft of thee I drift to east, I drift to west. Then I seem to see thee in the moonlight, and a peace beyond understanding comes over me.' The Jäger's precise calling here, as elsewhere in German poetry, is not clear, but the description rather suggests poaching. Schubert's sliding sixths in the right-hand part depict the ' schleichen ' of the first line. The song [1] was published in 1821 as Op. 3, No. 4.

The last of the Goethe songs of 1816 was *An Schwager Kronos* :

> ' Lash your horses, Time ! No dawdling for me ! I would devour life, not nibble at it crumb by crumb. Not for me the tedium of thrift and caution and the long defence. I would pack the thin life of many days into one day of glory and then—come what may, so the end come quickly.'

The song is the masterpiece of 1816 as *Gretchen am Spinnrade* and *Erlkönig* were of their respective years. The poem dates from Goethe's young days (1774), the days of ' storm and stress.' It was written in a postchaise. ' Schwager,' properly brother-in-law, was a nickname for postilion ; and so familiarly does Goethe address Chronos, the ancient of days. Arrogant youth never uttered words more reckless or superb. The verses describe the exhilaration of life in its first flush, the young man's delight in mere movement,

---

[1] Another setting, composed in 1815 and not included in the collected songs, was published by Mandyczewski in *Die Musik*, January 1907.

in merely breathing ; and the refreshment snatched from the girls at the wayside inn. Nothing else is worth having, so he cries in his pride ; and before the pace slackens, before jaws mumble and limbs totter, may driver and car over-topple and pitch him into hell ! He anticipates the end. So blow your horn, driver ; bring out Orcus, host of the netherworld inn, to welcome us !

Again, as in the great songs of the year before, the essence of the music is its dynamic character. The first thought conjured up by mention of the song's name is of the galloping of D minor quavers. The music springs from the ' rasselnde Trott ' of the poet's second line. Up hill and down dale go Time's horses, sometimes clattering heavily, sometimes almost dancing on the way, but on and on ; and the drinks and the kisses of the D major passage in the middle seem to be snatched on the wing, for the movement is relentless. It is not fast. ' Nicht zu schnell ' says Schubert's direction. An over-hurried pace robs the words of their due weight. A properly pointed rhythm gives the song dash enough. The composition is onrunning. On the basis of six quavers in a bar there is much artful variety. For the vision of the mountains in the third strophe there is a magnificent mounting and descending bass beneath crashing right-hand chords. The modulations here are of extraordinary boldness and effect. From Eb there is a plunge into B major (i.e. Cb) for the lines ' Boundless and beauteous the world stands open before us '—and it is indeed like some turn in an Alpine road that suddenly presents an unguessed-at prospect to the exhilarated gaze. ' There soars among the mountain tops the eternal soul of things.' In the tumultuous music the key rises by semitones—E minor, F minor, F♯ minor. Later the quaver movement becomes cajoling during the address to the girl at the tavern door. With the return of D minor, ' Downhill now, and quicker still,' we get a return of the theme of the second stanza (' Jog on and upwards, over stock and stone, into the way of life ! '). There is another wrench-ing chromatic progression in the contemptuous description of old age. The postilion's horn, mingling with the sound of the horses' hoofs, is a new element in the last section of the song, where the key changes to D major to announce the more bravely the wild spirits of the challenger at the gates of darkness. *An Schwager Kronos* was published with two other Goethe songs as Op. 19 in 1825, dedicated to the poet who was then enjoying in all serenity the old age he had so scouted in prospect half a century before. Schumann perhaps had a thought of *Kronos* in his mind when he wrote his *Wander-lied*, Op. 35 :

There comes down to us from 1816 a grievous relic, a fragment of a solo setting of Goethe's *Gesang der Geister über den Wassern*—and not an unfinished composition, but what must have once been an extraordinary song, now muti-lated by chance. As it stands, the music of the first strophe and most of the second are missing. It begins in the middle of a phrase. The next three strophes are intact, but the fragment ends in the middle of the word ' Wasser,' two lines before the end of the poem. The consolation is that two other settings by Schubert exist, both choral songs for men's voices. The first (four-part, unaccompanied) was composed in 1817 ; and the second (eight-part, with violas, violoncellos, and basses) in 1820–21. The latter, Op. 167, is one of Schu-bert's greatest choral works. The gist of the poem which so much appealed to the composer is in Omar Khayyám's line, ' I came like Water, and like Wind I go.' The remark-able fragment is for a bass of immense range (E below the stave to G above), and it is characterized by frequent leaps of octaves and ninths.

Schubert's first three settings of A. W. Schlegel belong to 1816. *Lebensmelodieen* with its interminable and rather absurd dialogue between the swan and the eagle was composed in one of his uncritical hours. He should have turned the poet's pages quickly. In *Die verfehlte Stunde* he begins an agitated love-song in the most promising way ; but the poet's stanza has a kind of refrain in which a change is made to three-footed instead of four-footed lines, and Schubert is evidently hard put to it here to avoid triviality. *Sprache der Liebe* is a fervent serenade, maintained by a great melodic impulse and artfully accompanied by gradually enhancing effects—simple quavers, then trembling semiquavers, then hammered semiquaver chords. The passionate melody ex-tends itself with ease to embrace a stanza of ten lines.   There

are four of these stanzas, that is, for Schubert's purpose,
three too many. With one there is enough and the song is
self-contained. It cannot be believed that Schubert thought
of his crescendo being repeated again and again.

We come to some songs written for the poets of Schubert's
Viennese circle. The text of *Leiden der Trennung* is a translation from Metastasio by Heinrich von Collin. This quiet
song tells of the nostalgia of inland waters for the sea whence
they came and whither they will return. It is very little
known, not being included by Friedländer ; yet the two
simple pages are memorable, they take our affections by their
brief expression of subdued regrets. The Schubertian who
has hitherto overlooked *Leiden der Trennung* will be grateful
for the indication ; he will admit that these pages have
served a purpose.

By the other Collin, Matthäus, is the text of *Licht und Liebe*,
which Schubert composed for soprano and tenor. As is the
way with duets, the music is principally interesting to duettists.
The one Schober song of the year is a very pretty one, *Am
Bach im Frühling*. The motive is ordinary enough : a hopeless
lover sighs by the stream where he had once known hope,
and with melancholy he plucks the blue symbolic floweret.
Above a tranquil flow of quavers there expands one of
Schubert's lovely waterside melodies, in C♯ (D♭) major and
minor. The middle section is recitative. Then Schubert
feels he cannot do better than give us the melody again by
a simple *da capo*. The pitch of the song is curiously low,
considering its mild idyllic character. It is, in fact, in
Schubert's key of D♭, a bass song, and goes as low as G♯.

Mayrhofer now begins to figure large ; Schubert composed
ten of his poems in 1816. The songs of this group have
little in common. They include the stately *Fragment aus
dem Æschylus*, a few lines from a chorus [1] in the ' Eumenides,'

> [1] ' Of Justice are we ministers,
> And whosoe'er of men may stand
> Lifting a pure unsullied hand,
> That man no doom of ours incurs,
> And walks through all his mortal path
> Untouched by woe, unharmed by wrath.
> But if, as yonder man, he hath
> Blood on his hands he strives to hide,
> We stand avengers at his side,
> Decreeing, *Thou hast wronged the dead :
> We are doom's witnesses to thee.*
> The price of blood, his hands have shed,
> We wring from him ; in life, in death,
> Hard at his side are we ! '   (Morshead's translation.)

which Schubert sets as a solo ; a longish, conventional ballad of the days of minstrelsy, *Liedesend* ; and also small pieces in folksong style like *Alte Liebe rostet nie* and the lively drinking song, *Zum Punsche*. Mayrhofer in *Geheimnis* pays Schubert the most handsome compliments—' Say, who taught thee thy beguiling songs, which bring to us spring in midwinter, yes, and a glimpse of heaven amid the oppressions of earthly life ? '—compliments which Schubert at once sets to music, like everything else his friend writes. *Abendlied der Fürstin* faintly foretells in its pastoral 6-8 melody the ' Rosamunde ' song, *Der Vollmond strahlt* ; but the thunderstorm in the middle section is not very well explained or convincing. The one familiar song in the group is *An die Dioscuren* :

' Eternal brethren, strong to save, grant your servant calm waters. O Castor, O Pollux, bless my passage ; and this my oar I will lay as thankoffering, holy ones, on your altar, so I make haven tonight.'

The song is short but substantial. Schubert gives it music of the full nobility of a hymn, although the believer is a simple boatman and his gods only stars. The rhythm swings slowly but powerfully. The fine unison phrase in the middle section is the confession of faith. When Ab returns, the chords of the hymn are heard softly from a distance, as on the dark waves of bass semiquavers the boat is lost to sight. The middle section is the occasion for the barytone singer to come out with a ring in his tone ; and the last stanza (the dedication of the oar) for an artful diminuendo. The song was published in 1826 as Op. 65, No. 1.

A curiosity belonging to 1816 is an aria, Dido's appeal to Æneas, from Metastasio's ' Didone,' composed on the Italian text. It looks like a pastiche, and as though Schubert —perhaps to recommend himself in Salieri's eyes—had painstakingly suppressed everything Schubertian in his style. He unquestionably imitates the grand classic manner very well. Here, in this large and formal piece, is the dramatic soprano's chance, including as it does a cadenza and in the penultimate bar a high C.

Mandyczewski included in the 1816 volume the two Rochlitz songs, Op. 81, Nos. 1 and 2, which were later on found to belong to 1827. Both are in Schubert's most dainty vein. The first is *Alinde*, a general favourite :

'O home-going reaper, have you seen my sweetheart ?
No ; the reaper has thought for none but the bairns in
his cot. And the fisherman ? He cares for nothing but
his catch ; and the ranger for nothing but his kill. Alinda !
There, echo, I have told you my love's name ; now help
me to find her. Alinda ! She has heard, she is here ! '

The movement is a gently swinging barcarolle. All is
peaceful and balmy in this trysting hour. The lover's
questioning is an idleness, he has no real apprehension. He
is simply passing the moments of waiting, and he frames his
affectionate fancies to the rhythm of the breeze in the boughs
and the lapping of waters. The music plays with the fondly
repeated name and, of course, with the irresistible responses
of the invoked echo. The call 'Alinda ! ' is increasingly varied
by the harmony, and the answers vary according to character.

As for *An die Laute*, it is a bewitching little serenade ; a flower
of song, a daisy.

VIII

THE SONGS OF 1817-1818

SCHUBERT continued to teach at his father's school until the spring of 1818. His heart was not in the work. When at last he threw it up, his father, full of misgivings about an artistic career, induced him not definitely to resign but to apply for a year's leave of absence. Schubert was now the centre of a group of admiring friends such as Spaun, Schober, and Mayrhofer. He made Vogl's acquaintance in 1817. Spaun collected a number of Schubert's settings of Goethe and sent them in April, 1816 to Weimar, but received no reply. Apart from some fifty songs, Schubert's 1817 compositions are distinguished by a series of pianoforte sonatas—-Ab (May), E minor fragment, (June), the Eb sonata published as Op. 122 in 1830, (June) the B major, Op. 147, published in 1843 (August), and the A minor published as Op. 164 in 1854. There were also three overtures for orchestra—in D (May) and the two in ' the Italian style ' in D and C, which record the influence of Rossini's sensational appearance in Vienna in that year. One of these overtures was played in public in the following March—Schubert's debut in the concert room.

Schubert began his sixth symphony in C in October 1817, and finished it in the following February, and to 1816 belongs the string quartet in E, No. 11, published as Op. 125 in 1830. Schubert's way of life during this winter is obscure, but he was teaching in his father's school at the Rossau house. In the summer of 1818 he obtained the post of music tutor to the two young daughters of Count and Countess John Charles Esterházy. The family spent the winter in Vienna, the summer at their country place at Zseliz in Hungary, whither Schubert accompanied them. The Zseliz compositions include, in addition to songs, an unfinished pianoforte sonata in F minor and the variations on a French air in E minor, for pianoforte duet, which Schubert dedicated to Beethoven and published as Op. 10. in 1822.

Mandyczewski's fifth volume contains forty-seven songs of 1817 and fourteen of 1818, which was a comparatively unproductive year. The masterpieces of this period are settings of Goethe, Schiller, Schubart, Claudius, Jacobi, and Schober ;

while there is a fine series of sixteen Mayrhofer songs all
but one of them belonging to 1817.

One of the grandest of Schubert's compositions, and incomp-
parably the finest of his Schiller songs, is the *Gruppe aus dem
Tartarus* :

> ' Lo ! Tartarus, the bottomless pit ; and the moans of
> the damned are like the sound of all the seas. Their tears
> swell Cocytus' bitter flood ; and their endless lamentation
> is this, Is there no end ? And there is none. From the
> eternal circle time is banished with his scythe in twain.'

The composition dates from September 1817, and was
published as Op. 24, No. 1, in 1823. As in the great Goethe
songs, the musician is here felt to have been transported by
the poet's vision ; to have been driven into the astonishing
utterance, so new at once and so natural, by burning inspiration. The form itself was the old one of different movements,
with a final brilliant allegro ; but this time the poetic content
brimmed. The ' muttering of an angry sea ' of the poet's
first line prompted the tumultuous sextolets of the opening
movement. Such a chromatic style must in Schubert's time
have seemed very audacious. Its effect is hardly dimmed
to-day. The tortuous progression is planned to create a
sense of long-baffled and ever less tolerable unrest, all tending
towards the desired resolution. This at length comes half-
way down the fourth page in a blaze of C major—it comes,
but with an appalling irony in its decision and in the triumphant shout ' Eternity ! ' for it celebrates victory over change
and time, and the perpetuity of damnation. If there is a
criticism of the magnificent composition, it is that the musical
content is not fully realizable in the sounds of a single voice
and pianoforte.

Hell has been found by all the artists from Dante downwards
to be a more manageable subject than heaven, and notably
by Schubert, who followed his *Tartarus* immediately with a
setting of Schiller's companion piece *Elysium*, but could not
produce music of a comparable intensity for the scene of bliss.
Still, the composition, which is in the older manner, is well
worth looking into. It consists of a chain of songs. There
is much repetition of the poet's lines, which extends the work
to the dimensions of a cantata (ten pages). If not inspired,
it contains admirable matter. Orchestrated, it would serve
the dramatic soprano as an imposing concert piece. Similarly
there is for the powerful bass singer a large and unduly

neglected composition, *Der Kampf*. The conflict it describes
is between principle and passion, and the latter is, so we are
left supposing, on the point of victory. The battlefield is a
lover's soul. Duty is defeated by the discovery that the
woman in the case is ready to return love for love. The inner
struggle is, all the same, agonizing, and there is despair in
the cry, ' Virtue, take back the wreath I won, and let me
sin ! ' The poem ends with the bitter thought that the
one reward worth having for the laborious upbuilding of
character involves that character's destruction. Though
rather highflown and abstract, it has genuine interest and a
reality not too common in Schiller. Schubert's setting points
to the kind of dramatic music he might have left us if chance
had helped him to give of his best to the stage. *Der Kampf*
is an operatic scena, and a fine one. It deserved to come at
the climax of a dramatic act. The music is rhetorical, but
good and bold, the D minor opening in particular, where the
voice has broad phrases above this energetic instrumental
theme—

a theme of rich symphonic implications.

Now Schubert returns to *Thekla : eine Geisterstimme*,
which we have seen him attempting before, in 1813. This
time the song of the gentle wraith is purely lyrical. The
melody, sweet and wan, fluctuates between minor and major
with a ghost's indecisiveness and is all contained within a
fourth. Monotony hardly is avoided if all six stanzas are
sung. There are two versions in Mandyczewski, the first in
C♯ minor and major, the second in C minor, with the difference that the alternate quatrains (2, 4 and 6) are given a slight
variation of the first melody. The latter song was published
as Op. 88, No. 2, in 1827. The remaining Schiller song
of 1817, *Der Alpenjäger*, is to be mentioned as one of Schubert's
out-and-out failures. Nothing, indeed, could have been
less inviting or tractable than the poem, which consists of two
poems in one, and neither good. In the first part the shep-

herd's mother makes three attempts to persuade her son to
look after the lambkins and cultivate the flower-garden ; but
each time the unruly youth declares preference for hunting
in the mountains.   Part II describes his ruthless pursuit of
a gazelle down gorges and up crags.   He has driven it to
bay on the brink of a precipice when the Spirit of the Alps
appears, taking the quarry into divine charge and denouncing
the hunter's cruelty—' Is there not room on earth for all ?
What drives you to spread anguish and death among my
flock ? '

Only two completed Goethe songs belong to this period ;
the first a setting of a celebrated poem, *Auf dem See* :

> ' Life is renewed in the air of this free world, and the
> lapping water is kind nature's lullaby. Shall I languish
> for an old dream's sake when reality is so good ? Morning
> comes down in the air from the hills, and the morning
> stars twinkle in the ripples of the lake.'

The verses were written by Goethe on Lake Zurich, in the
summer of 1775, in the course of a holiday with the Stolbergs,
undertaken to test (or perhaps to escape from) his sentiment
for pretty Lili Schönemann.   She is alluded to in the ' dream '
of the trochaic second stanza.   Schubert's song begins with
a charmingly graceful barcarolle movement, and it is possible
that he did not read deep enough, for though he makes a change
to 2–4 time to meet the changed rhythm of the third stanza, the
new movement is a little too jaunty for Goethe's exhilarate
greeting to morning in the hills.

A masterpiece of the period is *Ganymed* :

> ' It is spring, it is morning, it is heaven ! Soul of all
> things, come nearer. O sunlight, O Love ! The clouds
> open. God descends, and wraps his creation in his
> embrace.'

The poem belongs to the 1770's like ' Prometheus,' with
which we think of it as one of Goethe's finest renewals of
antique myth.   It is no empty exercise in a classic manner,
but a sheer discovery of modern poetry in the hoary theme.
Schubert sets out on the hymn with melodious rapture,
though the four-square structures—always more noticeable
in Schubert's instrumental music—is noticeable here.   Musical
thoughts crowd upon him.   The opening movement
in A♭ is full of rich and almost amorous contentment.   In

the middle section, in E, the voice part is more broken up, with pauses in which to listen to the bird-calls of the May morning. The movement animates ; and the F major finale is an outburst of enthusiasm with beautiful melismatic settings, each time more elaborate, of the invocation, ' All-loving Father ! ' The last of these is a searching test of the singer's stamina and technics :

all - - - lie- ben- der Va - - - ter!

The rambling key-design is a peculiarity of *Ganymed*, though *Prometheus* is similarly free. The song, which began deep among the flats (A*b*, C*b*, G*b*), ends with a soft, cloudlike drifting of F major chords upwards and away. *Ganymed* was first published as Op. 19, No. 3, in 1823.

The first of two fragmentary settings of *Mahomets Gesang* (Goethe) belongs to 1817. This, unlike the 1821 fragment which Schubert left unfinished, is believed by Mandyczewski to have been mutilated by chance like the *Gesang der Geister* of 1816 and Gretchen's prayer, *Ach, neige, du Schmerzenreiche* of 1817. The poem was written in 1773, and, like ' Prometheus,' was intended as part of a never finished play. It is not strictly ' Mahomet's song,' but is an ode in the prophet's honour, celebrating him with imagery drawn from the course of a great river. In the play it was to have been sung by Mahomet's cousin Ali and his daughter Fatima, Ali's wife. Schubert's magnificent 1817 fragment is of considerable extent (six pages) and includes about half the poem. Goethe begins, ' See the star-like gleam of the stream that springs from the rock ! ' and this gives Schubert his motive, a dancing fountain of semiquaver triplets which never ceases for a single beat all through the six pages. The composition must date from one of his most confident and brilliant days ; but we ask in vain whether he maintained and enhanced his music in Goethe's triumphant culminating strophes. The 1821 fragment is much shorter, including only the first twelve lines of the poem. It begins with great energy, in a rush of semiquaver scales and arpeggios.

If, indeed, the setting of Gretchen's prayer, *Ach, neige*, was once complete, its fragmentary state is a reproach to Schubert's friends and the inheritors of his papers, for here was assuredly one of the great songs. The three pages that survive include all but twelve lines of the poem, and since the last three lines

are repeated from the beginning there is every reason to
suppose that Schubert went (or would have gone) back to
his opening strain in B*b* minor. When the song was first
published (Posthumous Songs, Book 29) an *ad hoc* conclusion
was provided ; and a modern English composer, Nicholas
Gatty, has also written one, which should bring the song into
the light.

Gretchen is taken in the toils. The garden love-making
is over. The scene of the prayer comes between the colloquy
with Lieschen at the well and Valentin's tragedy. The lost
girl brings flowers to a shrine of the Virgin and there tells
her heartbreak. Schubert is plunged in sympathy. Gretchen
here is not murmuring her grief ; she cries it out on broad
phrases in which there are the beginnings of terror as well
as pathos. The pianoforte's opening motive is in itself a
gesture of appeal. In the syncopations of ' das Schwert
im Herzen ' Schubert seems to translate into notes his sympathetic and quickened heartbeats. At ' Was mein armes
Herz hier banget ' the voice and the accompaniment utter
different sobs :

There is no Gretchen music to compare with *Am Spinnrade*
and this song.

The Claudius songs of 1817 are insignificant with one
celebrated exception, *Der Tod und das Mädchen* :

> ' Away, away, dreadful spectre ! Spare my life ! Gentle
> spirit, spare me !—Soft, give me your hand. There is
> nothing to fear. I come simply to send you to sleep.'

This short page impressed from the first all who knew it.
One result of the admiration was the distribution among
collectors of morsels of the autograph, three of which survive
in the possession of the Vienna Gesellschaft der Musikfreunde.
The song was published as Op, 7, No. 3, in 1821. The

unforgettable picture is created by means of rare simplicity. Nothing better than the D minor ' death ' theme exemplifies Schubert's practice of taking up what lay nearest to hand, if it served the purpose. Death's naturalness, its inevitability, and, yes, its essential mercifulness are matchlessly expressed in this soft and solemn strain. The constituents were any composer's everyday material. It is, in fact, simply a bass. Yet Schubert had only to lay hold of it for infinite significance to be discovered. There was indeed depth below depth ; and years later, in 1826, he returned to the strain and revealed the implications in the Variations of the great D minor quartet. In the month (March) following *Der Tod und das Mädchen* Schubert composed a kind of pendant, *Der Jüngling und der Tod*, on a text by Spaun, who must have been prompted by the Claudius song. This is not a protest but an appeal for release by death. There are two versions, in the second of which (not in the first) there are a prelude and postlude to Death's answer based on the theme of the February song. The first version is ' for two voices.' In the second the answer is written up from B♭ to F, to bring it within the tenor compass of the whole. The music is good Schubert but not the equal of the other song. *Der Tod und das Mädchen* is for a deep contralto or bass voice, for it wants a low D at the end.

Schubert did not after 1817 return again to Claudius ; and similarly the last two settings of C. F. D. Schubart were composed in this year. *An den Tod* is another appeal to Death, this time a harrowing one, for it is on behalf (in the first stanza—the second is supererogatory[1]) of the untimely doomed, of the budding flower. The music exerts itself in passionate protest through a series of desperate modulations, as though the appellant were taking to one failing foothold after another. The technical means recall *Stimme der Liebe* (' Meine Selinde '). The sequence of keys is as follows : B, C, E minor, B♭, B minor, D, A, F♯ minor, B—within the two pages. *An den Tod* is the finest of the Schubart songs. The most popular is *Die Forelle* :

' Jolly little beast, trout. Nimbler than we are, for all our arms and legs. Wily as can be, too. They can spell " angler " as well as most folk. And that fellow with the rod thinks they can't see him ! Ha ! now he says he'll

---

[1] Schubart's poem consists of sixteen quatrains. The first two are used by Schubert as one stanza, and the last two form the second stanza as the song appears in Mandyczewski.

be wily too.   He's stirring the water up ; but it takes more
than that to beat a trout.   No, I'm wrong.   If he hasn't
landed one !   Well, I don't call him a sportsman.'

Schubert was critical enough to omit the poet's last stanza,
which contained the moral, namely a warning to maidens
to avoid fishy young men.   The song was popular from the
first, as witness the numerous autographs.   Mandyczewski
prints four versions ; the differences are slight, but the later
ones give an improved turn to the melody at ' Ich stand an
dem Gestade.'   The song was first published as a magazine
supplement in 1820 and then by Diabelli in 1825, as Op. 32.
The six introductory bars in Friedländer's edition are not
admitted by Mandyczewski.   Though the favour that *Die
Forelle* has received has been disproportionate, it remains
a charmingly pretty song.   The square and unpretentious
folksong-like tune is set off by the engaging sextolet figure
in the right-hand part, illustrative of the gliding fish.   The
song is essentially strophic, and Schubert seems to have roused
himself from his musical play to attend rather perfunctorily
to the trout's misfortune in the third stanza.   The sunny,
summery mood is very easily regained after the little dis-
turbance.   The *Forelle* tune was not done with.   Schubert
took it up again two years later for the fourth movement
(variations) of the favourite pianoforte quintet in A.   In the
sixth and last variation the sextolets of the song return with
charming, friendly effect.
    The Mayrhofer songs of the period have much diversity.
The poet wrote now of the heroines of antiquity, Antigone
and Iphigenia, and again of an idealized peasantry, as in
Der Alpenjäger, and for every scrap of his friend's verses,
so it appears, Schubert found music—not invariably
with the fullest success, but assuredly to the enrichment of
his thought and style.   Mayrhofer attempted to follow Goethe
and Schiller in tapping the themes of classical lore for new
poetry.   As songs, these efforts of his have unequal results.
The seventeen pages of *Uraniens Flucht*—a scene on Olympus,
containing a high-flown colloquy between Zeus and the
Uranian Aphrodite, who has returned home from her earthly
mission in disappointment with the ungrateful race of men—
leave us cold.   *Fahrt zum Hades* is a forgotten song, being
totally eclipsed by *Tartarus*.   *Antigone und Œdip* is a dramatic
fragment of stately character.   The scene is the road to
Colonos.   While the blind king sleeps, Antigone prays the
gods that they shift their fury from him to her innocent head.

Œdipus wakes ; he has had a vision of his end at Colonos, and to broad and solemn music he bids farewell to his glorious and ill-starred life. The piece is written for dramatic soprano and bass. It was published in 1821 as Op. 6, No. 2.

It was a far cry from any of Schubert's typical subjects to Mayrhofer's *Atys*, which is however not a translation of Catullus. It is a lament by the Phrygian shepherd for his lost home, whence the enamoured Cybele had ravished him in her lion-drawn chariot, to serve with deprivation a peculiar priesthood. Schubert was here not tempted a step from his everyday path. The opportunity which another would have seized on for something exotic, for some corybantic display, left him untouched ; and the piece is in fact particularly mild. *Iphigenia* again is an exile's plaint. Agamemnon's daughter, serving Artemis in distant Tauris, implores the goddess her saviour for yet another act of grace, namely, restoration to her southern home. The song should be attractive to a fine soprano singer ; the melody has large and noble curves and there are characteristic modulations in the sea music of the middle section. It was published after Schubert's death as Op. 98, No. 3, transposed from the original key of G*b* to F.

Philoktet again is derived from classic story. The Sopho- clean hero, Heracles' friend and the victim of Ulysses' wiles, was exiled on Lemnos while the Greeks laid siege to Troy. Philoctetes possessed the magical arrows, Heracles' legacy, which alone could reduce the Trojans ; but Ulysses has, so he complains, defrauded him of his weapons, and now he sits helpless on the desert strand, while birds fly past and deer rustle in the brake in immunity. The music begins outside the main key (B minor) in G# minor, with a striking agitato motive which one could imagine put to symphonic use. The whole is a vigorous little dramatic lyric, but perhaps fragmentary in effect. Philoctetes' remote plight really needs so much explaining.

We come to the finest of the Mayrhofer songs, *Memnon*,[1] and find the poet this time pouring a passionately subjective expression into the ancient myth. The theme is nominally the Egyptian statue that had the property of uttering a harp- like note to greet the sunrise ; but here in reality it is the poet's self whose days are a repression and who after nightlong and unbearable melancholy calls on the Dawn, Memnon's mother, to translate him from the mortal sphere. The thought of the unhappy Mayrhofer's end is not to be

[1] See p. 21.

banished ; it reinforces the poignancy of the yearning in
this and other poems of his. It is obvious how touched and
impressed Schubert was by the friend's dark sayings. The
music of *Memnon* seems to arise out of the depths of brooding.
It moves from noble melancholy to distraction and torment
in the declamatory middle section, and then, with the return
of D♭, to the longing appeal for the sphere of bliss. The
vocal part hovers with remarkable freedom between recitative
and lyric melody.   We see how flexible a style Schubert now
commanded in the natural change from the gloom and narrow
range of the opening phrases to the quickened lyricism
prompted by the thought of Aurora's purple in the sky.
The underlying music of the first two pages has the character
of an impassioned funeral march. The rhythm changes to
continuously throbbing triplets in the aspiring last page.
The noble song, a song for a barytone of power and range,
was dedicated to Vogl, and was published as Op. 6, No. 1, in
1821.

The subjects of the smaller Mayrhofer songs lay nearer
home. *Erlafsee* is a lightly worked sketch, in a limpid 6-8
movement, of the lake near Mariazell. This was the first
of Schubert's songs to be published. It appeared in 1818
as a supplement to Sartori's annual ' Picturesque Album for
Admirers of the most interesting Sites and most noteworthy
works of Nature and of Art in the Austrian Monarchy '
Dedicated to Count Esterházy, it came out later as Op. 8,
No. 3, in 1822. Schubert set only a few descriptive lines
from the friend's poem, leaving out the more personal stanzas
addressed to a ' Wunderfrau.' A more attaching little song,
also included in Op. 8, is *Am Strome* :

> ' Like thee, O river, is this my life, that has frolicked in
> youth, that has swollen in anger, and has known the lash
> of the storm. I too am passing, passing, and I too shall
> one day merge in the infinite ocean.'

The placid flow of the music is interrupted by a brief declamation ; then the mood of resignation, so melodiously
expressed, returns. Soft B major triplets in the accompaniment soothe the poet's weariness. The cantilena calls for
exquisite singing. It is justly a favourite among Schubert's
smaller waterside songs. *Auf der Donau* is more sombre and
contains more illustrative detail. The river rolls heedlessly
past the ruined works of the men of old, castle and tower ;
and bush and briar overgrow the crumbling sites. The poet

perceives something sinister in the obliteration and in nature's indifference ; and the Danube's flood seems a symbol of unrelenting Time. Schubert begins with a barcarolle movement in duple time. Oppressed feeling breaks out in the syncopated middle section. The resumption is, curiously enough, in F♯ minor, whereas the song began in E♭ ; and in F♯ minor it ends, carrying the voice to the low tonic in illustration of ' Downfall, downfall ! ' The song is hardly a favourite, the darkness of the scheme, of the bass voice and the low range of the pianoforte part is against it ; but it is a good one. *Nach einem Gewitter* is on the other hand positively naïve, and is surely not a song that Schubert would have wanted published. The attribution to Schubert can only be circumstantial, there is no particle of intrinsic evidence. Everything about it is rudimentary, and the accentuation very awkward.

One of the popular Mayrhofer songs is *Der Alpenjäger* :

' To live by your gun in the highlands is to be a man. The air of morning in the mountains ! It sends the blood racing, it makes the eye keen, the heart bold. It makes life worth living—that, and the air of evening in the valley, the soft air of the western valley where lives the prettiest girl in the world.'

The unpretentious piece jigs along cheerily. We are not, of course, convinced. This is the merry Swiss peasant of German chromolithography. ' The more risks, the jollier it is,' says Mayrhofer's mountaineer. That is the spirited holiday-maker's view, not the peasant's whose business is mountaineering. But we would not be without Schubert's song. Time has kindly lent a certain winsomeness to its undeniable banality. It engages us as a ' period piece.' The workmanship is perfectly deft. Observe the balance between the exuberant upward F major strain and the droopin F minor reference to the absent sweetheart. No one else would have done so irresponsible a thing half as well. The F minor–D major modulation of the middle section is the Schubert touch. The first version in Mandyczewski, in E, is without the introductory chords and has a slight melodic difference. The song, with two others in light vein (*Der Schäfer und der Reiter* and *Lob der Thränen*), was dedicated to Spaun and published in 1822 as Op. 13.

The hero of *Der Schiffer* again is inclined to pose picturesquely. There is sublime joy, declares this boastful boatman, in confronting the storm with manly bosom, and nothing is so odious as a life of comfort. The song is for a bass, the form is strophic, and the simple vigour of the movement is persistent. It sounds like a jolly drinking song. Schubert dedicated it to Mayrhofer when it was published in 1823 as Op. 21, together with two other settings of his verses, *Auf der Donau* and *Wie Ulfru fischt*. This last is a simple strophic song about a disappointed angler. The bold, uncommon tune marches enterprisingly into other keys before returning to its predestined D minor. There remains the *Schlaflied*, which appeared as a modest companion to *Gruppe aus dem Tartarus* in Op. 24 :

' Woodland and river murmur, Come, human boy, here is no place for sighing.—He lays him down on silk-soft grass, and soon he sleeps, lulled by the thousand voices of leaf and bird and brook.'

It is a placid and graceful lullaby in 12-8 time, with a melody that characteristically rises by octaves and spreads as it falls over F major chords.

In 1818 there was only one Mayrhofer song, but this was a dozen in one, being the cantata-like piece *Einsamkeit*, an affair of seventeen pages. Schubert wrote it in July at Zseliz, where, so says a letter to the bohemian circle at home, he was ' living and composing like a god.' ' Mayrhofer's *Einsamkeit* is ready, and I think it is the best thing I have done so far, for my mind has been free from care.' The problem of these enormous and unpractical compositions faces us again when so confident a word comes for once in a way from Schubert himself. Before now we have taken refuge in assuming that such pieces were usually of the nature of exercises, certainly not intended for immortality in the park-like pages of Breitkopf & Härtel's editions of the great masters. But here is Schubert at twenty, saying (true, only in the flush of finishing the composition) that this impossible *Einsamkeit* is his best thing. The fact perhaps is that litera-ture, which was Schubert's stimulus, was also his lure. For poetry he felt the same uncritical enthusiasm as men of letters often feel for music. The verses of the poets exhaled intoxications for the impassioned youth. He poured out music in their honour ; and sometimes it seems, in these early years, as though it were a matter of luck whether the chosen poem had the making of a song and we were bequeathed a masterpiece or whether the musical stream lost itself in a desert. *Einsamkeit* tells of the pilgrimage of a life. The hero is first drawn to the seclusion of monastic religion. Youthful blood runs too strong, and he seeks the world of activity. But neither the market-place nor joyful companionship satisfies his soul. He tastes the sweet and bitter of passion ; he knows the lust and horror of war. And, after all, he returns to solitude and communion with nature as the best compensation for the infliction of existence. The pilgrimage ends amid the sounds of rustling fir-branches, a cuckoo's call, and the plunging of a torrent through the rocky woodland. But Mayrhofer's hero is, after all, only an abstraction. We can take no personal interest in him. The musician never was who could keep such a composition alive. Schubert has his moments, notably in the E♭ minor love-episode. Best of all are the last three pages in G, the scene of the retreat with the cuckoo and the waterfall. Beginning with the words ' Gib mir die Weihe der Einsamkeit ! ' there is a self-contained and attractive song. Here, on a carpet of pine-needles and in sound of the woodpecker's drumming, Schubert was at home.

Two of the three Schober songs of 1817 are in praise of music. In *Trost im Liede* the poet faces the storms of fortune harp in hand, and the angry blast turns to sweet sounds on the sacred strings. The song, a neglected one, is pleasing in a modest way. The D minor beginning of the song proper, after the F major prelude, is one of the Schubertian touches. In the same month (March) was composed *An die Musik* :

'Music, my consolation and dear saviour, what would life have been without thee, home of the exile, love of the unbeloved, O music, earthly mirror of the heavenly kingdom ? Be thanked, dear and divine one, and be blest.'

The mood of this celebrated, this immortal page, is very different and deeper. Schubert was, we can feel, moved to his inmost being in the brief thanksgiving. Brief it could only be, and simple to the last degree, for here Schubert had all to say, the whole of gratitude, the whole of blessing. It was such a moment as even the golden-tongued have few words for, while most men bow and are mute. To pay a tribute of music to music's very self ! From Schubert, who drew existence thence as a saint from his deity, this could only be a religious act ; and *An die Musik* is essentially a prayer. Every particular of the song in which our composer was confessing his faith would be worth looking into. The poem consists of two quatrains of iambic pentameters, which are set strophically. Such long lines call for a broad melody. The germ of the music is the phrase shaped for the composer by the opening words, ' Du holde Kunst.' This passes between the bass and the voice imitatively. The first half of the melody droops by sixths and a seventh under the suggestion of ' grey hours ' and ' caught in life's toils.' The balance comes in the soaring second half, which reaches an eleventh above the lowest note and towards its end mounts above a chromatically rising bass. The melody has a codetta set to a repetition of the last four feet (in the second stanza, the first four feet) of the last line. This codetta is a subsidence from the exaltation of the climax (' rapt me to a better world ') and takes the form of a modification of the opening phrase :

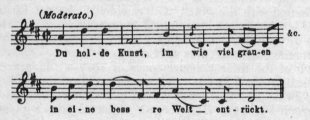

The right hand simply fills in the harmonies with repeated quaver chords that suggest the self-accompanying singer all engrossed, without thought for detail or figuration, by an ecstatic message. It is part of the single-heartedness of the music's effect that it adheres strongly to D major, with a chromatic touch or two and a momentary leaning to B minor, but none of Schubert's habitual play of picturesque modulation. Such a composition wins for the author a tenderness that is more than admiration from the coming and going generations. *An die Musik* was not published for ten years (Op. 88, No. 4).

There are but a few more songs of 1817. *Der Schäfer und der Reiter* (La Motte Fouqué) is a dialogue between a shepherd and a cavalier. It is all allegorical ; for we imagine no society in which shepherds urge passing cavaliers to give up errantry and take to amorous sport with Amaryllis, nor in which the cavalier would trouble to explain to the hind how a romantic vow was driving him ever onwards. The music sets in contrast a charmingly pretty pastoral in E against a galloping 6–8 movement in E minor. The song appeared in 1822 (Op. 13, No. 1), dedicated to Spaun. To the same period belongs No. 2 of that set, a very popular song, *Lob der Thränen* (A. W. Schlegel) :

> ' In the beauty and bounty of spring, in the raptures of youth, among the kisses and the rose-petals, is there not all the heart can wish ? No, unless there too is a glistening tear, the tear of tenderness and compassion.'

In the verses there is nothing but a pattering dance of double rhymes. The music is a delicious *Viennoiserie*. It is a waltz—only lightly disguised by the notation—half gay, half sentimental. It was just like Schubert to set his prelude coquetting one instant with G minor and the next with D. The song is a near relation of *Ungeduld* in ' Die schöne Müllerin.' Fetching though it is, only the caprice of publishers has made it one of Schubert's most familiar songs ; it has always been in their shop-windows, while nearly equally engaging songs, such as *Die Blumensprache*, have been kept in the dark. This latter, too, is an authentic example of Viennese cajolery. The verses (by Platner) came from a Keepsake ; which is just as it should be. It would be a courageous feat to-day to write a poem on the Language of Flowers ; but it was different then, and quite timid people did so without thinking twice. Schubert's music is as light as can be in texture, the pen that jotted this inveigling tune and the flutter of accompanying triplets must have skimmed across the paper ; it remains an exquisite valentine. Let a pleasant singer take it up, one able to suggest ardour under the cover of playfulness.

The two Széchenyi songs, both of 1817, are *Die abgeblühte Linde* and *Der Flug der Zeit ;* the former a recitative with air, somewhat pale, the latter a barcarolle in one of Schubert's favourite movements, which here tends to jauntiness, so that we see how he has only to go on hastening it to leave the suggestion of water traffic behind and to urge it into the wild ride of the D minor quartet finale. The two songs were published in 1821, in Op. 7, dedicated to the noble poet. *Der Strom*, a bass song in D minor, was dedicated to Albert Stadler, one of Schubert's Konvikt friends. He had been reading law, and at about this time he left Vienna for his home in Upper Austria, where in later years Schubert renewed intercourse with him. He wrote the libretto of one of Schubert's least lucky operettas, ' Fernando,' and the text of *Der Strom* is supposed to be his. The subject was a favourite one of the period, a comparison between the poet's life and the course of a river. A truceless semiquaver movement bears the music along with romantic vehemence and pessimism. *Der Knabe in der Wiege* was the last of the songs of 1817, a C major lullaby, graceful enough, but not especially characteristic.

Schubert's four Schreiber songs were all composed in 1818. All, though of rather less than the first intensity, have a safe place in the Schubertian's affections. *An den Mond in einer Herbstnacht* would never have been as neglected as it is if only it had consisted of four pages instead of six. The poet addresses the autumnal moon in a vein of quiet melancholy. He finds her the one old friend unchanged on his return to his childhood's home. The lightfoot lads are scattered, and the love of his youth has gone, gone where the dark and the moonlit nights are all one. The moon has seen many laughing and many weeping, and will see many more, but not these two. Against the soft and serene loveliness of Schubert's music is to be set the fact that, for him, the accentuation is more than once unfortunate. The principal melodic phrase, a beauty :

—suggests violin music ; it is rarely quite at home with the words, and at ' und erquickend wie das Wort des Trostes ' there is a plain misfit. Many details, however (the skipping child, the falling dew), show Schubert's engrossment in the poetic scene. The song, so little known, would reward an uncommon singer possessing art enough to maintain the interest for all its length. The next one, *Der Blumenbrief*, is a valentine :

' O posy, take my message, and say that one word from her will cure my ills.   You, red rose, will speak of my love. You, myrtle, whisper something about hope and the stars ; and you, marigold, hint at despair and heartbreak and a suicide's grave.'

The language of flowers again ; and the thing is a flower of song, an old-fashioned flower, prim and sweet.   It causes a smile, but the friendliest smile.   *Der Blumenbrief* is the paragon of its kind.   Passed between the right fond hearts, it must have been irresistible.   *Das Marienbild* is a little prayer at a wayside shrine, most delicately written, with tentative leanings towards many keys as though in devoted search of the most acceptable, sweet expression.   *Das Abendrot* is more of a parade piece, a rhetorical address to the splendour of sunset, rich in melody but depending much on the flooding tone of a noble voice.   It was composed in November at Zseliz, and Grove thinks it was ' evidently composed for the countess,' who sang contralto.   But when it was first published (true, this was not until 1867), it was specially designated ' for bass,' and Mandyczewski prints it in the bass clef.   Whoever sings it must have good, solid E's, top and bottom.   The musical interest dwindles in the last page unless the ear is engaged by a sumptuous voice.

The poignant song of the Virgin's suffering, *Vom Mitleiden Mariä* (F. Schlegel), may be associated with the *Litanei* and with *Das Marienbild*.   The G minor melody is oppressed by sympathetic grief.   The song is a piece of pure three-part writing with no filling-in, an exceptional texture in Schubert, though there is another example in the early Kosegarten song, *Von Ida*.   Here the pianoforte parts keep wandering as though driven to unrest by the thought of the subject, the Virgin's grief on Calvary.   The delicate little A minor song, *Blanka*, also has a text by Friedrich Schlegel.   It is for light soprano, a girl's song, precariously poised between major and minor—between the carelessness of first youth and the loss of peace of mind— and dipping apprehensively at last.

From the works of the other Schlegel, A. W., Schubert took and composed translations of three sonnets by Petrarch, in November and December.   Without being at a loss— for the music has a certain style—he seems to have felt the formality rather than the soul of this poetry ; and he wrote for it in the musicianly but not very characteristic vein of some of his classical and allegorical songs.   The first sonnet, *Apollo, lebet noch dein hold Verlangen*, is Petrarch's—

> ' Apollo, s'ancor vive il bel desio
> Che t'infiammava alle tessaliche onde,'

in which the poet likens his Laura to a laurel-tree, which he
begs the god to defend from foul weather. The music,
in which recitative and arioso alternate, is stately but hardly
affecting. The second sonnet, *Allein*, *nachdenklich*, is
Petrarch's celebrated—

> ' Solo e pensoso i più deserti campi
> Vo misurando a passi tardi e lenti.'

The poet avoids the paths of men, seeking to conceal from
all the passion that consumes him ; but whatever wild resort
he chooses, Love still bears him company. The ' dragging
footsteps ' of the original was embellished by Schlegel with
' as though lame with cramp.' The G minor opening of
Schubert's composition, serious and toiling, with syncopations
for the wanderer's halting steps, is the most striking part.
The third sonnet, *Nunmehr*, *da Himmel*, *Erde schweigt*, is
Petrarch's—

> ' Or che 'l ciel e la terra e 'l vento tace,
> E le fere e gli augelli il sonno affrena,
> Notte 'l carro stellato in giro mena,
> E nel suo letto il mar senz' onda giace.'

> ' Now that heaven, earth and the winds are silent
> And sleep holds reined both beast and bird,
> Night leads her starry chariot around
> And in his bed the sea lies all becalmed.'

In some unexplained way Schlegel or Schubert attributed
the sonnet to Dante, and Mandyczewski unsuspiciously
adopts the error, so that Dante's name has figured again
and again alongside Shakespeare's and Goethe's in lists of
Schubert's authors. There is a line in the ' Inferno '—

> ' Mentre che 'l vento, come fa, si tace '—

which may somehow have caused the confusion. Schubert's
setting is an extended piece. The description of nightfall
in the first quatrain was evidently welcome to him. But on
the whole he seems to have felt these sonnets of intellectual
love to be a little arid.

The romantic minstrelsy of *Blondel zu Marien* is unmistakable Schubert, a song for an impassioned tenor, rising
from deep gloom in Eb minor to an exalted major strain in
honour of the star of true love. The poem, erroneously
ascribed by Friedländer to Grillparzer, is by no known author.
The fioriture in the voice part look so strange to Schubert's

style that Mandyczewski takes them to be embellishments added by Vogl. We can see that Schubert associated them with an artificial expression from his lavish use of them in his graceful little Italian pastiche, *La Pastorella*, composed on a text from Goldoni in 1817.

IX

THE SONGS OF 1819–1821

SCHUBERT could not face a return to school-teaching at Lichtenthal. He broke with his father. Schober gave him lodging for a time in his mother's house, and then early in 1819 Schubert went to share Mayrhofer's roof in the Wipplingerstrasse. He set his hopes on the stage, and finished in January 1819 a ballad opera in one act, ' Die Zwillingsbrüder.' To this period also belong an overture in E, some choral songs, and a fragmentary piano sonata in C♯ minor.

The Esterházys went to Zseliz in April 1819 without him. Instead, Vogl took Schubert in July for a holiday in Upper Austria, where, at Steyr, he began the A major ' Trout ' pianoforte quintet, (published as Op. 114 in 1829)—the earliest of his generally known chamber compositions. The friends returned to Vienna in September. Schubert lived that winter at Mayrhofer's.

The Easter cantata ' Lazarus ; oder, die Feier der Auferstehung ' belongs to the spring of 1820. It has come down to us in imperfect form. The 1819 ballad opera, ' Die Zwillingsbrüder,' was produced at the Kärntnertor theatre on June 14 with Vogl in the principal part. Soon afterwards Schubert wrote incidental music for a fairy play, ' Die Zauberharfe,' which was produced on August 21 at the Theatre an-der-Wien. Another dramatic work of 1820, an opera, ' Sakuntala,' was unfinished ; and so, to our great loss, was the C minor string quartet, the opening movement of which is the beginning of Schubert's maturity in the composition of instrumental music.

In the spring of 1821 Schubert and Mayrhofer parted company. It was the year of Schubert's first publications— Opp. 1–7, all songs. In August he began an unfinished symphony in E, curious particulars of which are given in Grove's Dictionary. (The autograph belonged to Sir George Grove and is now in the library of the Royal College of Music. The symphony was at Grove's suggestion scored by J. F. Barnett and was performed at the Crystal Palace in 1883.) Schubert and Schober spent a country holiday together in the autumn of 1821, and the first two acts of the

opera ' Alfonso und Estrella,' to Schober's libretto, were
then composed. In this year began Schubert's friendship
with the two young painters, Kupelwieser and Schwind.

Twenty-two songs come down to us from 1819, eighteen
from 1820 and twelve from 1821. The masterpiece of 1819
was the setting of Goethe's *Prometheus*. The next year was
remarkable for some of the finest of the Mayrhofer songs,
as also for pretty settings of Friedrich Schlegel, and Uhland's
Frühlingsglaube. In 1821 Schubert went back again to Goethe
and composed a series of masterly songs, ranging from the
lightly erotic *Versunken* to the sublime *Grenzen der Menschheit*.

Prometheus is an extract from an unfinished drama begun
by Goethe in 1773-4. The monologue is in the third scene,
in Prometheus' smithy :

> ' Frown, God, and fume ! Tyrant, do your worst. The
> child that believed in you as protector and pitying father
> is a man grown. A pitying father, you ! I denounce you,
> sniffer of burnt sacrifices. I denounce your lovelessness,
> your petty everlasting spite ! Me and the men my sons
> you shall not have for slaves.'

In this magnificent ode, one of Goethe's most proud and
powerful compositions, the classic story took on a new life.
It became the voice of the actual revolt against theocracy,
echoes of which sounded throughout Europe for generations,
e.g. :

' Ah, thou that darkenest heaven—ah, thou that bringest a sword—
. . . Thou art smitten, thou God, thou art smitten ; thy death is upon thee,
    O Lord.
And the love-song of earth as thou diest resounds through the wind of her
    wings—
Glory to Man in the highest ! for Man is the master of things.' [1]

The Schubert of *Prometheus* and of such companion pieces
as *An Schwager Kronos* and *Grenzen der Menschheit* is a composer unsuspected by those who know only a few of the
Müller songs, and *Hark, hark, the lark*, *Die Forelle*, and the
like. He had a fist. How far he saw into the implications
of Goethe's lines there is no knowing. It is enough that
his generosity was stirred by the hero's defiance of the tyrant.
He found a music of revolt and challenge, of taunts and
of powerful optimism. Whether or not he knew the monologue as part of a play, he composed dramatic music for it

[1] Swinburne, ' Hymn of Man.'

(as indeed was the only way)—and this is the most successful of all his writings in that vein. It is not a song, but a dramatic scena. The form—recitative, arioso, allegro—was one that he used frequently but, as a rule, not very characteristically. But *Prometheus* should make us chary of deciding what were the limits of Schubert's genius, for, inspired by the appropriate poem, he is here seen to triumph in a field far from his normal lyricism. The recitative is the finest, the strongest and most apt, that is to be found anywhere in his work. It merges into arioso, and at points there is a prediction of Wagner's style. The terseness is remarkable. The poet's last seven words are repeated, and that is all. If there is a final allegro, it is in no way conventional, but is the closest interpretation of the poetic idea.

Prometheus has been injured by Friedländer's indication of 'allegro' at the opening, where 'maestoso' was wanted (Mandyczewski has 'kräftig,' energetic). 'Allegro' makes the challenging subject too jaunty. Simple as it is, it does well for the bold hero :

It begins confidently in Eb major, an indication that Schubert took Prometheus's defiance literally and not, like Wolf, as the wild audacity of despair. The heroic theme then turns towards G minor, the key of the powerful recitative, which in modified shapes (as in *b* above) it punctuates with bass octaves that seem to call for the sound of trombones. The instrumental part throughout is obviously not pianoforte music, but is the sketch of an orchestral accompaniment. At the words 'Nourished on prayers and sacrifices, your Majesty would starve but for children and beggars !' the music turns to a kind of arioso, and there is nothing in Schubert more like irony than the crawling of the part-writing. The second recitative, more angry still, comes in with crashing diminished sevenths—'Did any lend me help against the brute Titans? was any my saviour but my own courage?' The hero tenses himself to utter his supreme taunt—God no less than himself is the perishable creature of almighty time and everlasting destiny, 'My masters, God, and yours!' Schubert works up to these last words by an extraordinarily excited chromatic progression:

Enough said; Prometheus goes back to his job, and the short last movement sounds with doughty C major chords, his hammer-blows. The whole is one of the finest pieces of music available for dramatic bass. The other celebrated composition of the poem is, of course, Hugo Wolf's, a magnificent work which derives something from Schubert and also from Wagner. More even than in Schubert's setting, the pianoforte is in Wolf's felt to be inadequate to the storm and stress. There is a whole page of D minor thunder and lightning before the voice enters. The writing is altogether more elaborate and fin-de-siècle than is Schubert's, but that does not say that the intrinsic thought is superior. Both are great compositions, and neither is to be disparaged for the other's sake. It is curious how different are the heroes they depict. Wolf must have been thinking of Prometheus chained. The music is one wild storm. The tortured hero is desperate in defiance. The power he addresses may be evil, but must, to call for such a frenzy of denunciation, be a power indeed. Schubert's Prometheus is the confident artisan of a new order of things. He speaks in anger, certainly, but even more in scorn of the superstition that had imposed itself on his young credulousness. He ends rejoicing in a new liberty. Only C major, so Schubert felt, could properly celebrate the first freeman's, the first free-thinker's victory ; and in C major, in disregard of the remoteness of the key from his principal key of G minor, he ends. On another page was noticed Wolf's greater scrupulousness in his accentuation of certain words in Prometheus's last lines ; but whereas the sense of the lines in Goethe is, ' Behold me, then, forging a new race in my own image ! ' Wolf's last page of music rather represents the agony of the Caucasian martyrdom, and the victim seems to be crying in his extremity, ' Break me, twist and rack, but my spirit is my own ! '

Eighteen months (October 1819–March 1821) must here be skipped over to bring into association with *Prometheus* its pendant, the setting of Goethe's *Grenzen der Menschheit* :

' God speaks ; and man knows his own frailty. For who art thou, poor sport of time, that wouldst affront high heaven ? Man, bow down. Abase thyself, thou dis-appearing speck, thou drop that wilt in a moment be in-distinguishable in the flood, thou single ring in the ever-lasting chain of the life of God ! '

The poem was written at Weimar in about 1780. The mood of humility is sung as nobly as the arrogance of *Pro-metheus*. Let us admire the poet who lived so intensely in all his various days, and attempting no false synthesis seized for all he was worth on the truth of this one and of that. Schubert's song is again for bass ; and again the insufficiency of the pianoforte is felt in the realizing of the splendid music. The long succession of rich, low-lying harmonies seems to crave for the tones of horns, clarinets, and bassoons, and bass strings. If the composition, although one of Schubert's greatest masterpieces, as deep and beautiful as it is original, is too little known, it must be because in actual performance the many long, soft minims cannot be really sustained and the sound perhaps tends to dullness instead of a rich

darkness full of colour. This is not to go back on the
argument against scoring Schubert's lyrics. *Grenzen der
Menschheit* is for all its deep calm and *recueillement* not
an intimate lyric, but a universal hymn to the Author of
Being. Poet and musician both seem rapt by a vision of
all humanity abashed—not in dread, for what should
insignificance fear? but in self-forgetting wonder—before
the indifferent (' gelassen ') and all-embracing power. It
is not an individual's song.

The poet hears God's voice in the thunderstorm; and the
obvious thing for a composer would have been to begin with
storm-music. Schubert, however, and after him Wolf, are
both engrossed by the inner poetry; and thunder-clouds
and lightning can rarely have been so gently referred to as
in this first page. The composer's thought is all of the
divine majesty; and this is rendered by a progression of
massive bass harmonies which begin, with heavy sforzandos,
outside (in G) the main key (E) and subside—or, as we may
fancy, depart to a distance—before the voice, in low tones,
begins to express its solemn wonder. The eight-bar period
beginning ' I kiss the hem of his mantle ' is tenderly devout.
(In his haste Schubert here wrote ' *tief* in der Brust ' for
Goethe's ' treu '). Throughout the music we are conscious
of the imposing metrical foot—crotchet, dotted minim. The
movement hardly varies; but extraordinary modulations
lend the richest colouring. ' Would he raise himself to the
stars,' says Goethe, ' foothold on earth is lost '; and Schubert's bass advances chromatically and relapses. ' The
billows bear us up for a moment, but we sink, we are swallowed
up.' Here, with few notes but arresting harmonic trans-
formations, an effect is made of helplessness and collapse.
The modulation is from F♯ minor enharmonically to E♭ minor,
and thence to B :

The passion of such expressions is enhanced in the song by calm stretches of diatonic writing. *Grenzen der Menschheit* is no ordinary singer's song, but is meant for a bass of noble sonority, commanding the low E.

There was beside *Prometheus* one other Goethe song of 1819, a setting of the sonnet *Die Liebende schreibt*. Goethe felt for long no liking for the sonnet form, but in 1807 he retracted, and he wrote a sequence of sonnets, whose tender expressions are supposed to be related to Minna Herzlieb. Several of the sonnets are, like this one, given as a girl's utterances. Schubert no doubt had ' Die Liebende ' of the title in mind, and wrote a limpid music which flows through three pages with hardly a deviation from its key, B♭. He would surely have given different tones to an address from the poet himself. The song is modest, but is genuine Schubert. The two quatrains are treated to a repeated melody in 3-4 time, and the tercets similarly with a new melody in 2-4, repeated with modifications for the second half. There is an attractive setting of the poem in Mendelssohn's Op. 86.

Schubert's four compositions of poems from the ' Westöstlicher Divan ' date from 1821. A European vogue for oriental literature was started in the last quarter of the eighteenth century by Sir William Jones, the Persian and Sanskrit scholar. The immediate instigation for the ' Westöstlicher Divan ' was found by Goethe in Hammer's German translation of the Divan of Hafiz (1812). Goethe's first Divan poems were written in 1814 :

> ' Pendant les guerres de l'empire,
> Goethe, au bruit du canon brutal,
> Fit *le Divan occidental*,
> Fraîche oasis où l'art respire.' [1]

[1] Th. Gautier.

The word *divan* means a collection ; strictly, a collection of a poet's works in alphabetical order. But Goethe was, of course, not literally imitating Hafiz. The poet was at the time well on in the sixties. The ruling womanly influence was Marianne von Willemer, the ' Suleika ' of the ' Divan.' In later years she professed to be the author of the poems of Schubert's *Suleika I* and *II*. The ' Divan ' consists of some 200 poems in twelve books. Singers are familiar with a number of them through Mendelssohn, Schumann, and Wolf. The first one set by Schubert was *Versunken* from the ' Book of Love" (Uschk Nameh) :

> ' Curlylocks, give me leave to play in your tangles ; and pay out your streaming gold through my ten fingers, and take it back, and pay again ; and take my kisses on nape and ear, and pay me them back, curlylocks, with your lips, curlylocks.'

Schubert has here made a selection from Goethe's verses. The song is of the ' onrunning ' type ; not derived from recitative and aria, but from strophic form, become through the practice of ' modification ' ever more free and supple, while remaining lyrical. The incessant rush of the pianoforte's semiquavers seems to represent the rippling of the girl's loosened tresses through the playful lover's hands ; the movement is excited, and the tonality keeps on shifting as the lover finds ever new and delightful sensations. The key of the song is Ab ; but the opening harmony is the dominant minor ninth of Eb, and for long the animation of the caresses allows of only momentary glances at the tonic which, so unwelcome are its definiteness and stability, is put off again and again, until the fifth and last page. A pendant to this brilliant and delightful song of fortunate love is the yet more famous *Geheimes* :

> ' A glance from her eyes speaks volumes, volumes that are shut and sealed to all the world—but not to me, happy me ! '

The music is wreathed in smiles, half sly and wholly tender. Only at one point (' Lasset nur '), the lover, when he is telling people that they may guess and guess and never guess right, comes near giving his secret away through bursting self-gratulation. The inquisitive pianoforte persists with its questioning in bar after bar. At the end, as is the way with busily curious people, it has not heard the answer, and goes on putting its soft, pertinacious questions. The song is, of course, one of the jewels of all music. This and *Versunken* represent a new phase of Schubert's lyric art, further examples of which are in the Rückert songs of 1823. The compactness, the delicacy, and (shall we say?) psychological refinement of such writing were to give the cue to the later song-composers, Schumann and Wolf, with delightful and varied results, but nothing more lastingly sweet and engaging. Schubert dedicated *Geheimes* to Schober in 1822, when it was published as Op. 14 with another ' Divan ' song.

This was *Suleika (I)* (' Was bedeutet die Bewegung ? ') on Marianne's poem from the eighth book. Also composed at the time was *Suleika (II)* ('Ach, um deine feuchten Schwingen') which was not published till rather later (Op. 31, 1825, dedicated to Anna Milder, the opera singer). The enamoured woman in the first addresses the east, in the second the west wind. The east wind seems to her to bring messages from the absent lover, the west she charges with her voluptuous answers. The style is changed from the compactness of the first ' Divan ' songs to one of dreamy and enthusiastic extension. The winds blow softly, with numerous but suave modulations, in the pianoforte's pages of semiquavers, the east principally in B minor, the west in B♭. In both these beautiful songs Schubert has repeated words again and again as if in sympathy with the lonely Suleika's idle hours and desirous cogitations. In each there is towards the end a change of tempo and of accompanying figure expressive of quickened passion. The first is the more languorous, the second rather the more urgent. Both call for a rich quality of soprano tone. The first will hardly stand transposition downwards. It is seven pages long, the pianoforte part usually lies rather low ; sung by a contralto, it may sound monotonous. In *Suleika (II)* the right hand's broken octaves rise remarkably above the usual range of Schubert's pianoforte writing in the songs, and the voice is carried up to B♭. We have also in this year, 1821, Schubert's compositions of two of Mignon's songs in ' Wilhelm Meister,' which he had not hitherto attempted. They are *Heiss mich nicht reden* and *So lasst mich scheinen*. They are practically unknown through the fact of Schubert's having eclipsed them five years later with his celebrated Op. 62. The later music is more richly coloured, more passionately melodious. Yet if we think of the pathetic, childish Mignon, the earlier songs, with their slighter texture and high-lying vocal line, are seen to have an appropriateness of their own. They would certainly be sung, for all Schumann's and Wolf's settings, if Schubert himself had not

created supplanters. Both are in B minor and major, in
2–2 time, and are in other ways, too, a closely united pair.
The writing is almost cautiously delicate, as though Schubert
was continuously mindful of the susceptible waif. There
is a certain relationship perceptible between the two settings
of *So lasst mich scheinen* :

At about the same time as these ' Wilhelm Meister ' and
' Divan ' songs Schubert began the composition, on heroic
lines, of Goethe's ballad *Johanna Sebus*. The poem records
an actual event, the drowning of a seventeen-year-old girl in
a Rhine flood of 1809. She had rescued her mother and had
returned into danger to help some threatened children.
A dam burst and the brave girl was lost. Schubert set the
first two of Goethe's five stanzas in a rushing D minor movement ; there are six pages of it, then—a breaking-off. The
piece, like *Mahomets Gesang* of the month before, is a fragment ; there is no knowing whether the composer would
have been able to carry the immense undertaking to success.
With the tale only half told the piece is (like the 1817 fragment
of *Mahomets Gesang*) already as long as *Erlkönig*.
 A few Schiller songs belong to 1819. Three of them are
renewed attempts on poems already composed in 1812–15.
In *Sehnsucht*—which Mies assigns to 1817, probably rightly
—Schubert retains the theme of the finale of the 1813 song.[1]
The rest of the music is new. It is pleasant. If the song
remains formal and fails to move us to anything more than
a friendly regard, it is no doubt the fault of Schiller's frigid
allegory, which suggests nothing more intimate than a painting
on a palace ceiling. Mandyczewski prints two versions differing
only in very trifling points. In the one the voice part is in the
bass, in the other (which was published as Op. 39, in 1826)
in the G clef. The latter, curiously enough, takes the voice
rather lower than the former, e.g. at the words ' Gold'ne
Früchte.' The second setting of *Hoffnung* is a racy little song

[1] See p. 81.

in swinging 6-8 movement, with vivid chromatic touches
and a characteristic modulation. It makes the effect of
the wilder kind of drinking song. It was published in 1828
as Op. 84 in company with the third (1819) setting of *Der
Jüngling am Bache*, a poem on which we have seen Schubert
at work as early as 1812. This time, as also in 1815, he composed it as a strophic song. It is the popular setting ; a
sweetly melodious and plaintive piece. Only the fourth
repetition of the music is perhaps one too many. The
finest song in the group is *Die Götter Griechenlands* (' Schöne
Welt, wo bist du ? '). This is a setting of one stanza, the
twelfth, from Schiller's long ode in honour of the divinities
of the ancients. In a less judicious mood Schubert would
have undertaken all sixteen stanzas, impressing us more
perhaps by his courage and fluency than by the reality of
his regrets for the ousted Olympians. The lovely little song
that we so fortunately have names no god in particular, but
merely sighs in the true romantic way for a better land, a
golden age. It plays delicately with the cloud and sunlight
of alternations between minor and major modes—A minor
for the wistful question, A major for the ideal fancy and cheer-
ing gleam. This was Schubert's favourite means of pathetic
effect. A familiar instance is the minuet movement of the
A minor string quartet. Here its employment is exquisite.
Time and again consolation is attempted, but at the end the
questioner remains unsatisfied and the plaintive third and sixth
prevail. In the first of the two versions given by Mandyczewski the music is left half unresolved on the 6–4 chord.

Early in 1819 Schubert composed his two Silbert songs,
both of them expressions of piety evoked by nocturnal
nature. The stars in *Himmelsfunken* are God's signals to
adoring man. The song, a strophic one of the simplest
texture, acquires interest through its enterprising harmony
Abendbilder is a long stretch of music (seven pages), brimming
with a sense of nature's charms and benignancy. It is the
hour of dewfall and moonrise, and the only sounds in the
entranced air are the leaves' rustling, the nightingale's song
and the tinkle of a church bell in the valley. Such evocations
were just the ones to transport our Schubert into blissful
forgetfulness of the practical world. He poured out lovely
music (as later on he was in *Im Walde* to do in a really
extravagant way), not so much like a calculating artist
as a mystic. *Abendbilder* is largely composed of those
broken sixths which Schubert must have associated with the
movement of branches in the night wind. We get them

again in *Nachthymne* and as every singer's pianist remembers, in *Der Lindenbaum* :

The evening bell comes in, tolling F♯ minims. The moon shines on the stones in the churchyard ; and to the comfort of nature's sweetness in the summer night the poet adds thoughts of religious support, inducing Schubert to leave A minor (nominally the key, though actually the tonality has wandered freely to and fro) for a major ending. *Abendbilder* is a song too loose and also too persistently subdued for the public scene, but in private it will always be prized by Schubertians.

The six Novalis songs are extremely little known, for one reason because all are excluded from Friedländer's edition. *Hymne* (I) (' Wenige wissen das Geheimnis der Liebe ') and *Nachthymne* are extended compositions ; the others are quite small. The words of *Hymne* (*I*) are a passionate expression of eucharistic mysticism. The A minor opening of the music gives a slight hint of one of Wolf's most beautiful sacred songs, ' Wo find' ich Trost ? ' The song as a whole is stately rather than characteristic. *Hymnen* (II) and (III) (' Wenn ich ihn nur haben ' and ' Wenn alle untreu werden ') are both strophic songs, both in B♭ minor and major, and both express adoration in a sweet and tender tone hardly distinguishable from that of Schubert's village love-songs. The fourth (' Ich sag' es jedem, dass er lebt ') is another small strophic song, charming but almost naïve. *Marie* is a gemlike song of a score of bars. The melodious strain is the pure gift of a May morning. But this time it is beyond disguising that while Novalis has uttered a prayer, Schubert has paid a compliment. The sixth of the Novalis songs,

Nachthymne, belongs to the next year (1820). Here Schubert was not at his best. The copious repetitions of the words, necessary for the largely planned song, strike us as a little insensitive ; and although there are beauties in the music, the theme of the finale (in which the exalted poet welcomes the rejuvenation of death) must be set down as banal. Also to this period belongs *Widerschein* (Schlechta), a smiling village idyll about a fisherman who espies his girl's reflection in a brook.

The four Italian songs, later sent to Spaun's betrothed, Fräulein von Roner, belong to this period. They are *Non t'accostar all' urna, Guarda, che bianca luna, Da quel sembiante appresi*, and *Mio ben ricordati*. They were composed in January 1820. It is curious to see Schubert, with conscious demureness, writing in a foreign idiom. The poet's words were like Latin to a schoolboy—they appeared to him pompous and without vividness. We see from these songs how much the picturesque suggestions of native poetry counted in Schubert's art. There are tears, flowers and moonlight in Metastasio, but Schubert evidently did not recognize them as the real things—only as forms of polite expression.

Five Mayrhofer songs were composed in 1819 and five more in 1820. *An die Freunde* is the death-devoted poet's farewell. He bids his friends bury him namelessly in the woodland, where with spring's renewal the scene will have only delightful objects, flowers and greenery, to greet them with. But at this point in his resignation he rebels at the thought of utter obliteration and declares that the friends' affection will reach him even past the barriers of death. Schubert, to whom poor Mayrhofer was dear, must, knowing his melancholia unfeigned, have written the song with a certain ache. The music begins magnificently with a funeral-march movement in A minor. Everything points to one of Schubert's greatest tragic pieces. Half-way through, however, support from the poetic motive fails. The declaration of love's power over death is felt to be less real than the valediction. The music continues to be beautiful, but the development does not balance the exordium. An example sadder still of such a falling-away is the setting of the same poet's *Sehnsucht* (' Der Lerche wolkennahe Lieder,' Op. 8, No. 2). After Schubert's bewitching springtime melody of the first page, with its trilling larks and general air of holiday, it is a pity to see him compelled at Mayrhofer's behest to turn his back during the rest of the song on the sunny scene, and to find strains appropriate to an unseasonable woe.

Again the song *Beim Winde* fails to be all it promises ; and again the fault is clearly with the poet's flagging impulse. A scene is depicted of nature at peace ; the woods, the clouds, the river half asleep. Then the wind springs up and all is confusion. The poet proceeds to draw a moral : it is best to keep storms out of one's bosom. Schubert has set it all to music. The beginning of the song is charming. In *Sternennächte* Mayrhofer, gazing at the stars, gives up for once his quarrel with destiny. He submits to their calming influence. In those far spheres there are, he does not doubt, tormented souls and bleeding hearts, but the starry brightness is not dimmed ; and the poet concludes, not without humour, that even our unharmonious little earth, seen at a suitable distance, may well appear a gem in the heavens. Schubert's setting is a characteristic movement in 6-8 time, lightly flowing.

Nachtstück comes near the category of the great songs. The short accompanied recitative at the beginning is packed with music. The writing suggests the adagio opening of a string quartet. The air is hushed ; and the slow, chromatic unfolding of the harmonies makes us keenly expectant. This music introduces to the scene an aged minstrel. He comes into the moonlit woodland, feeling death upon him, to sing his last song to holy nature, the consoler of his life. He plucks soft arpeggios from the strings, above which his voice rises in noble melody. He prays for peace, and fancies that the trees, the grass, and the birds make answer, wishing him well. He expires ; and ghostly echoes of his harp-tones sound through the last page of the music. It is all as beautiful as could be ; only the situation is romantically vague and artificial. Not so gracefully do men die ; and aged musicians can no more than others make so sure of euthanasia. The intensity of the introduction and the gratefulness of the cantilena to a fine singer ensure a certain place for the song, but owing to the unconvincing subject it is rather less than a favourite. The *Nachtstück* was published in 1825 as Op. 36, together with another considerable Mayrhofer song, *Der zürnenden Diana*, of December 1820. This large composition of eight pages is an enthusiastic address from an Actæon-like victim of the chaste goddess. He has spied upon her and her nymphs at their bathing-pool, and he is dying, shot by an arrow from her vindictive bow. But death, says the inflamed youth, is not too much to pay her for the stolen privilege ; yes, it is a gratification to the victim to gaze upon her, still more beautiful in anger, even in her justiciary act.

Nothing was lacking in Schubert's impulse to make the song one of the grandest. It begins with a symphonic vehemence and sweep. The vocal part, for dramatic tenor, is drawn with exceptional breadth. Schubert, in fact, lent more eloquence to the dying adventurer than the poet had dreamt of. Lines had to be repeated again and again to provide words enough for the large musical design. Here we touch on the weakness of the song. It is too repetitive. A fresh thought, a dramatic development, are after a time badly wanted. None comes; but only a continued frothing of the youth's exaltation, which we begin to suspect as unnatural and picturesque.

The two noble Orestes songs, to Mayrhofer's text, belong to this period. In what we have called Schubert's ' stately ' manner there is nothing finer than *Orest auf Tauris*. It is a reminder that Goethe had made the hero a living character in German literature; and we think, too, of the schoolboy Schubert's enthusiasm for Gluck's ' Iphigenia in Tauris ' and for Vogl's performance—' I should like to know him, to throw myself at his feet in gratitude for his Orestes,' so he had said years before he dreamt of Vogl's singing Orestes music of his own. In *Orest auf Tauris* the tracked and weary hero reaches the Crimean shore (represented as bleak and unprepossessing as Spitsbergen); here, so the oracle has said, he will encounter that priestess of Diana's who will rid him of the parricide's curse. If it were another's case, the song or scena might appear fragmentary; but this hero's vicissitudes have been told often enough for the background to form in every listener's mind. At moments the music reminds us of *Philoktet*. It is serious, varied, and reasonably brief. A hint is here given us of what Schubert would, granted a favourable chance, have done in the way of classical opera. The pendant is *Der entsühnte Orest*:

> ' I see once more, yet hardly see for tears, that strand. The world is again, on this spring morning, what it was of old. It is enough. Goddess, my saviour, now let thy servant depart, and thy last mercy be that I, shriven, may now go down among my fathers.'

The scene is the Argolic bay. The old sins are expiated, the awful consequences of Clytemnestra's bloodshed at an end; the divine jealousy is appeased and mercy flows. The composition, one of Schubert's noblest, tells us with what passionate feeling he dwelt on the much-tried wanderer's return. It is ' onrunning ' with a mixture of song and recitative, the latter not of a formal type but merging into arioso, for instance in the fine period beginning ' Mycenæ hails me king,' which calls to mind the style of the first phrase in *Memnon*. The piece begins with a majestic billowing of bass arpeggios, and the hero's song spreads broadly over the scale with characteristic augmented fourths. The water-music becomes, in the middle part of the song, where Orestes opens his heart to the beauty of the morning, charmingly playful and dulcet. In the final prayer to Artemis the spreading vocal phrases have a more declamatory character, with punctuation by solemn dotted-semiquaver chords. The Orestes songs belong to September 1820, as also does the setting of Mayrhofer's *Freiwilliges Versinken* :

> ' Whither, O setting sun ?—I sink my glory in the western sea. Freely I gave my all, and I depart in splendour. Let there be night ! I lay down my crown upon the mountains. Now may the wan moon succeed to my once golden kingdom.'

The interrogated sun is felt to have already withdrawn, so hushed and solemn is the air. Ernest Newman has said that in Wagner the music tells us the season of the year and time of day of the dramatic action. So in these majestic pages of Schubert we fancy that without the text the hour would still have been felt to be nocturnal. Undue expressiveness is well avoided. It is not a tragic song. Simply a wonder at the mysteries of nature is conveyed, and a sense of encroaching cold. The music is assuredly one of Schubert's most remarkable inventions. The principal melody (' Ich nehme nicht ') is repeated (at ' Wie blass der Mond ') and yet the general impression is made of free dramatic arioso. From the very latest songs we guess how inviting a prospect Schubert more and more came to see in this style. There is indeed in *Freiwilliges Versinken* a hint of the *Doppelgänger* :

(*Molto adagio.*)   'Froiwilliges Versinken'.

Wie blass der Mond   wie matt die

This song is like *Memnon* and *Der entsühnte Orest* in being another expression of Mayrhofer's strange life-sickness and longing, which his friend, affectionate and no less impressed, translated into immortal music. It calls for a bass, or possibly a contralto, of exceptional dignity and rich tones.

Friedrich Schlegel was no great poet ; but his fluent verses well suited some of Schubert's easier moments in 1819-20, and all these Schlegel songs are worth knowing. *Die Gebüsche* is for light tenor—a flowing cantilena above a simple harp-like accompaniment. *Das Mädchen* is one of Schubert's most exquisite valentines. Her lover caresses her so tenderly, poor girl, to stop her complaining that in his heart of hearts he is not really in love. The thought is turned over in the light first of the major, then the minor mode. A little complaining, a little contentment, an appeal to the nightingale to say for her what she cannot find words for—that is all. The song has on mere paper the look of a flower. There is humour not without wistfulness in *Der Wanderer* :

> ' I owe this advice to the moon. Said she, Settle down in one place, and the fates have your address to visit you with any and every ill. So, she went on, keep to the road, keep moving like me, and you will slip out of trouble. Well, I took the hint and have never regretted it. Rolling stones gather no moss ? No doubt ; but I for one never could see fun in moss-collecting.'

In the first stanza the bass of the pianoforte is in unison with the voice—Schubert's frequent way of describing solitariness. The second stanza is reinforced by the moon's philosophy and by fuller harmonies. The genial little song is for barytone. Its title no doubt suggests to most the other and famous *Wanderer* ; but this one has only to be known to be liked. The music, moving so comfortably, conceals the difficulty

of the composer's feat in dealing with a highly unusual
stanza. If we set out a faithful translation it will be appreciated what the problem was, and how aptly Schubert met it :

> ' How clearly the new moon's ray
> Seems to say
> (For she shares the wanderer's passion),
> " Fix no settled habitation,
> Change the road and change the way
> You will find you
> Dread at last these bonds that bind you ;
> Learn of others
> Men are human, men are brothers,
> Leave the petty minds behind you." ' [1]

Der Wanderer was published in 1826 as Op. 65, No. 2.

Die Vögel belongs to the next year, 1820. ' Dwellers by
nature in darkness and like to the leaves' generations . . .
poor plumeless ephemerals, comfortless mortals,' so did the
birds of Aristophanes mock at men, and so do Schlegel's
birds, only in the humbler strain of German folksong. Schubert's music flutters and twitters. The neat and fetching
little song is just what it should be—a trifle for a light soprano.
To answer the assured encore, she has only to turn the page
and sing *Der Knabe*. This is the song of a boy in cherry-
time who wishes to be a bird ; another little piece as spritely
as it is delicately written. When selections from Schubert
are made for schoolchildren's singing classes, it would be better
to put aside inappropriate numbers (one has actually known
An Schwager Kronos chosen for massed performance by
London schoolgirls)—and to bring into circulation such songs
as these last two. If Schubert had not been so lavish with
his water-music, the next song, *Der Fluss*, would be more
prized. It is a river-scene after sunset, to which the music
responds with a romantic flowing movement and rich colouring
and sentiment. Little develops, however, in the thought or
feeling, and the song remains a lesser one, for all the impulse
with which it begins.

We have already met with Schubert's stately address to
the setting sun in *Das Abendrot* ; and to come later is the
beautiful evening hymn *Im Abendrot* (Lappe). The
Schlegel song *Abendröte* differs from both, being an affectionately detailed description of country sights and sounds
in the hour of sunset and twilight. The song begins in an
intimate way with close part-writing in 6-8 time. Roosting

[1] A. H. Fox Strangways.

birds twitter softly among the flowing quavers. The thought
of the sweet smells rising from the garden sets the music moving
more freely. At the mention of the mountains it broadens ;
and then the river's turning silver in the moonlight starts a soft
ripple of demisemiquavers which lasts out the rest of the
song. The detail of the earlier pages has faded with the
fading of day ; and the poet is left dreaming of the essential
unity of all nature's phenomena. *Der Schiffer* is a barcarolle
recalling a little *Auf dem See* (Goethe) and also pointing
towards *Am See* (Bruchmann). But whereas the latter is
charmingly animated, *Der Schiffer's* waters are nocturnal,
and the boatman is half asleep. He rouses himself a little,
with syncopations in B minor, to wish that his girl were there
in the boat with him ; but is soon lulled to contentment by
wave-like arpeggios.

All these are engaging and characteristic songs, but the most
delightful of the group is *Die Sterne*, to whose balmy air we
return again and again. The stars, according to the poet's
fancy, exhort mankind to emulate their harmony. Gracious
and blissful thoughts at once flow in upon the musician.
The slow 9-8 movement half dances and half floats. The
address of the starry spirit is tenderly playful. The sweetness of this music could not be excelled. In the middle part,
in A♭, the movement changes a little to describe the buoyancy
of the ideal existence. The melody is borne up and down
the notes of the tonic chord above a soft pulsing of quaver
triplets. Should the repeat marks be observed ? The
entrancing song is complete with one stanza. The poet has
really nothing to add in the second. After the softly rapturous
ending of the music it seems hardly natural to go back to
the condescension of the beginning again. On the other
hand the song is short ; and it is so little familiar that the
repetition may be needed if nothing of the music's charm is
to be missed.

The Schlegel songs have so far been small compositions ;
but now in *Im Walde* there is one of the most astonishing
and furiously impulsive things Schubert ever did, on a gigantic
scale. *Im Walde* occupies with one unflagging movement
fifteen of Mandyczewski's pages. It is no piecemeal composition like many of the extended songs, but is one gush
of wonderful, if unmastered, inspiration. The manuscript
(in the possession of the Viennese Society of Friends of
Music) bears signs, so it is said, of the composer's wild haste,
and the poet's text is far from accurately transcribed therein.
It is as though the spirit of music had whirled him, breathless

and half conscious, into some supernormal state. The copiousness is not in Schlegel's verses, which Schubert had to repeat very freely to match his musical outpouring. The words that so excited him tell of the exaltation brought about in a sensitive mind by the sounds and sights of the nocturnal forest, by the ghostly passage of the wind, the sighing firs, the splendour of the lightning. It is rather vague ; but the romantic abandon that is suggested must have seemed to Schubert on the day of *Im Walde* to be the highest of poetic states. The worship of nature, wild and free, was the new religious cult of the time. In the broadly rushing movement we have the Schubert of *Erlkönig* and *Mahomets Gesang ;* and the murmurs and thundering announce the forest and mountain music of ' Die Walküre.' After the midnight storm there enters in C the pianissimo song of the trickling springs, but the movement is the same, being always the movement of the excited poet's thought. On and on the music plunges through the night, as though there were intoxication in this communion with nature and strength were drawn from the infatigable wind. It is assuredly one of Schubert's greatest inspirations. The dæmon that possessed him in its composition was akin to the wild instigator of the finale of the C major symphony. All the same we have ventured to call it ' unmastered,' because the realizable sound is so much less than the musical conception. These fifteen pages of almost incessant pianoforte arpeggios strike dully after a time upon the ear. It has probably never been seen on a London concert programme since Bispham sang it. In turning Schubert's pages singers must often have passed it by in alarm at its look of impracticability. And it is for all that an intimate song, a piece of solitary lyricism without dramatic climax, so that an orchestrated version is hardly to be suggested. *Im Walde* is likely to remain the peculiar property of the private Schubertian and unlistened-to homely music-maker.

Berthas Lied in der Nacht, Schubert's one and only setting of verses by his friend Grillparzer, the celebrated playwright, was composed in February 1819. It is a slumber-song of much beauty, if possibly of a fragmentary effect. The dark, dreamy introduction is in *Eb* minor, and the rest of the song—the invitation to sleep—in the relative major, written as F . The texture is rich, with lulling syncopations and interesting inner parts such as the tenor counter-melody at 'und dem Schlummer dem lieblichen Kinde.' The song has not struck the amateur's fancy, for it lacks some word more to define Bertha and the circumstances of her lullaby. *Morgenlied* (Werner), composed in 1820, is one of Schubert's songs of innocence. In the naïve dialogue with the birds can be heard almost as really as in Mussorgsky the tones of an old nurse's ditty in entertainment of a child. The song was published in the next year as Op. 4, No. 2. The amiable serenade *Liebeslauschen* was composed on a text by Schlechta describing a picture (a cavalier playing the zither by moonlight beneath the fair one's window) by Schnorr von Carolsfeld. The song, a pretty one in a rather weak and languishing vein, was probably a good match for the picture. The pianoforte interludes echo the serenade in a way that points to the Rellstab *Ständchen* of eight years later. In the last page or two Schubert feels that the 3-4 movement is cloying and he makes an effort in 6-8 and 2-4 to revive the interest ; but it was an idle hour, and there is rarely found such indifferent accentuation in Schubert as at ' heimlich und von Liebe spricht.' Another inferior song is *Der Jüngling auf dem Hügel* (Hüttenbrenner) :

' He has gone out into the fields, poor fellow, to nurse the ache in his heart. The sights of spring mean nothing to him. The tolling of the village bell beats on his ears, and tears start again in his reddened eyes. But now day dies, now the quiet stars come out. He reads in their mild effulgence the promise of a happier hereafter.'

To glance at it is to recognise a weakness of Schubert's. The response of his sympathies was at moments almost mechanical. There was nothing real and true to be made out of Hüttenbrenner's commonplaces ; but the bad poet was a good friend, and Schubert's easy-going pen was the less able to refuse service since at its worst it could still charm. In effect, there are good things, notably the funeral procession, even in this unconvincing song. But as a whole there was nothing to be done with it ; and Schubert has set it bit and bit, and so nonchalantly that we doubt whether in beginning he had turned his author's page to inform himself of the situation. We have paused over *Der Jüngling* for the sake of fairness in a survey in which wonder has so largely had things its own way.

Schubert composed in 1820 his only setting of Uhland, *Frühlingsglaube* :

' This softness in the air, this new delicate tint in the landscape—ah, it is spring ! Come, bruised heart ! Come,

tearful eyes ! Surely there is balm for you in the turn
of the year.'

The song has, ever since it was published in 1823 (Op. 20,
No. 2), been affectionately prized. To some it seems the
very heart of Schubert. That is going too far. Schubert's
heart was more capacious than that, it was more vigorous.
But this *Frühlingsglaube*, so young, so tremulous with sadness
and with hope, is in truth something that belongs to him
alone. There was never another music so innocent at once
and so pathetically sensitive. It might be called ' adolescent '
music, if everything awkward and boisterous could be ruled
out of the associations of the word. Its poise is one of
unconscious grace and shrinking sensibility. The song, as
we open its page, looks like a discovered nymph.

Die gefangenen Sänger (1821) is a setting of verses by A. W.
Schlegel. ' As the caged bird hears its free brother's note
in the merry greenwood, so do men listen for the poet's song
that brings tidings of the ideal world.' The graceful, modest
6-8 rhythm calls to mind *An die Laute*. Such tunes sprang
into Schubert's thought at the suggestion of natural minstrelsy.
The listener might from the first page expect quite a short
song ; but the poet has five stanzas, and Schubert must
needs rouse himself to cope with them all. He does so
with admirable art, producing a chain of melodies, related
and yet different, in G major, G minor, B♭ minor, and so
back again. It is hard to say why so pleasing a song should
be neglected. The next, *Der Unglückliche* (Pichler), is one
of the few songs which Schubert is known to have sketched.
Mandyczewski's ' Revisionsbericht ' gives the original outline, the manuscript of which contains, he says, no corrections.
Once again there is nothing whatever to correspond to the
revelations of Beethoven's workshop. The sketch of *Der
Unglückliche* gives the melody precisely, and the bass very
nearly, as they appear in Mandyczewski's first version,
No. 390*a*. The latter in its turn differs only from the
published version (Op. 87, No. 1, 1828) in its time signature
(12-8, revised to 6-8) and in some quite trifling details. The
song, which is a revel of woe, is not the favourite it might
have been if Schubert had not so much surpassed it elsewhere,
notably in the incomparable *Aufenthalt*. For all the fine
music, it is not quite convincing. The final Andante carries
the mind back to Schubert's early formal pieces (cf. the ending
of *Die Erwartung*). The song is extended, and yet nothing
in the circumstances is particularized. The fatal reverse,

the bereavement, the despair, all seem abstract ; and there is something in the song that is more parade of emotion than emotion itself. We seek, it is seen, reasons for coolness felt towards a piece of music that contains no small measure of genuine Schubert. In the same year (1821) was composed *Der Jüngling an der Quelle*, the last and the most delightful of Schubert's Salis songs. This jet of melody and bubbling semiquavers is as beguiling as the forest spring to which the lover confides. His fair is called Louisa—old-fashioned but musical name. Louisa, he says, is prudish ; he attempts to forget her. But all he can do is to fit her name to the rhythm of the welling waters. May sunlight sparkles in Schubert's little fountain of music. In the charge of an accomplished lyric tenor the song is irresistible.

Der Blumen Schmerz (Mailath) is a song of sentimental fancy. The flowers' grievance is that they are born only to fade and so would have been better off if spring had never released them from winter's womb—a typical conceit of the valentine period. Never mind ; Schubert's music, springing up with none of the self-consciousness of Count Mailath's unnatural flora, covers any little weakness. The song announces the Müllerlieder. It is the Schubert of *Trockne Blumen* and of *Frühlingstraum*. The last song of the year was *Sei mir gegrüsst* (Rückert) :

> ' The song of my heart takes wing to meet thee and greet thee, to caress thee, to bless thee. Tremble, O Time, and Space, be you nought before Love's godhead who says that the soul is not your slave. O far-off soul, my soul yearns for thee, burns for thee, it holds thee and enfolds thee ! '

The celebrated song is in the nature of a serenade. We may well wonder where our Schubert found this strain of exalted amorousness. Rückert, the orientalist, was imitating Persian hyperbole ; but whence the passion of the music, in which the lover's desire is sublimated by sheer intensity and single-heartedness ? Schubert read literally this challenge from love to space and time. It inflamed the pure and poetic sensuousness of his character. There is a moment in youth when the fire of profane desire burns so clear as to be spiritual, and the carnal thing is sacred. In this glow the superb song was conceived. There are serenades playful, frivolous, persuasive, cynical. This one is noble. Of a commonplace of sensuous experience, Schubert by force of

feeling made a soaring aspiration ; of a waltz, a hymn. The
melody springs out of the poet's much-repeated refrain
' Sei mir gegrüsst, sei mir geküsst ! ' The waltz rhythm is
ennobled and transformed by the extremely slow pace. The
texture is enriched and the expression given a particular
voluptuousness by chromaticisms, such as the characteristic
augmented second in the first bar of the melody. Such
chromaticisms were overworked by the generation that
followed Schubert to the point of wearying the world ; and
only in the gradually clearing air is *Sei mir gegrüsst* coming
back into its own. The demands of the song are often
underrated by minor singers, who should never attempt it.
The voice must be noble and voluptuous to keep company
with the character of the music. A meagre voice will rob
the refrain of rapture and make the six recurrences seem too
many. There are two related melodies [1] in the song, and
both are freely modified in the different stanzas, always
with the same stately minstrel accompaniment of syncopated
chords. The date of its composition is not exactly known.
It is the 400th song in Mandyczewski. With another masterpiece, *Frühlingsglaube*, and a trifling merry song *Hänflings
Liebeswerbung* (Kind), it was published in 1823 as Op. 20,
No. 7, dedicated to Justina, wife of the merchant Johann von
Bruchmann, and mother of Schubert's Konvikt schoolfriend
Franz von Bruchmann, the poet of his *Am See* and other
songs. *Sei mir gegrüsst* was Schubert's first setting of
Rückert. The anticipation it arouses is not to be dis-
appointed.

[1] A set of variations on the principal theme is to be found in the Fantasia
for violin and pianoforte, Op. 159 (1827).

X

SONGS OF 1822-1823

'ALFONSO UND ESTRELLA' was finished early in 1822. Weber came to Vienna to conduct ' Freischütz ' and Schubert made his acquaintance. Some time in 1822 the frivolous young Bauernfeld joined Schubert's circle. This was the year of the immortal Unfinished (B minor) symphony, which was begun on October 30, and also of Schubert's fifth mass in A♭, the Kyrie of which had been begun in 1819. To the autumn of 1822 also belongs the celebrated ' Wanderer Phantasie,' for pianoforte, published in 1823 as Op. 15.

The year 1823 was one of illness and of furious creativeness. The records are equivocal about this illness, the first signs of which appeared in December 1822. In the summer of 1823 Schubert's state was serious. He went to hospital. He lost his hair. He believed himself doomed. His pathetic poem ' Mein Gebet ' (dated May 8) is a cry *de profundis*. But the work of composition never ceased. In the late summer Vogl took him again for holiday in Upper Austria, and his health and spirits improved. Weber paid another visit to Vienna in this autumn for the production of ' Euryanthe.' Schubert criticized the music for its lack of melody, and declared his preference for ' Freischütz.' The relations between the two composers suffered a chill. In this year Schubert did a bad stroke of business by selling outright to Diabelli the copyright of the works which had been published on commission.

The 1823 compositions included three more attempts by Schubert to conquer the stage. ' Die Verschworenen,' a ballad opera in one act (libretto by Castelli), was finished in April. The manuscript is in the British Museum. The theatre censor disapproved of the smell of conspiracy in the title, which was therefore changed to ' Der häusliche Krieg.' The piece was not performed until 1861. ' Fierrabras ' was a more ambitious work, a grand opera in three acts (libretto by Josef Kupelwieser, the painter's brother). The first act was written in May and June, the second between June and August, the third mostly at Steyr in August and September. The feebleness of the libretto doomed the work from the start.

When Schubert returned to Vienna, Schober, who had given him lodging, was away and the opera was finished at his father's. His health had improved, but his hair did not begin to grow again until the next year. In December he composed the incidental music for Wilhelmine von Chézy's 'Rosamunde, Fürstin von Cypern,' which was produced on December 20. The music pleased, but the play was a failure. The deplorable authoress had already, two months before, been responsible as librettist for the failure of 'Euryanthe.' Schubert's pianoforte sonata in A minor, published in 1839 as Op. 143, also belonged to this year.

* * *

The first of the 1822 songs was *Der Wachtelschlag* (text by S. F. Sauter) :

'That twittering bird seems to say " Fear the Lord ! Fear the Lord ! " It is the quail, the pious quail, in the stubble. Its song is three short notes, " Love the Lord ! Praise the Lord ! " Friend, modest bird, I will praise him with thee, and thank him for the fair world our home, thine and mine. When storms lower we will sing together " Prithee, Lord ! Prithee, Lord ! " And should war threaten our harvest fields, then, " Trust in God ! Trust in God." '

Unfortunately the quail has generally no such associations with us. Its song is not familiar in England in the way of Schubert's other bird-music—the nightingale in *Ganymed*, the lark in Mayrhofer's *Sehnsucht*, the cuckoo in the same poet's *Einsamkeit*, the cock in *Frühlingstraum*. The poor bird does not enjoy with us the reputation for piety suggested by the German poet, or the sympathy extended to it in Schubert's delicate little piece. The three notes of its cry form the motive of the song, which is strophic with a variation in the minor in reference to storm and war. It first appeared as a supplement to a magazine on July 30, 1822, and was published, with Italian text, by Diabelli in 1827, as Schubert's Op. 68.

Ihr Grab (Roos) is not one of the too facile meditations among the tombs which now and then jar on us in Schubert.

The harmonies are serious and dark. The prelude begins ambiguously outside the main key (E*b*). The melody is dictated by the fall of the much-repeated phrase, ' Dort ist ihr Grab.' The song calls for calm, sustained pianissimo singing, not too expressive but serious and resigned. It is obvious that Schubert undertook also in no light spirit to set Schober's *Todesmusik*, an extensive song in various movements, with interspersed recitatives in which the poet meditates on his last hour. This is no negligible piece even though Schober's glibness and complacent predictions of euthanasia have not made for strength in the latter pages. For the singer who may not appreciate who is the holy ' Kamöne ' invoked at the beginning, be it said that this is the eccentric Gothic spelling of Camena. She is the Muse who will alleviate her votary's death-agony. The *Todesmusik* appeared as Op. 108, No. 3, in the year after Schubert's death.

A finer piece of music is *Schatzgräbers Begehr* (Schober), a song of singular power, yet in effect hardly more than ' interesting ' because of the merely odd subject—a crazy seeker after a hidden treasure which may symbolize again the tantalizing Schillerian ideal. A striking figure stalks majestically about the bass of the pianoforte part. There is some fine, bold modulating (D minor, E*b*, F$\sharp$ minor, A minor) in the middle. The expression in the vocal part ranges from sullenness at the opening to a fierce outburst (' I dig and dig on, with glowing heart '), and then at the end to the pathos of madness (' Shall not a man be allowed to dig his own grave ? '). It is a song of broad design for a powerful singer. All that invalidates it is something puerile in Schober's intention—something would-be blood-curdling and grotesque, in the fashion set by ' The Mysteries of Udolpho.' The song was published in 1823 as Op. 23, No. 4.

Schwestergruss (Bruchmann) was composed at about the same time. It is another serious and considerable song, one on which Schubert has spent a wealth of ideas and, particularly, harmonic resources. The incessantly throbbing triplets are reminiscent of the *Erlkönig*. There is a magnificent bass movement during the description of the moonlit graveyard and the appearance of the phantom. Unfortunately, the poet (who is writing ' after the death of his sister ') commits an offence with nearly every line he writes. He describes himself as wandering by night among the graves and (so he says) the bones of the dead. His sister's ghost appears, tells of the heavenly bliss she enjoys, and

warns him he will know nothing of the sort unless he mends
his ways. The vision passes, the music relapses from F♯
to F♯ minor, and the poet returns home, singing the
Almighty's praise. There is something intolerably vulgar
about such German churchyard poetry ; but Schubert was
as oblivious of this now as when he had busied himself with
Eine Leichenphantasie in 1811. On the day he composed
Schwestergruss, as on that of the *Schatzgräbers Begehr*, he
was all disposed to write a masterpiece ; and on both days
he was frustrated by the sad versifiers his friends. This
Schwestergruss, the first of Schubert's Bruchmann songs,
remains virtually unknown. The second, *An die Leier*, is
relatively popular :

> ' Of the classical heroes, of Heracles or the celebrated
> Atridæ, I fain would sing. I strike a chord, but my song
> always turns into a love-song. Come, once again : some-
> thing impressive about the bloody plain of Troy. No
> good ! The harmonies melt under your killing eyes, you
> witch ! '

Bruchmann here imitates a poem of Anacreon's, a seventeenth-
century English version of which was delightfully set by
Purcell. An Englishman may be forgiven for comparing
the two songs and for feeling in Schubert's serious statement
of sentiment the lack of Purcell's playfulness and glancing
irony. Schubert has taken the poet's whimsical confession
of incompetency simply at its face-value. Purcell's music
is full of light mockery at the heroic conventions. Of what
should the enamoured poet sing save love ? Purcell knows
that all Anacreon cared for Alcides and the sons of Atreus
was that they could be made to serve a ballad to his mistress's
eyebrow.

Schubert sets the poet's heroic effort to recitative punctuated
by striking chords which bit by bit soften, leading to the
amorous cantilena that floats on the simple arpeggios of the
lyre. There is a second recitative, more strenuous ; and
a return to the cantilena, which is this time extended. *An
die Leier* is interesting to singers, calling as it does for bold
declamation and for a very finished legato in the dulcet movement. The song was published as Op. 56, No. 2, in 1826,
and with it (No. 3) *Im Haine* (Bruchmann) :

> ' Sunlight falls through the pines and with it contentment's
> balm. The breeze that moves so softly in the branches
> has wafted care from my heart.'

It is a beguiling little strophic song. No trace of care is left in its gently dancing 9-8 movement. The melody ramifies to the extent of fifteen bars. It is as though it typified for Schubert a sunny, indolent hour which he was unwilling to let go.

To be classed with these pieces are two more Bruchmann songs composed early in the next year (1823). *Der zürnende Barde* is the poet's cry of defiance to the hostile world. The wood of his lyre was cut from the father of all oak-trees, its strings were gathered from the rays of the sunset ; so shall its proud owner humble all disparagers, for the gods are on his side. The tone of the music is perhaps not extremely elevated. The indignant bard would be taken by anyone who did not catch his words to be delivering a rattling drinking song. It rolls along in 6-8 time, in the most spirited way. There is no jollier bass song in all Schubert. Its companion piece *Am See* (Bruchmann) is a barcarolle, likewise composed in holiday mood. If the poet chooses in his second stanza to become tiresome, leaving the splash and spray of the sunlit lake in an attempt to rise above the clouds, Schubert sensibly declines to follow him, but from first to last plays delightfully with his arpeggio figures in which we hear the regular gathering and breaking of billows. The charming melody is first given in the form of a sentence of nine bars. Its expansion on the next page over twenty bars is typical of the burgeoning and blossoming of Schubert's art.

The two settings of poems by his old school-fellow, J. M. Senn, both belong to 1822. *Selige Welt* is rather like *Der zürnende Barde*—a hearty bass song, the spirit of which would easily be taken to be convivial. The verses, however, tell of man's aimless and unpiloted voyage over the ocean of life. The song was published in 1823 as No. 2 of Op. 23, No. 3 of which was Senn's *Schwanengesang*, a serious, expressive piece, which exemplifies within a small room Schubert's ever-growing delicacy and suppleness of harmonic style.

The Mayrhofer songs of 1822 include *Im kalten, rauhen Norden* and *Fels auf Felsen*, both texts being extracts from the poet's 'Heliopolis.' The sentiment of the former had been better put by someone Mayrhofer never heard of :

> ' Ah, sunflower ! weary of time,
> Who countest the steps of the sun ;
> Seeking after that sweet golden clime
> Where the traveller's journey is done. . . .'

It is a characteristic aspiration of Mayrhofer's, this longing for a different clime, a different world. A few years before Schubert would assuredly have set some of these lines to recitative ; but he was now master of a style of concatenated melody. This *Heliopolis* song flows without a break from the sombre E minor opening, in which the poet asks hopelessly for the way to the city of the sun, on to the bland E major consolation uttered by the emblematic sunflower. At the beginning we observe in the bare unison of voice and pianoforte Schubert's favourite means of expressing forlorn solitude. The second *Heliopolis* tells of a romantic landscape of waterfalls and windy crags amid which, says the poet, the mind can rid itself of trivialities and can rightly give rein to the passions. There, in the free air of nature, they are grand and beautiful. Schubert has made of it a fine, blustering bass song in C minor, rather like *Selige Welt*, but more extended and more earnest in its plunging energy. We are reminded a little of *Muth* in the ' Winterreise.'

But only a little. These songs of Schubert's maturity, while they naturally have a family resemblance, are one after the other most unmistakably individuals. Schubert did not start on a vein and methodically exploit it. The different days and their events brought to him particular images, and his keen eyes appreciated the multiformity of the procession. These beings of his fancy must have been simply collected from the evidence of his senses, only so can we say, seeing the impossibility of a man's inventing by labour such a fairy progeny. In his flower-pieces, for instance, the flowers of nature revive each according to its kind. We come upon *Nachtviolen* in which the poet, Mayrhofer, gave him hardly anything to go upon except the flower's name (the ' Nachtviole ' is the flower we call dame's violet), and a word about its velvety blue ; but for Schubert, with his delight in flowers, it was enough—he responded, he reflected. The music is as delicate as the flower. It expands modestly in close treble harmonies. It has a luscious chromatic chord or two, because dame's violet smells sweet. Schubert's musical translation of the name ' Nachtviolen ' haunts the piece and when the voice has gone on to something else the pianoforte keeps playing on the four notes as on a chime of little bells.

Another flower song of the same period is *Die Rose* (F. Schlegel) :

' This is the life of a rose. The sun has beguiled me. His soft ray kissed me and I put out a bud to greet him. But

he grew fierce, he grew burning. He has scorched me ;
I wilt. Ah me, I shall breathe my last before evening.'

Again a song so compact and consummate that it might be
thought the result of a month of chastening. The close high-
lying harmonies again suggest the delicacy of a flower and its
plicated petals. The principal melody consists simply of
two sections of four bars, but a little surprise is afforded by
a one-bar interlude where the obvious thing would have
been one of two bars or none at all. The key is G major,
but verges tremulously on the minor, into which (after the
middle section in the dominant key, which has a ramification
of the melody and a delicately agitated accompaniment)
the song definitely lapses. Only at the end it turns back into
the major, as much as to say, ' After all, only a rose ! ' This
exquisite song seems to foretell certain small and highly
wrought songs in Schumann and Wolf (compare the latter's
Citronenfalter im April). It first appeared (in F) as a supplement to a Viennese magazine on May 7, 1822, and was
published (in G) in 1827 as Op. 73. The higher key is
preferable, the song being one for light soprano. If the
lower key is used, correct Mandyczewski's misprint in the
last bar of the voice part.

Two flower songs composed in the next year (1823), settings
of Schober's *Viola* and *Vergissmeinnicht*, are only for the out-
and-out Schubertian. It is one thing to be presented with
an exquisite flower ; it is another to be inveigled into a tour
of a horticultural show. The latter of these floral pageants
is a matter of eleven, the former one of fifteen pages. Both
contain charming things, more especially *Viola ;* yet the two
songs are no more than curiosities. Schubert, whose writing
could be as compact and concentrated as any man's, was
occasionally led into these impossible adventures by possessing
an unequalled facility. He could more light-heartedly risk
failures than another man, for if to-day's ideas were squandered,
there were always plenty more where they came from. An
economical composer would have taken to heart the lesson
of experience that after a certain time the listener loses interest
in any piece of music that consists simply of voice and pianoforte. A song must in fact be short ; and the smaller and
daintier its theme the shorter. But here Schubert set out
to tell of snowdrops and pansies on the scale of a tale of
Troy. The delightful music is wasted. In the light of
' Die schöne Müllerin ' we can see what was wanted, namely,
a sequence of little poems that would have made a song-

cycle. A cycle of flower songs by Schubert ! That would have been worth having. And all the material was here in these two long pieces ! But Schubert's invention did not work in that way. The suggestion of the form had to come from without ; and in this respect it was equally by luck that *Viola* turned as it did, and ' Die schöne Müllerin.' *Viola* was published in 1830 as Op. 123. The charming E major movement in *Vergissmeinnicht* might well be treated as a self-contained song.

Schubert's two Platen songs were written in 1822. The music of both is astonishing by force and concentration of passion. The first is *Du liebst mich nicht* :

> ' Disaster and anguish ! To be paid for love with scorn !
> The free gift of my all to be thrown aside ! The whole flowering world and the star-flowered heavens are a mockery.
> Disaster ! Anguish ! '

The poem is a *ghazal* on the Persian model. A *ghazal* consists of a short series of self-contained couplets. The rule of the form is that the two halves of the first line of the poem rhyme together, and the other couplets all end on this same rhyme. Platen has simply worked out a difficult puzzle, analogous to the ballades and rondeaux of Austin Dobson and his circle ; but Schubert took the poem in deep earnest. His song is built on the terse rhythmical phrase of the prelude. This is made to persist with the effect of a desperate ache. The constituent notes alter again and again. The phrase is dragged through rending modulations. It rises slowly to a shattering fortissimo and at length dies away ; but always its fatal beat underlies the song. The lover would wish the truth he speaks not true, and hopes against hope. But the rhythm hammers home the truth. There is no escape. Schubert here, in a burning hour, forged a lyrical form which was to serve composers of a much later generation. The song vividly suggests Hugo Wolf. His beautiful and poignant *Mühvoll komm' ich und beladen* obviously derives from *Du liebst mich nicht*. It is a pity that Platen's prosodic exercise was not quite worthy of the music. The lover's enumeration of the flowers (rose, jasmin, narcissus) which, he says, may for all he cares as well not blossom, seems rather petty when the acme of suffering is being touched by the music. The song defies the translator ; and it is not a favourite with singers because of the ungrateful vowels in the ten-times-repeated ' Du liebst mich nicht ! '

It was published, together with three of the Rückert songs, as Op. 59 in 1826, having been separated from its companion piece which appeared in 1823 as Op. 23, No. 1. This latter is *Die Liebe hat gelogen* :

> ' Love is a lie. Eyes, rain your tears, you cannot wash it away. Heart, if you can, take in this truth, that truth is not, love having lied.'

This music similarly expresses relentless suffering. It seems that Schubert is again going to persist with an ostinato figure ; but the one he starts with is not quite so characteristic as before, and in the middle of the short song he drops it, the mention of the victim's tears setting up a sobbing syncopated figure which calls to mind the ' Winterreise.' This song, so tense with resentment and distress, is even more telling than the other, when sung by an accomplished tenor or high barytone. Schubert indicates a great reinforcement of tone just before the return to C minor, then a pianissimo, and afterwards another climax. The singer may, if his voice is properly controlled, allow himself an almost operatic vehemence of expression.

A fresh group of Goethe songs was composed in December 1822, first of them *Der Musensohn* :

> ' Up hill and down dale I go singing and piping. I find a rhyme for everything, and everything goes into my rhymes. I sing in the spring, and when spring is long past I sing its memories to cheer up winter. I sing ; and hobbledehoys and the awkwardest wenches give ear and step to my tunes, and start dallying and dancing.
> ' But now I ask you, dear saints of song, am I to go on like this for ever ? Will your old minstrel never have earned a rest from his singing ? '

The song is perfectly captivating ; and Goethe's verses will never be dissociated from its dancing melodies which seem to come to us from over the hills and far away and to depart as they came, back to the land of immortal youth. There are five stanzas, and Schubert sets them alternately to two closely related melodies, one in G, the other in B, which leaves the fifth stanza to finish off the song in G. Nothing could be simpler. But the movement has a gay poetry of which we never weary. The change of key, to and from B major, can hardly be called a modulation, for the music each time simply dives into one key or the other. These changes make the effect of a new infusion of energy at the beginning of each stanza. The two melodies are so much alike that the flow of the music is quite unbroken ; but they are delicately differentiated in shape, as may be seen at a glance by the different disposition of the repeated words. Goethe has set the musician a problem when, in the last three of his thirty lines, he makes his merry minstrel suddenly turn weary of it all and ask for relief. It is too late for Schubert to pay heed ; or at most he is willing to indicate a pianissimo. The tuneful wanderer can surely never tire— can beg for nothing better than to pipe and sing—so long as breath is in him. Schubert does not believe in the last three lines—surely the old poet does not honestly mean them ! The *Musensohn* was Goethe, but has now become Schubert. Mandyczewski's two versions of the song differ only in insignificant details. No. 1 is in A♭, No. 2 in G. The latter was published with two other Goethe songs as Op. 92, No. 1, in the spring of 1828.

An die Entfernte is as neglected as the *Musensohn* is popular. Only chance can explain this. There is no reason why the song should not be a high favourite among the more intimate and tender of Schubert's pieces. It is perfectly written for the lyric tenor voice. The poem, a gentle appeal to an absent mistress, is supposed to date from 1789 and to refer to Charlotte von Stein. Schubert's music is remarkable for its ranging modulations. Beginning in G, the first quatrain ends in F. The middle part of the song is in F minor. Here again we get a hint of the 1827 ' Winterreise.' Every phrase of the consummate little piece deserves looking into.

Schubert had most likely forgotten his 1815 setting of *Am Flusse* when now, nearly eight years later, he wrote the second setting in D major. The earlier song was more poignant ; but one may for all that be very fond of the later one. It is simplicity itself. It might have been written to demonstrate the art of using few notes. The stream into which the lover casts his despised songs is the most equable in Schubert. The melody which floats above it, and which is beautifully expanded over twenty-three bars, is expressive of no more than gentle melancholy. There is little in the song to catch the eye when the pages are being turned. But it stands the test of acquaintance. No one but Schubert could have written it.

There is a lively contrast in the galloping and palpitations of the next song, *Willkommen und Abschied*. The poem

dates from Goethe's Alsacian days (1771) ; and the Juliet
to whom young Romeo-Goethe so boldly rides through the
night, whom he clasps and whom he leaves at dawn with her
kisses on his lips and in his heart, was the hapless Friederike
Brion.   These verses might have been composed on horseback, and as much could be said of the song.   The music
keeps up a spirited, cantering movement in 12-8 rhythm
except for a moment when the lover's heart stands almost still
at the thought of his bliss.   ' It's all too good to be true !   Ye
gods !   I never knew life had such happiness ! '   There are
four stanzas.   For each Schubert has a different melody ;
but one borrows morsels from another, the 12-8 rhythm
binds all together, and the whole seems cast in a single piece.
There are striking modulations to depict the phantasms of
the romantic night-ride.   It is a capital song for the barytone
who has good resonant tone for the low-lying first and
second stanzas and brilliance for the last page.   He will sing
it in C, the key in which the song was first published as Op.
56, No. 1, in 1826.   Op. 56 was dedicated to Carl Pinterics,
a civil servant, pianist, singer, and ardent Schubertian, who
left at his death in 1831 a collection of 505 MSS. of Schubert's
songs.   Mandyczewski prints another version of the song in
D, the only difference in which is the briefer dwelling on
the word ' doch ' in the last page.

The last song of the year 1822 was *Wanderers Nachtlied*
(' Ueber allen Gipfeln ') :

> ' How silent are the hills !   The tree-tops hardly stir,
> and the birds are hushed.   Soon, soon thou too shalt
> rest.'

There is no more celebrated poem in German.   It is called
' Ein Gleiches ' in Goethe's works.   The eight short lines
were written by the poet on the bedroom wall of his chalet
on the Kickelhahn, in the Thuringian hills, on the night of
September 6, 1780.   He renewed the writing thirty-three
years later, and in the late evening of his life he read the
epigraph there again, with tears.   Schubert's marvellous
composition consists of fourteen bars.   The beauty of evening
is in the simple B*b* harmonies.   ' The tree-tops hardly stir '
—the harmonies take up the suggestion in soft syncopation.
(Observe that Mandyczewski gives the turn on the word
' balde ' as optional, and that Friedländer omits it.)   It was
all something that no one before Schubert had done—this
compact, epigrammatic style of musical composition, ' a

World in a grain of sand, and a Heaven in a wild flower.' *Ueber allen Gipfeln* appeared twice in Schubert's lifetime— first as a supplement to a magazine in 1827, and then with three other songs, dedicated to Princess Kinsky, in 1828. A Leipzig firm also issued it a month after the composer's death. It is numbered Op. 96, No. 3. Schumann's setting of the poem was, curiously enough, his Op. 96, No. 1. There are also settings by Loewe and Liszt.

Schubert's first Leitner song, composed in 1823, was *Drang in die Ferne* :

'Like the clouds and the birds and the waves in the river, let me be off and away. My dear ones, you cannot say no when my blood and my breath are craving for air and movement and the wonders of the seven seas. They are stronger than I. Let me go ! '

The piece is in compound waltz measure, and the spirit of it is sublimated Viennese gaiety. Hardly has the pianist's left hand indicated the movement when the right hand melody is off like a bird. The voice of the would-be wanderer comes in like another bird, they dart away together, they part company, they cross each other's way. What buoyant, madcap music ! It subsides a little when the pleading words take on a sentimental tone ('and if the worst comes to the worst you can always say I had my heart's desire ')—a tone not to be taken too seriously—and then again it is up and off, and this time disappears into the blue. The song is Schubert all over. No one else has had just such a gaiety, so reckless and so delicate. *Drang in die Ferne* first appeared in a magazine on March 25, 1823, and was published as Op. 71 in 1827.

The ballad *Der Zwerg* (Collin) is a singular composition. The subject is a piece of insufferable nonsense. It is the story of a court dwarf who is enamoured of the queen and strangles her on board a ship : a piece of the romantic scaremongering so fashionable at the moment. This same year, 1823, saw the typical production of the kind in Victor Hugo's 'Han d'Islande.' Schubert did not take it too seriously, if we may believe the unreliable Randhartinger's account of the composition of the music. This friend had called on Schubert to invite him to a stroll. The composer accepted, but asked for a few minutes' delay to set Collin's ballad. While talking and joking with Randhartinger he wrote out the music at lightning speed, and was soon

ready for the walk. A piece so recklessly thrown off might
be thought to have small interest. It is, on the contrary,
one that excites the fancy in regard to Schubert's frustrated
future. *Der Zwerg*, it is not too much to say, is a link between
Beethoven and Wagner. We peer into the prophetic pages
and fondly wonder what would have been the outcome if
Schubert had lived to know Wagner's operas. The peculiarity of the music resides in the use of two terse and pregnant
themes :

—the first of which expresses the overhanging tragic fate,
and the second the dwarf's anguish of mind. The pianoforte
part is here obviously a mere sketch of the orchestral music
Schubert had in thought. The two themes are unfolded in
a way that derives from the free fantasia of the symphony,
but also looks forward to Wagner's representative motives.
Observe the drop of the ' fate ' theme by a diminished fifth
when the dwarf pronounces sentence of death, and the
diminished fourths when he stares at the dead woman. It
would be interesting to hear an orchestrated version of the
ballad. *Der Zwerg* was dedicated to the poet, and was
published in 1823 as Schubert's Op. 22, together with the
next song, a setting of Collin's *Wehmut* :

> ' Beauty's transitoriness and the doom of the flowering
> world ! The thought wrings my heart, it kills my joy in
> the morning of the year. They pass, the strong in life
> and the beautiful ; all things fade in the fading of man's
> awareness in which they have their existence—fade and
> perish, and are soon as nothing.'

The short song is rich in sounding D minor harmonies and
a grateful cantilena. There is something luxurious in its

expression of grief, bringing back to mind *Erster Verlust*. Schubert lovingly embraces the beauty whose doom the poet foretells. The mood is characterized by the sumptuous thirteenth in the farewell cadence.

The next song, *Lied*, by Stolberg (' Des Lebens Tag ist schwer '), dated April 1823, likewise expresses voluptuous melancholy. The beautiful music is, however, weighed down by a muddled poem, and is not generally known. It is a churchyard piece ; and the text jars on us by confusing the thought of the repose of the departed with images drawn from the burial-place, the moonlight on the graves, the dew in the grass. There is a further jar between the reference to a mourner's hopes and the poet's own contemplation of oblivion in the bosom of mother earth. This *Lied* might benefit by a very free translation. It is one of the most abstract of Schubert's songs. The composer has found in the text no picturesque suggestion. The page looks Brahmsian rather than Schubertian. Nothing, on the other hand, is more characteristic of our composer in a charming holiday mood than the next Stolberg song, the last and the most celebrated of his settings of that poet—*Auf dem Wasser zu singen*. The piece is all graceful indolence, a swaying of skiffs, a ripple of waters flecked by the sunset. Was music ever before so care-free and so warm-hearted ? The song is purely strophic, but three repetitions are not too much. The key is A♭ minor, there is a lazy swaying to and from C♭, and an almost triumphant ending in A♭ major, as though the sunset were flooding the scene with ruddy light. The song is the idealization of Viennese river-pleasures. It first appeared as a magazine supplement at the end of 1823, and was published in 1827 as Op. 72.

Another barcarolle, a more sentimental one, is the setting of Schober's *Pilgerweise* (April 1823). This piece has earned less popularity than a ' Song without Words ' of Mendelssohn's (likewise in F♯ minor, Schubert's key), which was composed about ten years later and looks as though it might have been derived from Schubert :

SCHUBERT: 'Pilgerweise'.

MENDELSSOHN: Op. 80. № 6.

Schubert is the more adventurous of the two in his roamings. There is already in the prelude a surprising deviation towards G major. This is one of numerous incidents that speak of Schubert's devotion in attempting to buoy up the friend's long and sentimental poem. The song remains secondary Schubert. It is gracefully pretty, but languishes in the long run.

Another pilgrim song of the same period was the setting of Schiller's celebrated stanzas, *Der Pilgrim*, a companion poem to his *Sehnsucht*. The verses tell of the hapless idealist's career. His life is one hopeless quest for the Golden Gate beyond which the Earthly becomes Divine. But no way leads thither—there is no point where earth touches heaven—*there* (so Schiller lamentably discovers) is never *here*. Schubert did not attempt to follow the allegorical images with detailed illustration, but based his song firmly on the idea of the pilgrim's wandering. This he renders by a square, hymnlike tune, or rather by a chain of three or four such tunes, all closely related, which he only abandons in the ninth and last quatrain to express with a complete change of rhythm and tempo the pilgrim's disillusionment. The first four stanzas remain steadily in E major. The increasing distractions of the quest are then represented—while the serious march movement is maintained—by an extraordinary play of modulation. In the eighth stanza the dominating rhythm is loosened and dispersed in response to the pilgrim's loss of touch with his lifelong object. Schubert has, then, spared no pains to do justice again, almost for the last time (this is the last but one of the Schiller songs), to the poet of his boyhood. If for all its beauties the song fails to rank with the greatest, the fault must be put down to the poet, whose quest is ill defined and whose long-deferred conclusion makes the effect of bathos. *Der Pilgrim* was published (in D) as Op. 37, No. 1, in 1825, dedicated to Schnorr von Carolsfeld, the painter. Just before it was composed Schubert's second setting of the love-poem, *Das Geheimnis*, one of those addressed by Schiller to Charlotte von Lengefeld, his betrothed. The Secret is the lover's nocturnal tryst in a beechen arbour, which is expatiated upon in four long stanzas. The poem had first, in 1815, been treated by Schubert as a simple strophic song. The result was music of great charm and tenderness ; but Schubert probably felt (if he remembered the song of eight years before) that it did not well support the whole poem, and notably the stanza which describes the sounds of toil in the town and the sordid business of the day. The 1823 song is laid out on much more ambitious lines, but with all its bolder beauty we miss the delicacy of the lover's sentiment in the earlier setting.

XI

1823—'THE MAID OF THE MILL'

THE year 1823 was for Schubert one of repeated failure, of illness, and of terrible dejection. Yet it was to bequeath to charmed posterity the May-time music of the sun and showers, the brook and watermill, and the fond and fickle hearts of ' Die schöne Müllerin ' :

'Prentice days are over. I am a journeyman miller, and to-day I set out to see something of the world. Where there's a stream there's a mill. Let's see where this one leads to.

'What a snug little mill-house all among the greenery ! One might go farther and fare worse. Brook, you know a thing or two. I believe you brought me here on purpose. Brook, I believe you knew the miller's daughter.

'If only I had the strength of water and the bellows of the wind ! I would do all the work of the mill, and then she couldn't help but notice me. Has she noticed me ? Does she care for me ? There is nothing in the world I should so much like to know. Yes ! I'm in love, madly, sadly, gladly, gloriously in love.

'The sun is up, and why not she ? Why doesn't she give me a glimpse of herself ? I don't ask her to come near,— only to know that she is about, to catch a little glimpse of her. Forget-me-nots, you, with dewdrops for tears, speak to her for me,—tell her to forget me not.

'The moon came out and the stars. I saw them mirrored in the water, them and someone else too. And in someone else's eyes I saw the stars mirrored. Heavens ! she is mine !

'Since then my zither has never been taken down from the wall. Somehow such happiness as this is unsingable. At times the strings get brushed in passing and they sigh. An echo of my old sighing ? or the prelude to a new song ? She has asked me for the ribbon from the lute. It is a green ribbon, green is her favourite colour, green is the colour of hope.

'That black-bearded game-keeper in his green coat hangs about the house far too much, until I can't bear the sight of him. Be off! There's no one wants you here! But isn't there? Am I so sure? Brook, brook, go and tell your mistress not to,—what? Not to look out of doors when fellows like him are about. And you may tell her that nothing at all has upset me,—that I am enjoying myself nicely. Oh, my heart!

' Green was her favourite colour, and green shall be mine, the green of the weeping willow, the green of the church-yard grass. I would go off into the wide world, but the hateful colour would stare me in the face everywhere. I am going, yes, going where ears never hear the hunts-man's horn, and eyes see no colours at all.

' The flowers she gave me shall be buried with me. They or their like will grow up again in another spring, a spring that will be hers and not mine. She may give me a thought then.

' My heart is breaking. Brook, old friend, what is the cure for a broken heart? You whisper and I understand —yes—under your waters,—no more fever or pain,— I understand, I am coming.'

The origin of Müller's little lyrical sequence was a family charade. His poems were first published in 1821. Benedikt Randhartinger gives a (very probably fictitious) account of how Schubert came across them. Randhartinger had been a school-fellow of Schubert's at the Konvikt. In 1824, he was private secretary to Count Louis Széchenyi. Schubert, calling on him at the count's one day in that summer, picked up a new book of verse while waiting for his friend, and read Müller for the first time. He saw in a flash what could be done with him; and at once hurried home with the book. The next day as an excuse to his friend, he showed him some of the mill songs already completed. Grove opines that the first ' Mül-lerin ' songs were written in May. Then came a break, owing to the opera ' Fierrabras ' (Acts I and II). Then a spell in hospital, where more mill songs were composed : and then Act III of the opera. *Eifersucht und Stolz*, the fifteenth of the mill songs, is dated October 1823. The cycle was published as Schubert's Op. 25 in 1824. It was dedicated to Baron Schönstein.

The debt to Müller is not that the Mill and the ' Winterreise ' songs are unmatched in Schubert. Taken separately, there are not many among them to be included in a first general choice of favourites. But they are not properly to be taken separately. Müller's glory is that he prompted Schubert to two large and quite unexampled compositions. If Schubert had set nothing of Müller's, we should be the poorer by more than forty-four songs. The two cycles are greater than the sum of their parts. A chain of happy circumstances helped Schubert to make a second new musical form just as, a decade before, he had with hardly any logical toil made a new thing of the single song. A frown from fortune, and 'Die schöne Müllerin' might have been but another of those rambling tales, extended beyond every lyrical propriety, with which Schubert now and again, as cannot be disguised, has fairly bored us. Thanks to Müller, it was something quite different—new and endlessly engaging. The all-important advantage is that the interruptions in the recital afford a succession of new standpoints in time : a drama is revealed to us in a series of lyrical moments.

Schubert had not consciously to think much of what he was to do with Müller. If 'Die schöne Müllerin' had depended for existence on anything like Wagner's conquest of an intractable form or on Beethoven's onslaughts on the very material of music, it would have been where now are all Schubert's unlucky operas, which are evidence enough of his inaptitude for feats of logic.

The peasant in Schubert, and the tender heart also, were touched by Müller's naïvety and pathos. His fancy flew to the rustic scene. There, there was the air in which he, the exile in the city, revived his spirit. There were the folk whom he, awkward and humble, understood and felt at home amongst. Possibly he understood Müller's peasantry rather better than the real sort. He himself was a peasant once removed ; he had a townsman's softness. He had lost the true countryman's gnarledness and long-suffering. The rude fishermen and rangers and mountaineers in his songs are rather frequently conscious of the picturesqueness and pathos of their situation. We cannot forget the modish Rousseauism —the idealization of rural and inarticulate men—which was the very air breathed by the literary and artistic folk of the time. It is in Goethe. To it is due a certain quaintness in 'Die schöne Müllerin,' a certain small element in the sentiment not universal but fashionable, which it would be uncandid not to admit along with our recognition of the abounding genuineness of the thing and its innumerable charms.

How Schubert embraced the simple Müller's book there is hardly need for Randhartinger and Kreissle to tell. Almost as much could be guessed from the welling music, which fondly takes in, along with the major joys and sorrows, so many details in the homely picture—the forget-me-nots with their naïve appeal, the bee that brushes a string of the neglected lute, and above all the babbling mill stream, this last such a hint as Schubert never in all his song-writing could resist. Dare anyone say that too much can be made of the impulse imparted to this music by external suggestions ? True, the man who has it in him to make music will apply his art, if not to this, then to that. True, it was chance that gave to Schubert as subject a lovesick lad in a green valley. Is that to say that he would have done as well with sheikhs and caravans ? Some assert that the musical mind's sole concern is music, with which it deals like an engineer who applies himself to the problems of a gasworks or a cathedral in an identical spirit. Well, as much may be true of some musicians, but it is irreconcilable with Schubert— Schubert, the bosom friend not of musicians but of painters and poets ; Schubert, who learnt to approach instrumental forms by song-writing ; Schubert, for whom the visible world existed. Did Schubert, for that matter, ever apply himself to a problem ?

What we know of his heart's private affairs is practically nothing. He may not in 1823—he may never at all—have been in love. But it is impossible that he never pictured to himself the figure he would cut in love : this Schubert, so little imposing, so negligent, so inconquerably shy. And it is almost impossible that in composing the mill songs he did not think of himself as the fickle Müllerin's sweetheart. Our utterances flow by the way our experiences and sympathies go. Schubert simply did not know what to do with the bold and the bad of the earth. But he lent his luckless young miller tones that he could not have bettered if he had wanted them for himself. And surely just such a one would he himself have been if he had fallen to such a milleress's charms ; timid and rapturous, flower-plucking and star-gazing, a fount of tenderness, a gulf of despair.

Schubert omitted, as well as the Prologue and the Epilogue of Müller's sequence, three of the miller's song—one of each period, joyful, jealous, and despairing. ' Das Mühlenleben,' which in Müller follows *Der Neugierige*, gives us further glimpses of the girl—of her picking flowers and berries and of her coming into the mill and demurely distributing a word of praise here and there. After *Eifersucht und Stolz*, Schubert left out ' Erster Schmerz, letzter Schmerz,' which carries on the ' Eifersucht ' theme. The miller sits by the brook piping to the children and inwardly convulsed, for behind the window panes that are shining in the sunlight as brightly as on the day of his arrival he knows that his sweetheart holds her new lover in her arms. Before *Trockne Blumen*, Müller put in another poem about forget-me-nots, ' Blümlein Vergissmeinnicht.' Schubert had enough desperate stanzas without these; but the miller's phantasy of the odourless, colourless flowers of the sunless world and his ironical cry ' Shut fast behind me the garden door ! ' would otherwise have suited the musician well. The name of the first song, which Schubert altered to *Das Wandern*, is *Wanderschaft* in Müller. The composer here and there departed slightly from the poet's text : once (in *Der Müller und der Bach*, where he inserts ' und ' in Müller's ' halb roth, halb weiss ') for the sake of his music but elsewhere more in haste apparently than by design.

' Die schöne Müllerin ' tells us how little Schubert was preoccupied by technics for their own sake. Feeling, the right feeling, was everything to him. The skill and ingenuity of his pen had by this time become prodigious ; but there is nothing in ' Die schöne Müllerin ' of the extraordinary novel refinements of the Rückert songs of 1823. It tells us how little he thought about himself that now, at twenty-six, a celebrity in a way and the inventor of unheard-of musical expressions, Schubert never once in these twenty songs dreamt of showing off. Probably no such notion ever crossed his mind. Still, the limpidity of the Müllerin music is remarkable when account is taken of all Schubert's spiritual adventures since 1815. He who had explored philosophies and passions in the company of Goethe and the rest, still could turn back to simple things with the candid gaze of his boyhood.

The right style for the Müllerin songs came to him through rapt concentration on the represented scene. In a moment, by force of frank feeling, he put out of mind Goethe's intellect, Schiller's allegories, and Mayrhofer's introspection, in engrossment in the simple relations in the millhouse and the pitiable young journeyman. So fixing his gaze, he instinctively, as it seems, reached out his hand again to the primitive forms of song in which he had delighted in 1815–16. Naturally rather than consciously he could now handle them far more exquisitely. There are songs of the earlier period which have the look of exercises for ' Die schöne Müllerin.' Thus *Daphne am Bach* (1816), a song that Schubert had probably forgotten, turns up recognizable but transfigured in *Wohin ?*

Eight of the twenty Müllerin songs are simply strophic, or
nine, if *Thränenregen* is included, which has only a minor
variation in the last stanza. Again and again there is a feeling
of folksong, typically in *Das Wandern*. But Schubert was
formulating nothing. Limpidity was the one general characteristic to be maintained. Where strophic form would do,
it was well : but he was ready with every other resource.
The strophic melodies are as apt as possible (allowing perhaps
a reservation in regard to *Die liebe Farbe*), and equally so such
ramifying melodies as *Wohin?*, *Halt !*, and *Eifersucht*. Schubert's old practice of resorting to recitative on occasion now
serves his purpose again ; but the little interjected declama-
tions in *Am Feierabend*, *Der Neugierige*, and elsewhere are
much less formal than was the recitative in such a song as
Am Bach im Frühling of 1816. With much art they are
kept in the closest touch with the cantilena. It is almost by
sleight of hand that in the passionate movement of *Die böse
Farbe* Schubert brings in the declaimed ' Horch, wenn im
Wald ein Jagdhorn schallt '[1] without loss to the lyrical
tension.

Let us in all this admire the great artist for whom skill was
for its own sake nothing, and who seems never to have been
tempted to go farther in his practice than was needed. He
knew how to leave well alone. He knew even how to relin-
quish. The strophic song *Die liebe Farbe* has sometimes
been criticized because the music suits only the first of Müller's
three stanzas. But observe the beauty of its psychological
fitness. The broken lover has fallen out of love with life,
and one thought, Death, Death, Death, beats in his brain.
The music with its incessant muffled tapping of the dominant
is a little funeral march. Pain, Pain, Pain, says the monotony
of the song, and one, one, one the way of escape. Note also
that *Die liebe Farbe* occurs between two transports, one of
jealousy, the other of despair. It is a spell of numbness. The
words that are said are of little account ; they are said mechanically to fit the funeral rhythm of the mind. The fact remains
that some of the lines in the second and third stanzas do
disturb the melody. Schubert has indeed relinquished
something for the sake of the essential impression. *Die
liebe Farbe* should be sung numbly, quite without expressive
vividness.

That is but one example of the way in which the 'Müllerin'
songs hang together and set one another off in delicate contrast.
In the earlier pieces *Wohin ?* represents a free holiday between

[1] In Müller the word is not ' schallt ' but ' ruft.'

the young journeyman's two jobs ; and there is unmistakable in the music a different poetry from the cheerful opening song—a sense of sheer nature sweet and wild. The piano-forte in *Das Wandern* tells of the brook in harness to the mill machinery. In *Wohin ?* it has escaped from man and rambles at its own sweet will. In *Halt !* it sobers down again, and there is a hint in the bass arpeggio figure of the new-found millwheel. The brook flows very demurely in *Danksagung*. *Am Feierabend* is one of the most engaging of these little miniatures in which the scene is perceived with the lively colours of a magic mirror. After a tug and a wrench, the work is got going with a swing. ' But oh, my arms are too weak by half ! ' says the young fellow as he takes a breather, and the pianoforte tells the thuds of his heart. The master-miller, however, says, ' Well done,' the daughter of the house smiles good-night ; the sluice is shut, the wheel slows down.

The detached performance of any of the ' Müllerin ' songs is not commendable. Any disarranging of Schubert's order is to be condemned, and the edition which prints these songs all higgledy-piggledy is a disgrace. Still, the exquisite sixth Müllerin song, *Der Neugierige*, may be allowed to be one which, unlike some of them, can stand transplantation from its native flower-bed. The form of this song, *a a b x b*, is singular. The *x* stands for the declamatory phrase already referred to (' On one of two little words, Yes or No, hangs for me the whole world's future '). The first two stanzas are set tenderly but playfully ; but when the lover turns with his question to the friendly brook the whole tone seriously changes—not, indeed, the key, but tempo, metre, and melody. It is a most engaging example of Schubert's sensibility and responsiveness. There is in all the ' Müllerin ' no more searching test of the singer than *Der Neugierige*. The tone must be both soft and warm ; and the extremely slow 3-4 movement demands a faultless legato style. The oracular brook meanwhile murmurs to itself almost inaudibly.

With the swiftest of turns, the music becomes in *Ungeduld* a frolic, an outburst of confidence, laughter, and joyful anticipa-tion. The four stanzas of this strophic song are not too much. Never was there such a music of youth's racing blood. The song is a daisy : it is a bird ! The ' *rather* fast ' of the direction is to be observed. English singers often incline to gabble the German words. In English,[1] a quicker tempo may be risked. There follow three strophic songs of courtship, the plainest and simplest of all the set. The

[1] Fox-Strangways's version in ' Schubert's Songs Translated ' is first rate.

aubade *Morgengruss* conveys the sweetness and emptiness of the world in the early summer morning. The forget-me-not song, *Des Müllers Blumen*, falls naturally into a 6-8 movement as homely as the flower. *Thränenregen* carries on the same key and movement, with a rather more pensive sentiment. These three songs, each of which has four stanzas, are best not dawdled over by the singer. The eleventh song, *Mein !*, is the climax. The brook and the millwheel and the birds in the bushes are all bidden to join in the word's triumphant sound. The exuberant melody runs on for twenty-nine bars as though trying in vain to encompass all the joy of the situation ; then, after a breath, it makes a start in quite a different place (B*b* instead of D), then returns. All the world seems to be dancing and carolling.

In *Mein !* we have the first fortissimos in ' Die schöne Müllerin.' (They are also the last except a singular and not very explicable one in *Pause*, and those in the distraught *Böse Farbe*.) The singer who does not go through his tone will give pleasure by some ringing F♯'s here. After this song, and nowhere else, is the proper place, when the cycle is being performed, for an interval.

The twelfth song, *Pause*, is the subtlest, and some would also say the most beautiful of the set. Schubert saw that the verses could only be treated by a free and various melody. He therefore bound the song together with a strongly characteristic pianoforte theme :

This is used a little in the manner of an ostinato. The first of these quoted bars recurs eighteen times in the song, and, transposed and slightly varied, eight times more. This we may call the lute motive, suggesting as it does the thrumming of strings by a casual hand. The general tone of the song is a hush, an ambiguous hush in which anything may happen. The lyrical movement is twice held up by phrases of quasi-recitative. The form is *a b a c* and coda. The particular charm of the song lies in the use of the lute motive and the half unquiet questioning in the last section. The motive has gone as far afield as A*b* and A*b* minor. ' An echo of my old griefs, or a prelude to new songs ? ' asks the lover. The harmonies hang on the words with a touching solicitude.

Under 'griefs?' there is a 6-5 chord on B♭. '. . . old griefs or'—which way will it turn? The seventh surreptitiously changes to an augmented sixth—' or a new prelude?' —and almost before we know where we are, we are back in the daylight of B♭ major again after those obscure F♭'s and the C♭ chord that was half expected, but was evaded. Sometimes, in effect, the B♭ has been known to come back, leaving the singer still in the dark. It is a trap for the careless. But nothing could be more perfectly in place than this little progression. Schubert has not done with it. The musing lover, getting no answer to his questions, must needs ask them again. The lute motive then leads back (G minor, A♭ minor) to the 6-3 chord in F♭, for the miller to go over the same ground. In the end he feels pretty well satisfied, so says the B♭ postlude.

Before the clouds gather, there is one more happy, affectionate little song, *Mit dem grünen Lautenbande*, the song of the green ribbon. The girl's words are in B♭, to which the miller answers in F. In the fourteenth song, the 'Jäger' comes on the scene. Exactly what is the Jäger of these German poems is a puzzle. He seems to be a peasant with unlimited shooting rights; he is at times a gamekeeper or gillie, and at other times apparently a poacher. *Der Jäger* is an excited, scherzo-like song in C minor, based on the huntsman's horn-call. The young miller is all bristling with annoyance and uneasiness. Admirable is Schubert's skill in prolonging the expression of irritation and enhancing it over a period of twenty-four bars.

Uneasiness has become acute apprehension in *Eifersucht und Stolz*. The brook is angry and tears along its course in G minor semiquavers with a movement it never knew before. The lover is in torment. Schubert's music takes on wonderfully the tone of his moods—the reproaches, the pathos. The song is one of the most ingenious pieces in the cycle. The pathos is expressed by a longing return to the major. In the next song, *Die liebe Farbe*, there is an invasion of despair. The unremitting F♯'s (the note is struck 536 times) are like a dull ache. It is hope's funeral. 'My love was so fond of green' is the haunting thought, repeated again and again, first with a major third in memory of the bright past, then with a fall to the melancholy minor.

The rushing movement of *Die böse Farbe* in B major seems to be carrying the unfortunate away on its stream. He begs for a word, a gesture of farewell; but he cannot stay for it— he has to cry out his good-bye to the prevailing tune. Phantasms come and go in the music, notably the huntsman's tally-ho. The general tone is feverish. In *Trockne Blumen*, our miller is simply dying of a broken heart. The theme is an old-fashioned one—the language of flowers ; but no one will smile at this song. The dried flowers are no doubt the forget-me-nots of the first radiant period. The dead flowers of the spring are to be buried in the suicide's grave, but in another May others are bidden to appear with a message of remembrance. The music is elegiac in tone, and march-like in rhythm : an elfin funeral march for the dead forget-me-nots.

Let us, let the singer in particular, observe the delicacy of Schubert's touch in this extremity of sorrow. There is no longer a question of appeal ; and the singer must be very careful with his *f*'s in the E major portion of the song, remembering that the exhortation is a purely fanciful one to the flowers of an unborn year. The affecting E minor melody ends with a noteworthy interrogatory cadence (' Dead flowers, whence your dew ? '). The minor sixth that occurs in the accompaniment after the melody has veered towards G major is one of several touches of refinement. The phantasy of the coming spring calls for the major key and a more active bass to the march movement. This brighter colouring dies away at the end. The last song but one, *Der Müller und der Bach*—the miller's last song—is a pathetic colloquy with the brook. In answer to the lover's poignant G minor melody there is a ripple of semiquavers and the brook endeavours in C, G, and D major to bring comfort. The rippling continues, but the miller's answer falls back on G minor. The brook can, he says, bring comfort—not, however, by its friendly-sounding surface, but in the silence of its depths.

The twentieth song is the brook's lullaby for the drowned lover ; a strophic song of five stanzas, tender, placid, and monotonous. Lovers come, and lovers go, their wounds may smart, but are before long assuaged : such things had already happened and were likely to happen again, and are taken compassionately but equably by the brook—the brook that goes on for ever.

XII

SONGS OF 1823-1827

MANDYCZEWSKI'S eighth volume begins with a few songs
attributed to 1823 and includes at the end one or two that
were composed at the beginning of 1827.

The year 1824 began miserably enough. Schubert was still
not really well, and he was penniless. He could not live
permanently at his father's. He took a lodging, at No. 100
auf der Wieden, near St. Charles's Church. Necessity made
him return to the Esterházys, with whom in May he went to
Zseliz for the second time. Early in the year (in February),
while in the depths of depression, he had written the celebrated
and delightful octet in F, Op. 166.

At Zseliz an old friend was a guest of the Esterházys—
Baron Carl von Schönstein, the singer, who in later years
was to introduce Liszt to Schubert's songs. Schubert
dedicated to Schönstein 'Die schöne Müllerin,' which was
at this time being published in Vienna in instalments. The
Esterházys were gracious to the modest music-teacher, but
he never felt at home in their society. He was homesick for
Vienna and his bohemian friends. His health, however,
improved during the summer, and he composed busily. The
Zseliz works of 1824 included the lovely string quartet
in A minor, which was published the same year as Op. 29
under the title 'Trois Quatuors,' and a series of outstanding
compositions for pianoforte duet, thus, the two sonatas in B♭
(Op. 30, published 1825) and in C, (Op. 140, published in
1838, and later scored by Joachim), variations on an original
theme in A♭ (Op. 35, published in 1825) and the 'Divertisse-
ment à la Hongroise' (Op. 54, published in 1826). Schubert
returned to Vienna in November.

The winter was more cheerful than the last had been.
Schubert had hardly any money and there was something
wrong with his health ; but he received some small sums for
the compositions that were pouring from the press, and he
made new friends. Then in May 1825 he joined Vogl for
the summer in Upper Austria, and these months (May to
October) were among the happiest in his life. Steyr was
Vogl's native place. There and at Linz Schubert acquired

numbers of fresh admirers. Vogl and Schubert made excursions to Salzburg and to Gastein, where the lost ' Gastein ' symphony is supposed to have been written. (The evidence that it ever existed is slender, resting mainly, as it does, on the flighty Bauernfeld.) In the autumn Schober returned to Vienna after his theatrical adventures at Breslau. Schubert might now, if he had so wished, have obtained a modest court appointment. The post of second court organist was vacant, but Johann Hugo Worzischek was appointed and Schubert was left, mercifully for us, with liberty for creative work.

The 1825 compositions are distinguished—apart from the songs—by three pianoforte sonatas: in A minor (No. 9, Op. 42, published 1826, dedicated to the Archduke Rudolf, Beethoven's Archduke), in D (Op. 53, composed in the autumn and published in 1826), and the magnificent C major sonata, the last two movements of which were left unfinished. There was a funeral march for pianoforte duet, Op. 55, written on the death of Alexander I of Russia, a pendant to which was the coronation march, Op. 66, for his successor, Nicholas I, in the next year. 1825 was also the year of twenty-two songs.

In the winter of 1825–26 there recurred signs that Schubert's health was undermined. The great composition of the previous year was his fourteenth and most famous string quartet, the D minor (' Death and the Maiden '). It was first played by his friends the Hackers at their house on January 29, 1826, but was not published until 1831. During ten days of the following summer (June 20–30) Schubert wrote the great G major quartet. This, his last string quarrtet, was not published until 1852. There were also a number of choral songs, and then in the autumn the pianoforte sonata in G, Op. 78, dedicated to Spaun (published 1827), the celebrated rondo in B minor for violin and pianoforte, Op. 70, (published 1827), and the great pianoforte trio, No. 1 in B*b*, Op. 99 (published 1836). The trio was first played at a bachelors' farewell party given in honour of Spaun, who was now back in Vienna and was about to be married.

This year Schubert got no farther from Vienna than Währing, just outside the city, where he spent some weeks with Schober and Schwind. His financial position showed no improvement, and now he himself made an attempt to obtain a salaried post. Salieri had died in the spring of 1825, and was succeeded as court choirmaster by Josef Eybler. Schubert applied for Eybler's old post of secondary choirmaster. He failed. Eybler was unfavourable. He said he had never

heard any of Schubert's compositions. The post was given
to Josef Weigl, formerly conductor at the court theatre.

*   *

*

The last songs of 1823 are four settings of Rückert, every one
of them entrancing. The eighth volume opens with *Dass sie
hier gewesen* :

> ' Beauty has known this spot, and love : your beauty and
> my love. There is fragrance in the air, there are my
> tears in the grass. They tell that you have been here.'

The form of the music is ordered by the poet's syntax.
Rückert begins with a subordinate noun-clause—' That
there is fragrance in the air proves,' etc. With a sensitive
flexibility of style before him unknown in music, Schubert
delays the statement of his key (C) until he reaches the poet's
main clause. The song begins outside the key with a sighing
of ambiguous sevenths, thus:

Nearly at the end of the century such an opening could
still, by its strangeness and poignancy, serve Wolf for one
of his truest masterpieces[1] :

[1] Spanisches Liederbuch, (I), 9.

They say that Schubert did not develop, that at the beginning he was already all that he was at the last.[1] This can simply not be maintained. There is a peculiar refinement and mobility in the writing of *Dass sie hier gewesen* unknown before the 1820's. The ' Divan ' songs of 1821 are the first typical examples. Schubert had then already composed 400 songs. It is true that *Versunken* and even *Dass sie hier gewesen* are still not very well known. The latter was published in 1826 as Op. 57 with other Rückert songs, which included one supremely celebrated, *Du bist die Ruh'* :

> ' O bliss and fount of peace, thou who awakenest the eyes to blessedness and closest· them in satisfied sleep, take in dedication all that I am. Be with me and the world is not. Thou dome of heaven's brightness, let me live wholly in thy light.'

Rückert addresses Love as the double giver of desire and its assuagement. The poem, idealizing the gratified lover's peace, is pitched in a key almost of mysticism, in the oriental way. The diction remains perfectly restrained. Schubert, noticing nothing extravagant in the erotic hymn, felt at once and wonderfully matched this modesty of style. ' Sehnsucht ' was this time left aside ; and he simply embraced the idea of peace in a singularly pure and beautiful spirit. The first few words were, we can see, what charmed and held him ; and from his murmuring of them, ' Thou who art peace,' the whole melody sprang. How close and humble are the harmonies, how hushed the air, not to scare off the holy visitant ! The song is in three parts, the second being simply a repetition of the first. The third is, as it were, the stretching of tired limbs in the luxury of repose. ' From horizon to horizon thou art the only light,' says the text. The broad suggestion of the word ' Augenzelt ' (one of Rückert's orientalisms) sets the music slowly climbing the scale up to A♭, with a crescendo for the first time in the song. But the light is peace ; and the over-bold music pauses for an empty bar, and then resumes, pianissimo again, with the cadence of the other strophes. With a repetition of this ascent and relapse (only enriched towards the end by imitations in the pianoforte part, which for the rest of the song has kept very close to the voice) the third stanza ends. In

[1] E.g. Paul Landormy, (' Schubert,' Paris, 1928)—' Chez Schubert point de renouvellement, point d'évolution. Du premier jour il est tout lui-même et il restera jusqu'à sa dernière heure ce qu'il fut à 17 ans.'

the last page of *Du bist die Ruh'* there is a discrepancy between
Mandyczewski and Friedländer, a matter, it is true, of only
a couple of notes, yet considerable in the melody of so famous
a piece of music. The latter editor, following the original
publication of the song, takes the voice up a fourth (C*b*–F*b*)
at the repetition of ' von deinem (Glanz).' The former
believes the F*b* to have been a misprint in 1826, and he gives
D*b* again as in the first occurrence of the scale. Singers
frequently attempt *Du bist die Ruh'*, having only the lightest
notion of its requirements. The music is, of course, limpid-
ness itself ; the scope obvious. It remains one of the most
difficult songs in existence, taxing the technical control as
severely as the singer's taste. An exquisitely refined *mezza
voce* is called for in the greater part of it, and then a power
of expansion on the two scales. There is no cover for a
fault ; and the more accomplished the artist, the more seriously
will he consider the undertaking.

Du bist die Ruh' was No. 3 of Op. 59, its companion, No. 4,
being *Lachen und Weinen* :

> ' To be in love ! It means laughing one moment, crying
> the next. Why, this morning I was jumping for joy and
> tonight I am sobbing my heart out. And all for no
> reason ! Heart, are you crazy ? '

This was composed in a lucky hour. It is a quick and
voluble song, it is light, excited, and girlish. ' And all for
no reason ? ' No ; there is more reason than is admitted.
There is probably a pretty reason, a hope and a doubt, with
decidedly more of hope. The song is rather in the vein of
Geheimes, than which it is only a little less charming, being
more gay and flighty. It talks of tears, but we think it means
pouting more than weeping. How graceful is its gaiety,
how Schubert must have noted the fling of some tempestuous
petticoat ! The song smiles in A*b* major ; it pouts in the
minor, in different places in the two stanzas. Apart from a
momentary leaning to D*b* there is no modulation, and to
this perhaps is due some of the effect of bright thoughtlessness
in the mood—to this, and to the extreme lightness of the
texture. The handling of the few notes could not have been
prettier.

After the young girl, the ageing amorist. The last of the
Rückert songs is *Greisengesang* :

> ' I was not ready for winter, but it has come, it has caught
> me unawares. Ah, but I shut my door, I draw close the

curtains, and here in the room of my heart I still hug the
ghost of delight. O memory, lingering perfume of the
lost summer of life ! '

The poem, called in Rückert ' Vom künftigen Alter,' is
from his book of eastern lyrics, ' Östliche Rosen.' The
thought of age hardly enters into Schubert's song ; the composer has simply seized on the idea of the sentimentalist's
consolation in dreaming. Memory he depicts as bathed in
the loveliest harmonies, and love's ghost as sweeter than
the reality. The second half of the song nearly repeats
the first ; only there are questions for answers and harmonies
now where there were unisons before, the dreamer having
peopled the solitude with his evocations. It is written for
bass, and the singer is justified in descending to the low F♯,
where Schubert has written the middle one, at ' all' gegangen
einander nach ' ; for the repetitions of the phrase that immediately follow in the pianoforte part show what Schubert
had in his mind. A peculiarity of the song are the tender
and lingering melismata at the end of each stanza, principally
on the word ' desires ' in the first and ' dreams ' in the second.
With the *Greisengesang* was published, in Op. 60, Schubert's
last Schiller song, *Dithyrambe*. The poem was paraphrased
by Coleridge, beginning thus :

> ' Never, believe me, appear the immortals, never alone ;
>   Scarce had I welcomed the Sorrow-beguiler
>   Iacchus, but in came Boy Cupid the Smiler ;
> Lo, Phœbus the Glorious descends from his throne.
>   They advance, they float in, the Olympians all !
>   With Divinities fills my terrestrial hall ! '

Schubert sets the ode strophically, for bass voice, in the
most spirited way. It is the sublimation of a students' song.
In the crashing prelude there is a brilliant rhythmical invention. Bacchus is the first god mentioned ; and, as has
happened before, we suspect that the musician's fancy took
fire from a phrase caught by a glance rather than from the
study of all the poet's verses. Since Bacchus was leading
the heavenly rout, Bacchic the whole song had to be, and to
our advantage. The swinging tune has tremendous vitality
in it. At the end of twelve bars it comes to a close in the
subdominant, and thence with new vigour it continues its
course. ' They come, they are nearing ' ; and the music
mounts with excitement on a chromatic bass. Schubert
had in earlier years toiled and toiled over Schiller, but now

that he was saying farewell it was with no ceremony, but
rather in a reckless breaking-up spirit.

The last Mayrhofer songs were composed in March 1824.
They are a group of four, beginning with *Der Sieg* :

> ' World beyond the clouds, realm of the ideal, I hold
> your key ! I, the poet, know the way of escape. The
> might of thought can break the bondage of the flesh.
> Eden's curse is wiped out, and I with my own hand have
> dealt old serpent his death-blow.'

It is again a variation on Mayrhofer's haunting theme.
The verses might have been thought intractable, but Schubert
seized on the musical thought that was suggested by the
poet's longed-for, unbenighted life—or perhaps just by the
simple and sounding epithets, ' so rein und tief und klar.'
The thought took the form of the soft and solemn F major
harmonies that are the making of the song. The middle
section is energetic, telling of the poet's spiritual victory ;
then a return is made, not without an impression of pathos,
to the deep calm of the beginning. The song is for bass.
Generally neglected, it is known to English audiences through
Plunket Greene's singing. Pathos, we say, is felt to underlie
the desperate assertiveness of *Der Sieg* and the poet's heavenly
mirage. In *Auflösung* Mayrhofer is a stage farther on the
road of revelation or illusion :

> ' Wither, O earthly spring, and thou, O sun, get thee gone ;
> for the old world is sinking, it yields place to the non-
> world, and already my being thrills with the bliss of non-
> being, and already (O life, be silent !) there steal upon me
> inexistence's eternal harmonies.'

Past protest and defiance, the death-dedicated poet has
worked himself into an ecstatic state. What could Schubert
know of anything so strange and morbid ? Well, he was
inclined (as seems a good musical policy) to let the words
that had no bearing on the music in him take care of themselves, so long as there was something he could lay hold
of. Here was the idea of ecstasy, and Schubert knew
ecstasies, although purely as a lover of life and not, like his
friend, in life's despite. He was able therefore in *Auflösung*
to write a masterpiece of buoyancy and delight and, such being
the nature of music, we can read into it either the suicidal
poet's exaltation or the musician's glorying in the very earthly

spring that the other contemns. The song is built on a great arpeggio figure that ranges over the keyboard. This and the broad and soaring vocal line make *Auflösung* one of the grandest of the songs, appropriate only to a good pianist and a noble voice. It calls for a superior artist to give it full-throated tones and at the same time an expression of rare spiritual exaltation.

By its side there is one of the smallest and most exquisite of the Mayrhofer songs, *Abendstern* :

> ' Why so solitary, star of eve ?—I am Love.—Join, then, join your starry companions.—Not so, for true love's lot is to sorrow apart.'

The writing is pellucid. The fewness of the notes makes a chilly air, an empty scene. It is all, says the music, a mere wistful fancy. The simplicity and delicacy of the touch are everything. The key veers between A minor and major in a way that is this song's own ; let us call it a disheartened way. A pathetic little attempt is made to reach the larger third. It is grasped for an instant, and at the next it slips from love's chilled fingers. The fourth song of the set, *Gondelfahrer*, is farewell to Mayrhofer. It is a rather sombre barcarolle, much more Viennese than Venetian in sentiment. The gondolier hears midnight striking in St. Mark's Square, and he feels himself alone in the romantic city, while the reflections of moon and stars dance in the waters like ghosts. The soft striking of the hour in A*b* is a picturesque incident of the quiet little song.

The memory of an obscure poet, Carl Lappe, was perpetuated by Schubert's setting in this year of his lines *Im Abendroth* :

> ' Author of light and life, Father ! Thy glory shines in the beauty of the evening. The heart swells in the bosom, humble and adoring. Ah, evening glory, presage of God's light in paradise ! '

Mandyczewski tells us that Schubert's manuscript is ' extraordinarily neat and most lovingly written ' ; and well we can believe it. The music is in every strain an outpouring of humble and thankful love to the Creator of the world of beauty. The western splendour is not depicted, but simply a trance of gratitude and wonder. The song is ' quiet as a nun, breathless with adoration.'—A poet has to be called in

to give a hint of the poetry of Schubert's music. Words-
worth's sonnet is its match and nothing less. To stare at
the page—at the simple spread of A♭ chords, at the tonic-
dominant bass—is to find nothing explaining how such beauty
came to be. Music is here felt to be not so much a medium
of expression as something more intimate, the very emotion
itself miraculously manifested. *Im Abendroth* is one of the
most difficult songs in Schubert, only to be essayed by a singer
in command of a singularly pure and serene legato. The
other Lappe song, *Der Einsame*, was composed in 1825 :

> ' A book and a pipe and the cricket on the hearth—I
> ask for no better company. Perhaps the book drops, and
> I sit staring into the fire and turning over my fancies.
> What has a man to do bustling up and down the world ?
> He can never be more than himself. Here by my fireside
> I revolve within my head the whole world, or as much as
> I want of it, and my friend the cricket seems to be doing
> the same thing.'

The music ambles contentedly along with engaging humour.
The making of the song is the whimsical use in the pianoforte
bass of a little semiquaver figure borrowed from the cadences
of the vocal part :

The stay-at-home's thoughts wander at ease among the
keys—into A one moment, into F the next. In the last page
the jumps of a ninth in the vocal part are not far off a comic
effect. Schubert's eyes twinkled, we cannot doubt, he must
have rubbed his hands together in the composition of this
pleasant piece. The high G's in the last page were an afterthought. They appeared in Diabelli's edition, with one or
two other trifling modifications, in 1826, a year after the
song had been issued as a supplement to the ' Wiener Zeitschrift für Kunst.' The song was numbered Op. 41.

The three Craigher songs also belong to 1825. *Totengräbers
Heimweh* might, with a fractional difference in the revolution
of its fortune's wheel, have been one of Schubert's greatest
masterpieces. The music was grandly conceived. It begins
in F minor with an imposing funeral movement. The right
hand has heavy repeated chords, while in the darkness a

magnificent bass strides with tragic state. The misfortune is that we cannot feel touched by the situation. The morbid gravedigger, out of love with life, and yearning for the earthy abode to which it is his duty to consign others !—we hardly believe in him, his peculiar woe is forced, he is a figment of fashionable romantic gruesomeness. The case is, at any rate, too odd for a lyric, the vogue for graveyard poetry having collapsed ; and all the musical richness of *Todtengräbers Heimweh* does not hide a certain absurdity in the grave-digger's distress.

The next song, *Der blinde Knabe*, is on a translation from Colley Cibber, a name curious to find associated with Schubert.

> ' O say, what is that thing called Light
> Which I must ne'er enjoy ;
> What are the blessings of the sight,
> O tell your poor blind boy !
> . . . Then let not what I cannot have
> My cheer of mind destroy ;
> While thus I sing I am a king,
> Although a poor blind boy.'

The pages, considered without regard for the text, suggest a graceful and placid brook song. The arpeggio figure is one of the prettiest of its kind in Schubert. All is delicacy and suavity. Unfortunately the subject renders the song intolerable. For the sighted complacently to put smooth words into the mouth of the blind, and to make a comfortable song of unimagined disaster is a sentimentality and an impertinence. The English text fits Schubert's melody.

The song by which the otherwise obscure Craigher is remembered and will be, so long as our music endures, is *Die junge Nonne* :

> ' What a fearful night ! The thunder makes the whole house rock. Outside it is as dark as the grave. Once my life was just such a storm as this. No light but mad flashes of lightning—the lightning of passions.
> ' I have come out of that storm into peace—out of that night into the eternal morning. I am the bride of the heavenly Bridegroom. Dear bell, you ring sweet and clear above the raging noises of the world. You call my soul. I come.'

We find again after ten years the Schubert of *Erlkönig*. Here is just such another nocturnal landscape with a great

movement of wind and storm-clouds. It is the very heart
of romance, this awed admiration of nature's wild revelry.
Schubert loved the thought of the untamable elements and
their free play out of man's reach. *Die junge Nonne* comes
strangely near being a hymn to the storm. We hear the
weather's formidable soughing from end to end of the song.
The storm is never close at hand. To be observed is the
subdued tone of the music. It leaves us with a notion of a
tremendous billowing and buffeting and yet it has rarely
risen to *f* and has for the most part been pianissimo. The
sense of grandeur is created by the strength of the first F
minor theme, and by the symphonic breadth of its treatment.
In the first page it is in one form or another heard seven
or eight times ; and when, after the tonic has been so
massively established, the theme starts on its adventures in
F♯ minor, every listener is aware of some powerful spirit at
work. None who heard will ever forget Arthur Nikisch's
rendering of this muffled storm in the days when he used
to play for Elena Gerhardt. It was a discovery of
the depths of Schubert's poetry. Half-way through the song
the mode changes to the major and the air clears, but the
music of the weather is not shut out. The nun sings a variant
of the storm melody which continues with developments to
the end. Schubert does not draw a contrast between nature's
raging and the nun's spiritual peace. Rather does he suggest
in the turn of the music from the dark and awesome minor
mode, a reconciliation, a larger understanding of nature's
ways, a recognition of the essential benignancy of the forces
of the wild night. While the end is calm, while the chapel
bell rings out its F's and C's, and the nun sings her ' Halle-
luyah !,' the air is still alive with the quivering wind (right-
hand tremolo), and bass octaves depict majestic looming
rain-clouds.

The immortal song was published in the year of its composition as Op. 43, together with *Nacht und Träume*, which
is another of Schubert's hymns to nature. The text is not,
as some editions say, by Schiller, but by Schubert's friend
Collin, who had died the year before. The verses are a
simple greeting to the falling night, bringer of dreams to tired
humankind. The song is a hushed adagio. The first bar
is marked pianissimo, and there is no dynamic modification
at all indicated in the two pages of the pianoforte's equable,
lulling semiquavers. This is not to say that the voice part
is to be sung in an absolutely level tone. It was Schubert's

principle not to give the singer expressive directions. The text, he said, was direction enough. The lovely melody appears among the semiquavers like moonlight that breaks through clouds. It cannot be too slowly sung ; for in this dreaming hour time and circumstance are forgotten. Again Schubert has, all unthinking, composed one of the severest tests of the singer's technics. A perfectly calm and steady flow of beautiful tone is wanted in *Nacht und Träume* ; and not a moment's agitation or constriction, nor a misshapen syllable, can be forgiven. Schubert has avoided monotony in his almost motionless music by what is not a modulation but a simple drop from key to key (B to G) half-way through the song. It is as though the dreamer, still sleeping, unconsciously changed his attitude for still greater ease. In *Der Musensohn* we saw Schubert similarly interchanging these two keys without preparation.

The ' Lady of the Lake ' songs were composed in 1825. Schubert used a translation by P. A. Storck. It was excessively free, so that considerable editing is necessary if the music is to be made to fit the original text. Sometimes Storck departed from Scott's metres, or again he would take the liberty of expanding a poem. Nevertheless, Artaria, Schubert's publisher, sought to interest the English public by giving Scott's text above the German in the 1826 edition of the songs—to all of them, that is, except Norman's song, in which nothing but a rewriting could make Scott and Schubert come to terms. Ellen's first song, *Soldier, rest ! thy warfare o'er* (' Raste, Krieger '), is an extended composition of eight pages. The graceful D*b* lullaby comes over three times. There are two considerable episodes, one in A on ' In our isle's enchanted hall,' the other in F♯ minor on ' No rude sound shall reach thine ear.' In the first of these Schubert had eight lines of Storck to set, expanded from four of Scott's. In the second, too, there are departures from the English, rendering adaptation difficult. Schubert has here, for the sake of musical variety, directly contradicted the sense of Ellen's—

> ' No rude sound shall reach thine ear,
> Armour's clang or war-steed champing,'

by coming in with a spirited martial strain. Similarly in Ellen's second song, *Huntsman, rest ! thy chase is done* (' Jäger, ruhe '), the music is all the time echoing with horn-calls. The two pieces, while very agreeable and mellow, have not the firm character of first-rate Schubert. Ellen's third song is the *Ave Maria* from the third canto. From the first, as we know from Schubert's correspondence, all ears and hearts were won. Writing to his father from Steyr on July 25, 1825, he said:

> ' Especially have my new songs from " The Lady of the Lake " earned me success. Much have I surprised people by the religious feeling I have expressed in a hymn to the Blessed Virgin, by which, so it seems, all are struck and solemnly impressed. The reason, I think, is that I never force myself to think religiously and never write sacred music unless something stronger than myself urges me to it ; but then that, surely, is more likely to be genuine religious feeling.'

The exquisite song is not so much a proper ecclesiastical ornament as an ex-voto, hung not for fitness but for its preciousness at the shrine. It is in itself no more liturgical than one of Chopin's nocturnes ; but there need be no doubt of the spirit in which it was dedicated. The criticism has been known that it is too sweet, too graceful and secular for a ' hymn to the Virgin ' and that its adequate performance is too much a mere question of technics. One should remember, however, as Schubert remembered, that Ellen is singing a harp-song, not reciting the Angel's salutation.

> ' It is the harp of Allan-bane
> That makes its measure slow and high,
> Attuned to sacred minstrelsy.
> What melting voice attends the strings ?
> 'Tis Ellen, or an angel, sings.'

The thought of the harp's thin and quickly evaporating accompaniment naturally suggested to the musician, as counterpoise, a tense and noble melodic line. Schubert's harp-figure might seem to have been derived from Bach if it were at all likely that he knew the Bell cantata :

BACH: 'Schlage doch'.

SCHUBERT: Op. 52. N̰o 6

A peculiarity of Scott's prosody here is that in the first stanza the lines are mostly trochaic, while in the second and third they have a syllable more, becoming regularly iambic. The German translator made the first stanza conform to the rest and he used double rhymes freely ; hence some little discrepancies when the English is sung. Schubert's ' anacruses ' must not be interfered with. It is better to supplement Scott's lines with ' O,' ' for ' and so on.

But nothing of the sort will help in Norman's song *The heath this night* (' Die Nacht bricht bald herein '), for Storck has entirely recomposed Scott in longer stanzas of shorter lines. The young bridegroom has been separated from his Mary at the church door, summoned to the rallying of Clan-Alpine by the messenger with the fiery cross. He loyally sets off without ado to carry on the signal ; and sings his song on the way. A military movement of dotted semi-quavers springs into Schubert's mind, suggested by :

> ' The manly thirst for martial fame,
>   The stormy joy of mountaineers
>   Ere yet they rush upon the spears.'

He keeps this movement going without truce, through all the eight pages of the song. There are a principal and a secondary melody, both in C minor. Both are modified in the repetitions, and the first appears finally in C major when Norman anticipates a victorious return to home and beauty. What happened to the spirited groom and maiden-wife Scott forgot to tell ; but probably nothing good, to judge from the account of the ensuing battle of Beal' an Duine. The fifth

of the ' Lady of the Lake ' songs is the ' Lay of the Imprisoned
Huntsman ' (Lied des gefangenen Jägers), beginning *My
hawk is tired of perch* ('Mein Ross so müde '). Ellen, on
her mission to Stirling, overhears it sung from a turret in the
castle, and recognizes her lover's, Malcolm Græme's, voice.
Scott's iambic lines became anapæstic in Storck's German.
The music can nevertheless be fairly well adapted to the
original. The song is a polonaise in D minor and major.
The chivalric rhythm and the bold tune start well ; and yet
the song is cloying. The voice part is, for one thing, contained
wholly within an octave. The pianoforte never rises above
the D of the treble stave ; and all modulation is denied. The
' Ivanhoe ' song, ' The Crusader's Return ' (*High deeds
achieved of knightly fame*)—in German called ' Romanze des
Richard Löwenherz ' (*Grosse Taten tat der Ritter*)—was
composed in the following year, 1826. In the novel the king
sings the song for Friar Tuck's entertainment in the forest
hermitage, accompanying himself on the anchorite's harp.
Scott's translator turned iambs into trochees, so that the
English text and Schubert's music cannot be made to agree.
The music, in B minor and major, is all built on a spirited
dotted-quaver rhythm. Its fanfares suggest brilliant pagean-
try. Such music as this and Norman's and Malcolm's songs
from ' The Lady of the Lake ' should surely have been saved
up by Schubert for use as instrumental finales. This B minor
' Ivanhoe ' song in particular might have served one of the
1928 composers who attempted to finish the ' Unfinished '
symphony. As a song, it does not, in its seven pages of
hammered quavers, altogether avoid monotony.

Schubert's two compositions on verses by his clerical patron,
the Patriarch Pyrker, were written at Gastein in August 1825.
They were *Das Heimweh* and *Die Allmacht*. They were
published as Op. 79 in 1827, dedicated to the poet. The
first is a piece of eight pages, one of Schubert's cantata-songs.
The subject was a very favourite one in the early romantic
period, namely the nostalgia of the exiled highlander. Here
the simple mountaineer expresses in hexameters his yearning
for the snowy peaks, the sunsets, the flora and the musical
cow-bells of his home. There exist two versions of the
song. The second is revised in a radical way very rare in
Schubert. Both are given by Mandyczewski in A minor.
The musical material is the same—an opening movement of
symphonic stateliness in the minor, and a scherzo-like 3-4
movement in the major. But whereas in the first version

the minor movement is recalled at the end only in a brief postlude, in the second it comes back in state and is newly developed in the last two pages, the 3-4 movement now being correspondingly shorter. Although Schubert does not succeed in really touching us with his homesick highlander, the song is likable in its old-fashioned way, suggesting as it does an engraved frontispiece in a contemporary edition of 'Waverley.' It is full of good music, which at moments verges on greatness. When the exile dreams of the black pine-forest and 'mountain on mountain piled in dizzying majesty' the fine surging of the music calls to mind *An Schwager Kronos.* The song, however, is altogether over-shadowed by its companion-piece, *Die Allmacht* :

'Heaven and earth proclaim Thy Being ! The storm and the torrent are Thy Voice. The leaf and the golden sea of corn are Thou, and Thou art the starry floweret and the flower-field of the stars. Great God, Thou art the firmament and beyond the firmament and art the pulsing heart in me.'

Schubert, exhilarated by his tour in the hills of Upper Austria, his thoughts—as is shown by the letters he wrote home at the time, the longest and most characteristic that have been preserved—all set quivering by so many revelations of nature both benign and magnificent, found in this song the outlet for overflowing feeling. The patriarch's verses could not have been happened on at a better moment. The subject, God apprehended in nature, went straight to Schubert's heart. There, with the hills round about him, he poured forth his blessing upon the health-giving air and thanks to the Creator of life. The magnificent song is any-thing but a formal piece. It is not to be judged on the assumption that Schubert was composing for solemn general devotions and should therefore have restrained himself. It is intensely personal and rapturous. Schubert's temple was the hill-side ; and he brought all the sounds of the open air, the torrent, the forest's murmur, the thunder-roll, into his hymn of praise. So far from withholding himself, he clearly set himself to make the music as Schubertian as possible. After the general majesty of the movement and the exultancy of the great vocal line, the characteristic of the song is the harmonic richness, as seen for instance in the almost Wagnerian crescendo on 'He speaks in the thundering storm, in the river's reverberant roar,' where the bass mounts

chromatically through fourteen bars from C to A♭. Contrast
of dynamic extremes also helps to give the sense of poetic
rapture. A powerful and brilliant voice is indispensable here.
No song of Schubert's is less tolerant of meagre singing. The
fortissimos are to be truly generous. The last of the climaxes
(of which there are about ten), Schubert marks *fff*. For all
his strength the singer is to be a fine artist, penetrated
by the poetry of the song and respectful of the numerous
pianissimos. The key is C ; and it is improper to transpose
it for the use of contraltos. It is best in charge of a dramatic
soprano. The pianoforte part is sometimes played on the
organ, but only with deplorable effect.

Three songs on poems by Baron Schlechta fall within this
period. *Des Sängers Habe* (1825) is rather in the vein of
Der zürnende Barde, being the defiant song of the proud
minstrel whose lyre is his all-in-all. Life can do its worst,
so it leaves him the instrument of his art ; which after death
is, he says, to take the place of a gravestone, that his ghost
may continue to pluck music from its strings. The song
is spirited to the point of jollity. It is strangely neglected
by singers, seeing how effective it might be made by a bright
barytone. The chivalric triplet figure that is so much used
in the pianoforte interludes calls to mind the first subject
of the B♭ trio, Op. 99. *Fischerweise* was composed in
March 1826, and was published in 1826 as Op. 96, No. 4 :

> ' The fisherman's life suits a hardy young fellow. I am
> up before the lark, singing like him for sheer high spirits.
> Hard work means health, and health is my wealth. A
> sharp eye and a strong arm are wanted for my job. And
> wily fish make wily fishermen. Girls before now have
> tempted me with bait. Thank you ! I know all about the
> hook.'

Schubert sets the quatrains to alternating tunes, both of them
rustic and cheerful, while the same plain accompaniment
figure continues throughout. There is a slight modification
in the setting of the last quatrain, in which the damsel is
seen on the bridge angling for the fisher. An odd quatrain
of Schlechta's which did not fit into the *a.b.a.b.* scheme was left
out. In contrast to the extreme plainness of this song is the
remarkable modulatory style of *Totengräberweise*. This is
a grave-side elegy, in F♯ minor and major, the movement
suggesting a funeral march. As in the *Pilgrim* of 1823
Schubert may be fancied here as consciously charging the

page with harmonic riches to compensate for the squareness
of the rhythm. Compensation was wanted also in *Totengräberweise* for the altogether unprepossessing angularity of
the melodic line. The song is singular in lacking charm,
while at the same time being so stamped with Schubert's
ingeniousness and originality.

Schubert's nine settings of the romantic poet Schulze were
all written in 1825–26. The majority are compositions of
some length, not, however, in the piecemeal manner of the
cantatas of his youth but in a way we recognize as specially
characteristic of the 1820's. In this mood Schubert gave
the reins to his music with a kind of recklessness now wild,
then gay. The initial movement races on sometimes as
though it were out of hand ; and whereas in such a song of
the early days as *Sehnsucht* (Goethe, 1814) we saw Schubert
breaking up his music in his attachment to the poet's text,
in Schulze's *Im Walde* we find the poet's mild intentions
borne down fiercely by ten pages of a musical torrent. ' I
wander,' says the poet, ' up hill and down dale, and with me
a companion, Sorrow, there's no escaping.' Schubert at
once reads it as being a passionate pilgrimage, instead of a
rather pensive one. He launches off with a powerful swinging
movement in B♭ minor and a melody that cries out on repeated
top G♭'s. This melody is heard four times in all, and a
secondary melody of much the same character twice, while
the driving triplets never cease. The poet would fain linger
to envy the bee that he sees stealing kisses from the flowers ;
but Schubert's dæmon has taken charge, the flowers are
trampled down, the songbirds unheeded in the wild ride.
The companion song *Auf der Bruck* with which *Im Walde*
was published (at Graz in 1828, Op. 93) is rather similar in
moving by a single over-mastering impulse that never relaxes.
Here, however, as in *Willkommen und Abschied*, the lover is
on horseback, and it is natural that the composition should
be dominated by the regular thudding of hoofs. It is a
happy journey, a return to the beloved after three weary
days. This same separation was the cause of the distress in
Im Walde. From Schulze's ' Poetic Diary ' we know, in
fact, that the two poems were written at an interval of three
days in July 1814. Schubert filled the song of home-coming
with blissful impatience as the other with restless unhappiness.
The thought of *Auf der Bruck* and its emphatic melody is
something to be avoided in train-travel, for. allying itself
with the rumble and rattling over the rails, it can become an
obsession. It is a fourfold strophic song of six pages, with

slight modifications in each repetition. The title (sometimes misprinted ' auf der Brücke ') refers to a holiday resort, Die Bruck, near Göttingen ; and near there, too, is the scene of the poem of *Im Walde*, which in Schulze is called ' In the forest behind Falkenhagen.'

Another of these romantic songs, *Über Wildemann*, has again an impetuous and persistent driving movement. Pace is given at times by the absence of all harmony, the voice part being doubled by bass octaves while the right hand has broken octaves on the same note. The mood is once again agitated and overcast. The poet is wandering high among the hills (Wildemann is a township in the Harz). They are snow-covered while in the valley spring is already at work. But, unhappy in love, he anticipates no good in the pleasant season and gives his preference to winter. Already we catch the note of the ' Winterreise.' It sounds more clearly still in *An mein Herz*, a song of harrowing grief, with syncopated A minor chords for the agitation of the heart. Although the song is of Schubert's prime it is not a familiar one. The admirer of the ' Winterreise ' who has missed it will feel in coming across it that he has found a lost flower from the chaplet.

As for *Tiefes Leid*, it goes still nearer. Not only does the song seem in character and mood to belong to the ' Winterreise ' ; it is in actual material closely related to one of the songs of the cycle, namely, *Rückblick*. Perhaps when Schubert came to set *Rückblick* the words ' du Stadt der Unbeständigkeit ' recalled Schulze's ' als in der unbeständ'gen Welt ' and hence the music of *Tiefes Leid* returned to mind and pen. The song, in E minor and major, is an expression of weary and inconsolable grief. From the minor melody with its complaint of the burden of life, the music turns to the major at the thought of the way of escape, the one sure haven, the grave. It is simple and pathetic in a kind of humbled way, as though the singer were worn down by suffering.

Der liebliche Stern is, for all its plaintiveness, the song of a lighter mood. A dainty accompaniment figure trips persistently throughout the piece, reflecting the dancing of the stars in the rippling lake. The song gives us in G major the charming air of the spring evening and then with an inclination to G minor and B♭ the poet's wistfulness—his own star, his affinity, is missing from the host. It is a little pearl of song ; but the prettiest gem of the whole group is *Im Frühling* :

' Spring is here on the hills in blue and green and gold.
It was never lovelier. But there is a difference, for last
spring there was no one so content as I, but this year love
has not come back with the swallows. Oh, if I were a
bird ! I would stay here all the summer, singing of my
love.'

The song is a little set of variations. Schubert arranges
the six short stanzas in pairs and sets each pair to two linked
and recurring melodies. The pianoforte prelude is based
on the second of them. This ingenuous and captivating
strain was later on to make the fortune of Tchaikovsky's
' Chant sans Paroles.' Schubert's device is simple but
successful. He gives us four bars of *b* in the prelude, and
then the voice enters with *a*. When charming *b* comes in
(expanded to seven bars) with the second stanza it is the more
welcome since we thought it possibly lost sight of. The
whole is now repeated for the third and fourth stanzas with
the variation of a semiquaver figure for the right hand. In
the setting of the next pair of stanzas *a* is in the minor with
syncopated right-hand chords and *b* has a syncopated bass.
In this enchanting song of spring Schubert has admitted
hardly a thought of the poet's plaint. It is full of the sweetness of the meadows on a May morning. The song was
published at Leipzig a month after Schubert's death. It
had appeared in September 1828, as a supplement to the
' Wiener Zeitschrift für Kunst.' Elena Gerhardt first made
it a favourite with London audiences.

Um Mitternacht was composed in the same month (March
1826). It is a placid song of hymnlike cast and also, if all
the repetitions are sung, of hymnlike monotony. *Lebensmut*,
also composed in that month, is similarly overdone with
repetitions and is of inferior interest in spite of a brave
beginning.

There was only one setting of Friedrich Schlegel in this
period, namely, the ardent love-song, *Fülle der Liebe*—
Schubert's farewell to this poet. The song calls to mind
Du liebst mich nicht in its relentless play with a single rhythmical motive. In the Platen song it was :

(a)

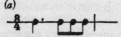

In the Schlegel song it is :

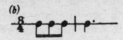

And again Schubert calls on all the magic of his harmonies
to compensate for the possible baldness of effect. There
are not only richly coloured modulations but also a succession
of sudden drops into foreign keys. The poet's theme is
high romantic passion—anguish, fire, a flood of tears, a star
from paradise, the sanctity of pain. This reads uncon-
vincingly in the lack of any particulars ; but the composer
has unified it by music of a noble ardour. The song is,
however, not all that Schubert might have made of it
in a luckier hour. We are much taken by the first page or
two, we admire the third ; but before the end the song has
cloyed—the result, in part, of the jingle of Schlegel's con-
tiguous rhymes. Grieg was indebted to *Fülle der Liebe* for
the melody of one of his favourite songs, ' Brown Eyes,'
Op. 5, No. 1.

Schubert's two last settings of A. W. Schlegel belong to
the same period. They are much slighter, *Wiedersehn* being
indeed one of the least of the songs of Schubert's maturity,
though a very pretty one. Above a soft thrumming of
simple four-part crotchet chords a slender, graceful melody
rises. It is a song of happy love, for a light tenor. All is
transparent as can be. The four stanzas are too many.
Abendlied für die Entfernte (published 1827, Op. 88, No. 1),
is a return once more to the 6-8 pastoral measure in which
Schubert was inexhaustible. The writing is charmingly
graceful. The song is akin to the Romance in ' Rosamunde.'
Only, unfortunately, the tiresome Schlegel induced Schubert
to sprawl. Although there was nothing in his evening meditations to interest us he composed out of them six longish
stanzas, and of these Schubert left aside only one.

The two incidental songs, *Florio* and *Delphine*, written at
this period for Schütz's play ' Lacrimas,' by an error ascribed
to Schlegel, were in the first edition, which Friedländer then
followed. They are dated September 1825, like the two last
Schlegel songs. *Florio* is a serenade, set by Schubert with easy
grace and not too much attention to the lover's more desperate
expressions. It is a pretty song, rather in the vein of *Who
is Silvia ?* but of less intensity. *Delphine* is on a much larger
scale (nine pages). The same movement is kept up throughout the whole song, as was Schubert's frequent practice at the

time ; and the right-hand semiquaver figure is almost invariable from end to end. By the rustle of these semiquavers, as also by the subject of the piece (an amorous woman's rhapsody), *Delphine* is related to the *Suleika* songs of 1821. By the extraordinary development, too, of the piece, which is impracticably prolonged. At least, one never hears *Delphine* sung. But is it really impracticable ? The music is rich in harmonic colour ;- and what should afford relief in effect is the bold writing for soprano voice. The song is of the rare ones that Schubert obviously composed for a grand dramatic soprano. The music soars to B*b* and to C. A fine artist with a sumptuous voice should not fail to sustain the interest in *Delphine*.

The last Goethe songs were composed in January 1826. They are a group of four settings of lyrics from ' Wilhelm Meister.' The group was published in 1827, as Op. 62, dedicated to Princess Mathilde zu Schwarzenberg. It includes the two last settings of a poem which, as we have said, Schubert set, in all, six times : *Nur wer die Sehnsucht kennt :*

> ' Who knows what I suffer, that has never known the pangs of love-longing ? I look round on an empty earth, up to an empty heaven. The beloved is far away. My brain swims, my very being quakes. Who that has never loved and longed can know what suffering is ? '

To these celebrated lines Schubert returned now, more than ten years after he had first composed them. The beautiful 1815 setting would have been surpassed by Op. 62, No. 7, if Schubert had not, here following Goethe too literally, written it as a duet. ' At this moment Mignon and the Harper began to sing a kind of irregular duet, with the most touching expression.' So is ' Nur wer die Sehnsucht kennt ' introduced in ' Wilhelm Meister.' It was not a very happy hint on the part of the great poet. How can he have thought, he the author of a lyric so intimate, a sigh from the secret heart, of its being shared and separated with the imitations and formalities proper to duet-singing ? The lyric must, of course, have been written before the juncture in the story ; and there it was tossed more or less by chance, because a song was wanted and this one came to hand. The fact remains that Goethe gave the hint ; and that Schubert, acting on it, produced in *Mignon und der Harfner* (so is the

duet called) a characteristic and most lovely piece of music.
It is more measured, more deeply felt than the flowing music
of the solo song, Op. 62, No. 4, which is the famous setting,
the only famous one of Schubert's six, of the lines in question.
The duet is for soprano and tenor, in B minor, in 2-2 time.
The principal melody is broadly phrased and expresses a
deep pensiveness. The setting of ' Ach, der mich liebt,' in C,
very remarkably conveys a sudden sense of emptiness. ' Es
schwindelt mir ' is recited by both voices in alternation, with
the inevitable diminished sevenths. At this moment in
particular the duet form is felt to be regrettable, the
sentiment being so much one of forlorn solitariness. But
if the sense of incongruity can be overcome (and then there
are those, too, whom the text and its associations do not much
preoccupy) the piece becomes endearing and much prized.
Compared with it the charming A minor song seems rather
lightly felt, for all its plaintiveness.

The two other songs of Op. 62, both masterpieces, are
settings of Mignon's *Heiss mich nicht reden* and *So lasst mich
scheinen*, lyrics which Schubert now composed for the second
time. The 1821 songs are eclipsed. Mignon in the first
poem protests the inviolability of her life's secret. Fate has
sealed her lips. Another may pour out his heart to a friend.
The lover shares his every thought with the beloved. Alone
the strangely fated one is bound to silence by an oath that
God alone can absolve. The poem is merely appended
to the fifth book of ' Wilhelm Meister.' The simple but
terrible words, obscurely indicative of some tragic destiny,
moved Schubert now more deeply. He could not think
of Mignon's childish tones and at the same time of the poet's
unbearably pathetic thought ; and the song, though called
' Lied der Mignon,' is taken clean away from the child and
is given a voice of passionate experience. This attitude is
reflected on the merely technical plane by such a feature
as the powerful crescendo in the seventh bar of the voice
part and again at the end—a crescendo that makes a sudden
call on vocal experience and control. The second and third
quatrains are set to very free and subtle modifications of the
first melody. Infinitely touching is the E major variation
(' ein jeder sucht ') where a glimpse is caught of the un-
attainable happiness. The pathos of *So lasst mich scheinen*
is resigned. It is Mignon's last song. She has found a haven
in Natalia's queer orphanage (all this is in the fantastic eighth
book) but her heart is broken (' Let it break ! ' are her last
words. ' It has beaten too long '). The ' white robes '

of the song, the chaplet and the girdle, are the disguise with which Natalia provided her to appear as an angel bearing gifts at a birthday celebration. The dying child clung to the dress, and sang her ' So lasst mich scheinen.' Mignon's thoughts are no longer of earth. ' Sorrows here have aged me before my time ; oh, may I there be born again to ever-lasting youth ! ' Schubert, it has already been suggested, had not quite forgotten his first setting when composing this affecting song. He also felt that there was still something more to be done with the rhythmical figure of *Fülle der Liebe*. In effect that song limped, while *So lasst mich scheinen* is perfectly articulated. The four quatrains are treated in pairs. The second half of the song repeats the first, but with some notable modifications, especially the wrench to D minor in the crescendo (' tiefen Schmerz ') whereas we had D major the first time, which was already a surprising enough break-away. Again the music is no doubt too rich and passionate to belong truly to the ethereal Mignon. For one thing, it keeps moving in full-bodied chords. It is no less sweet than sorrowful. The renuncia-tion it expresses is felt to have a background of earthly delights. Schubert, in fact, sang as he was, of what he knew.

Ten settings of the poet Seidl were composed in 1826. One or two of these are compact and intimate, such as *Am Fenster* ; others are expansive, rather in the way of the Schulze songs of the time. Schubert lets loose in *Sehnsucht* (' Die Scheibe friert '), a movement of winged and roaming triplets, although the poet states that on this bitter night he is shut in his chamber. He stares forlornly through the frosty window at the glittering sky ; he is, he says, loveless and (until near the end) songless. We shall shortly find in the ' Winterreise ' (*Erstarrung*), Schubert's finest use of such a movement. This *Sehnsucht* might indeed be fancied a rejected number from the ' Winterreise.' Another expansive song, in a happy mood, is *Im Freien* :

' What brings me abroad, this balmy night ? The moon is amazed, she cannot understand. Look you, moon ; pour out your shining silver on river and tree and house and I will tell. Look you, moon, if you can, behind those shutters. You will see there someone so delightful that she makes the whole place delightful and me in love with its every stick and stone. So no wonder I cannot tear myself away ! '

The pianoforte's incessant semiquavers are perhaps the
moon-flecked river ripples and the glistening willow leaves.
Schubert was, we can see, simply enchanted by the effect
of their quivering reduplication of the singer's melody. After
a moment he brightens the charming sound by giving the
right-hand octaves, and these are kept going throughout
the six pages of the song. It is thus decidedly the pianist's
piece. On his musical performance of the babble, now soft
and again excited, with which these semiquaver octaves
echo and encourage the contented lover, depends the effect
of the song and in particular its success in avoiding what
will be the reproach of an indifferent performance, namely,
a too luxuriant length. In the later stages Schubert brings
in the upper treble of the pianoforte—tones that are curiously
rare in his song-writing. *Im Freien* was published with
two other Seidl songs as Op. 80, in 1827, dedicated to a
good friend in the Schubertian circle, Joseph Witteczek.

Op. 80, No. 2, is the most beautiful song of the group,
Das Zügenglöcklein :

> ' Toll for the weary, O mourning bell. Resolve the
> separations of true hearts ; and may thy summons not
> sound fearful to the departing voyager. Toll for the
> weary, toll for the strong in faith. But, tolling bell, be
> quiet and call not one who is in love with life and love and
> the happy sunlight.'

The music is bathed in rich sunset colouring. The bell
tolls on the dominant (E♭) in nearly every bar of the three
pages. There are five stanzas all set to the one melody,
which is, however, never quite the same twice. The fourth
time is most nearly like the first. The others have minor
inflections, and modulations into C♭, a key Schubert could
hardly ever resist when in A♭. The song is sung in a soft
mood when sadness is almost a luxury. It is full of pity and
of submissiveness ; and at the same time so suffused with
the beauty of the passing world that we cannot believe in the
relinquishment that is its theme. There are pieces in
Schubert more grand, more poignant and rare, but nothing
more obviously signed. Here is Schubert the compassionate
and trusting, for whom all things worked together for beauty.

The other song in Op. 80, *Der Wanderer an den Mond*, is
slight. The wanderer compares his lot with the moon's.
He and she are for ever on the move ; only he is homeless
while she has all heaven for a home. There is a distinct

category of such walking songs, with tunes sprung from the rhythm of the stride. *Am Fenster* is a song of quiet and rustic character, made into a gem by delicate, loving workmanship. The subject is simple, yet a little unusual. The poet addresses the walls of his old home. Once they knew him an isolated and unhappy youth. No doubt, seeing him return home, they expect him to be the same melancholy creature. He tells them no ; life has treated him better than he thought possible. He has found sympathy, has made friends. The music is placid and particularly intimate. The flattened seventh of the principal melody is a peculiarity ; it virtually puts each phrase in which it occurs into the subdominant. This melody occurs with modifications three times (once in the minor) ; and there are three others near of kin. The material is all very modest ; but during the four middle stanzas Schubert cunningly accumulates interest first by a little semiquaver movement, then by syncopation, then by a bold modulation, which lands in A. At this point we have a feeling of quite considerable experiences behind us ; which is just what the poet intended. And still Schubert has kept it all on the small scale of a modest, cheerful meditation. He now uses the penultimate stanza to prepare the way home again, with tactful hints of the original F major and a reminder by the pianoforte of the principal melody, for which, on its reappearance at last, we find a real affection.

The four so-called ' Refrain-Lieder,' published in 1828 as Op. 95, are all settings of verses by Seidl. The publisher, Thaddäus Weigl, announced them gleefully as a new departure by Schubert, a descent into the composition of comic songs. Two of the set are rustic ditties such as Schubert might have written for a ballad opera. These are *Die Unterscheidung* and *Die Männer sind méchant* (*sic*). In the former a village maiden, warned by her mother against love-affairs, archly tells her young man that while she may not give him her heart she counts very certainly on retaining his. In the latter the girl is deceived. She has, so she pours it out to her mother, overheard and overseen the young man with another. *Bei dir allein* is quite different. It is a warm-hearted, expansive love-song, not unrelated to *Sei mir gegrüsst*. One might have expected it to be among the most popular of Schubert's songs, so frank and effusive is the melody and so animated the accompanying movement of triplets ; but singers no doubt find the tessitura embarrassing. The interpretation presents no problem, given the voice.

The song is simply a lover's enthusiastic declaration. But the voice (tenor or high barytone) must have full resonance on the lower C and also upwards to A♭. The fourth song of the set, *Irdisches Glück*, is a jovial piece with a typical ' walking ' or ' wanderer's ' tune. The subject is workaday philosophy. Take life as it comes and don't cry for the moon ! The sturdy tune, in D minor and major, would make a capital march. There are musicianly touches in the writing ; but the song was no doubt meant primarily for conviviality.

The remaining Seidl song is the *Wiegenlied*, which was published with three others as Op. 105 on the day of Schubert's funeral. It is a long, sweet, sleepy lullaby, so repetitive that it seems as though in writing it the musician had charmed himself into a doze. The suave melody comes over again and again, five times in all, making a song of six pages. This is altogether too much, unless one is actually courting sleep ; but the softness and the tenderness of the music are Schubert's own. Another lullaby of the period is *Der Vater mit dem Kind* (Bauernfeld) ; the singer, a fond father. *Das Echo* (Castelli) is a light song for an arch singer ; the subject, a peasant girl's confidences to her mother.

Schubert's three settings of translations from Shakespeare were all composed in July 1826 at Währing, which was then a village. Of two of them, the Drinking Song from ' Antony and Cleopatra ' and Cloten's musicians' song, in the second act of ' Cymbeline,' (*Hark, hark, the lark !*), does legend tell of Schubert's writing the music on the bill of fare at an inn table. The drinking song (*Come, thou monarch of the vine*) has not enjoyed the universal fame of the other two. It recommends itself by a bold and jovial tune which happens to fit Shakespeare's lines well. There is a curious suggestion of Handel in these few bars of solid C major music. It is vaguely akin to the drinking songs in ' Serse ' (' Del mio caro Bacco ') and ' Belshazzar ' (' Let the deep bowl '). The theme seems to promise developments, but of course there are none. The song in Shakespeare is only six lines long. A later hand added a second stanza to Mayrhofer's German. The English singer may as well simply repeat the song as it stands.

A second German stanza was also provided after Schubert's time for *Hark, hark, the lark !* In ' Cymbeline ' Cloten says : ' I am advised to give her music o' mornings ; they say it will penetrate. Come on ; tune . . . First, a very excellent good-conceited thing ; after, a wonderful sweet air, with admirable rich words to it.' The music Schubert chose to give her o' mornings was a kind of ländler or rustic waltz, and a very pretty one. Yet the song is hardly one to be very fond of. Not a lifetime of familiarity with it can bridge the gap that yawns between the Elizabethan's verse and the Austrian's tune. Imogen would have been altogether too startled at being bidden arise by the interval of a seventh, and could only have taken the aubade for a brawl. It is only fair to remember that for Germans Shakespeare is not Elizabethan but, thanks to the Schlegel and Tieck translation, a contemporary of Goethe's and Schiller's. Perhaps we too ought to call the song a ' Ständchen ' and sing to it ' Horch, horch! die Lerch'.' If, like *Die Forelle*, it has generally been a trifle overrated, Schubert's *Who is Silvia?* is irresistible, however little Shakespearian all its sevenths, dominant and diminished. The melody is a perfect fit for the stanza (true, as much must be allowed of the ' Cymbeline ' song). The pianoforte part is the idealization of a rustic music—plucked bass strings for the left hand, thrummed strings for the right. Even in so light a pastoral compliment Schubert could not help opening his heart. For the moment, at least, he is all in love with Silvia. Her name, which the bass seems to keep saying with its falling intervals, and which is sighed by a couple of treble notes during the singer's two bars of rest,[1] has surely bewitched him. The music acquires vivaciousness not so much from any general characteristic vivaciousness in the composer as from the exhilaration of the heart's new emotion. Could any shepherdess resist such a pure and eager flame ? The ingenuous Schubert has ousted the gentleman of Verona and made Silvia his own. The song was no doubt the inspiration of another Shakespearian setting, Arthur Sullivan's delightful ' Orpheus and his Lute,' one that might have been passed for Schubert's if Sullivan had cared to plan a hoax. *Who is Silvia?* was published shortly after Schubert's death, together with three songs of 1827 (later called Op. 106), dedicated to Marie Pachler, Schubert's kindly hostess at Graz.

Hippolyts Lied (Friedrich von Gerstenbergk) is another little song that was composed at Währing. The plaintive A minor melody—nearly all contained within a fifth—is embellished by a graceful accompaniment figure quite peculiar to this song, with a characteristic inverted mordent. At the end of Mandyczewski's eighth volume are two settings of Schober composed early in 1827. *Jägers Liebeslied* is insignificant,

---

[1] The first of these (in which the pianoforte echoes the E–C♯ of the voice) is shown by Schubert's MS. to have been an afterthought.

except that the text throws light on the Jäger's activities. He is an out-and-out sportsman, shooting at every living thing he sets eye on. *Schiffers Scheidelied*, a song of enormous length, is not very good Schubert, and is yet unmistakably Schubertian. The romantic sailor bids farewell in alternations of E minor and B major. He is, in the most unsailorly way, full of apprehensions about the coming voyage, and he urges his young woman to renounce a tie with one so almost certainly doomed. The minor melody comes over (with the slightest modifications) five times and the major one four times. Both are characteristic, and there is a fine clangour in the pianoforte's stormy water music ; but there is no development. It is impossible, of course, to refuse a certain sympathy with the distraught sailor ; but it is one of those appeals which we feel rather at a loss in listening to, the obvious comment being a brutal one—that the poor fellow was simply never cut out for seafaring. We can make a guess at the charm such a song must have had in the days of the novelty of the romantic movement. The rush of the semiquavers and the song's self-surrender to the pathos of the minor mode no doubt seemed noble and audacious. But after a deluge of emotional art the world has become less inclined to admire effusiveness as such. By integrity and intensity all Schubert's principal work stands well apart from temporariness. Only now and again in a slack mood a flimsier piece was produced that too easily pleased the taste of the moment and was in fact sentimental.

In 1827 Schubert wrote the last of his Italian songs, a set of three for bass, on texts by Metastasio, dedicated to Lablache, and published as Op. 83. *L'incanto degli occhi* is an agreeable cavatina, *Il traditor deluso* a dramatic scena, and *Il modo di prender moglie* a buffo air, in Rossini's manner. Schubert is here deliberately working outside his natural style, but he does it uncommonly well. The *Traditor* is conventional in design, but Schubertian harmonies creep in. The *Incanto* has an obsequious accompaniment quaint to find in Schubert, but it is an ingratiating song for a really fine voice, and the third piece is quite brilliant. The bass singer will find all three first-rate studies.

XIII

1827.—'THE WINTER JOURNEY'

MANDYCZEWSKI'S ninth volume begins with the ' Winterreise '; it includes a number of other songs of 1827, and also those of 1828, Schubert's last year.

On March 26, 1827, Beethoven died. Schubert was a torchbearer at the funeral. The two had in all probability never met. The year was one of splendid compositions and of unimproved material rewards. Schubert sold twenty-one compositions to the Viennese publishers in 1827 for wretchedly small payments. Mayrhofer, Spaun, and Bauernfeld all tell us of his sombre moods in this year of the ' Winterreise.' In September, however, he spent a delightful holiday on new ground, at Graz in Styria where, as in other years in Upper Austria, he was made much of by a circle of Schubertians. It was the year of a number of beautiful choral songs, the beginning of another opera, ' Der Graf von Gleichen ' (to Bauernfeld's libretto), and among instrumental works the superb pianoforte trio No. 2 in E*b*, Op. 100, which was composed in November and published in the following autumn just before Schubert's death. Some of the favourite Moments Musicaux and Impromptus for pianoforte also date from the autumn of 1827.

*   *

*

The first twelve poems of Wilhelm Müller's ' Winterreise ' were published in a literary annual in 1823, and the whole sequence appeared in book form in 1824. As in ' Die schöne Müllerin,' we set out on a journey, but with a difference :

' Goodnight !—a bitter night. Maytime welcomed me here. December freezes the farewell.

' The weathervane is the right sign for that house. And there a fool thought to find a loyal heart ! The fool has wept, wept burning tears. Does he think to melt the iron world ? Freeze, tears ; freeze, heart ! Winter has killed the happy earth I knew.

' There was a tree where I carved her name. Its branches

are creaking in the wind, they whisper like a ghost. An absurd fancy strikes me, of a brook made by the tears I have shed, which will thaw in spring and trickle past her house. To-night my heart is frozen hard like the river. Under the ice there is a mad torrent.

' I hurried from the town, hating its very name. Then the thought of the past pulled me up, and I nearly turned back again. I stumbled on ; a will-o'-the-wisp led me off the track. But right ways and wrong ones are the same to me.

' A charcoal-burner gave me shelter. My limbs rested, and my heart started aching more furiously than ever. I dreamt of spring and fields of flowers. I woke : never was winter drearier, and the only flowers were the frost-flowers on the window pane. I dreamt, too, of love.

' A still morning after the storm. I could stand the storm better. There is the postman's horn. It has set my crazy heart thudding. Fool !

' The hoar-frost on my hair made me think for a moment I had grown old. Better old age than this, better the grave ! That raven has been keeping me company for hours. If there is constancy among birds he shall have my bones to pick.

' A last leaf is fluttering there on a twig. How like hope ! Ah, it falls.

' The watchdogs bark while the village sleeps, each man dreaming he has what he has not. Only I am past dreaming. There is nothing I would have, dreaming or awake.

' Day has broken in a rage. Good for you, winter ! The more you howl, the better I like it. A curious gleam is dancing before my eyes, and I follow it, though I know it spells illusion. I have been rambling crazily off the roads where the sign-posts are. Now I see my proper sign-post plain. It leads somewhere whence there is no turning back. There is an inn there that is never full up and that no one ever wants to leave.

' " Blow, blow, thou winter wind ! " Sing, man, and choke that whimpering in your breast. Take things as they come, and anything you have a mind to. If there're no gods on earth, who's to say we shouldn't take their places ? Ha ! a curious sight—three suns in the sky. Mock-suns are scientifically known as parhelia, which amounts to the same thing. Mock-suns make me think of Faith, Hope and Charity. They don't last long.

'Poor, wretched old hurdy-gurdy man! I'll make up to him, for I never saw anyone in a worse way   I will sing, and he shall play for me.'

The poet's premature death occurred in 1827, the year of the composition of the music, the proofs of which Schubert corrected when himself dying in the following autumn. Schubert made certain alterations in Müller's 1824 order of the poems.[1] The principal are these : *Die Post*, which had come immediately after *Der Lindenbaum*, was relegated to the thirteenth place in the cycle, *Frühlingstraum*, which had been fourth from the end, became No. 11, *Das Irrlicht* and *Rast* were given earlier places than in Müller, and *Der Wegweiser* and *Das Wirthshaus* later ones, and *Die Nebensonnen* was delayed by Schubert to separate *Mut* from *Der Leiermann*, *Mut* being in Müller the penultimate poem. These alterations justify themselves beyond a doubt. There are also a few insignificant departures from Müller's text.

Schubert composed the first half of the cycle in February, the second in October. Spaun has left an interesting account of some of the circumstances :

'Schubert had seemed for some time moody and run down. To my questioning he replied, You will soon understand. One day he said, Come to Schober's and I will sing over a bunch of ghastly songs to you. I shall be curious, he went on, to hear what you think of them— they have taken more out of me than any other songs I have written. He then sang to us the whole Winterreise through, with much emotion in his voice. The gloom of the songs quite nonplussed us, and Schober said there was only one he cared for, the *Lindenbaum*. All Schubert answered was, I like them all more than any of the other songs, and the day will come when you will like them too. He was right ; we were soon full of admiration for these mournful songs, which Vogl sang like a master.'

And Spaun goes on :

'After he had finished the Winterreise, Schubert was run down in health, if not to any alarming point. Many believed and perhaps still do that Schubert was a thick-skinned fellow who could stand anything, but we who

---

[1] He followed that of the 1823 publication, in which the order was not that of the 1824 volume.

were near and dear knew how much the creatures of his mind took out of him and in what travail they were born. No one who ever saw him at his morning's work, glowing and his eyes aflame, yes and positively with a changed speech . . . will ever forget it. . . . I hold it beyond question that the excitement in which he composed his finest songs, the Winterreise in particular, brought about his untimely death.'

Mayrhofer goes farther, and suggests that Schubert was led to the melancholy of the ' Winterreise ' by his own melancholy. ' The very choice of subject proved an increased seriousness in our musician. He had been long and severely ill, he had suffered one discouragement after another ; life had lost its rosiness, winter was upon him.'

Spaun's sound sense is more attractive than Mayrhofer's theory. If Schubert composed the sombre ' Winterreise ' because, at thirty, he felt himself to be entering on the winter of life, we may ask how there came to be an array of compositions of 1827 and 1828 all glowing with the spirit of spring. There is no need of material circumstances to explain the ' Winterreise.' It is enough that Schubert found the lyrics, more lyrics by the poet of the ' Müllerin '—more lyrics of a homely scene and of a suffering heart, only this time with a change of season, December for May, and a deeper core of pain, the difference between the heartbreak of a youth and a man. There is no need to seek in external vicissitudes an explanation of the pathos of the ' Winterreise ' music when the composer was this Schubert who as a boy of seventeen had the imagination to fix Gretchen's cry in music once for all, and had so quivered year by year in response to every appeal, to Mignon's and the Harper's grief, to Mayrhofer's nostalgia. It is not surprising to hear of Schubert's haggard look in the ' Winterreise ' period ; but not depression, rather a kind of sacred exhilaration, goes to the making of such a poetic art, which must leave its author worn and panting, no doubt, but also exalted by the discoveries and conquests to which the spirit drives and urges. When all account is taken of Schubert's sickness and the discouragements of existence, we see him practically gasping with fearful joy over his tragic ' Winterreise '—at his luck in the subject, at the beauty of the chance that brought him his collaborator back, at the countless fresh images provoked by this poetry of fire and snow, of torrent and ice, of scalding and frozen tears. The composer of the ' Winterreise ' may have gone hungry to bed, but he was a happy artist. No dejected imagination ever invented and invented thus.

Schubert this time left nothing out. He set all twenty-four of Müller's poems, although with its unrelieved cry of ' Woe's me, woe's me ! ' the ' Winterreise ' might have appeared a less manageable whole than the ' Müllerin.' It is just as well that he did not come across the poems earlier, for he was always learning about life and music, and he, even he, might not have coped in younger days with such enormous variations on the one theme of misery. The ' Müllerin ' cycle had its diversions, its radiant hours. The young miller was not alone on the scene ; we caught glimpses of the minx of the mill, of the father, of the shaggy rival. But at the very beginning of the ' Winterreise ' the door is shut in the face of the luckless lover and unfriended roamer whose solitary tracks in the frostbound country-side we are to follow. The jilt is not only not presented ; she is very barely referred to in the victim's monologue. The songs of the ' Winterreise ' are hardly love-songs. Something other than an amorous misadventure, in fact any of the disasters of our precarious life, might almost as well have started this outcry of scorched sensibility, of rage, of wounded pride that dashes frantically up and down the room of the mind and at last finds an escape only in madness.

The objection has sometimes been made that Schubert did not in the ' Winterreise ' repeat his charming success of the ' Müllerin.' But such an artist does not repeat successes after the manner of the fashionable portrait painter. He is a lifelong adventurer ; and a happy enterprise can only, by the rule of his honour, lead to another more hard and hazardous. Schubert is not to be imagined as stopping to weigh up the risks of the ' Winterreise.' Visibly he flung himself into the attack. Müller helped him with plentiful pictures and fancies, but not with any characterization or dramatic encounters. The winter journey is vague. We do not know how long or far the outcast wandered or how many nights he spent on the road. Himself we do not truly know, though we hear the tale of his soliloquy from the ironical farewell, through storms of reproaches, regrets, and plaints, to the final fancies of the unhinged mind. We guess at a character more mature, more introspective and egoistic than the young miller. But we could see the miller. Here only an outline is visible of the form that goes off staggering into the snowstorm. Schubert, however, saw enough. He saw pictures of the wintry land, all blank with

snow, the brooks all iron, the lovers' linden bare. He saw
in this landscape the victim of some unkindness and heard
a repeated plaint. Enough. We think of Schubert as modest,
and so he was in relation to society. But the artist in him
was a lion of audacity. The enterprise of the ' Winterreise '
was unique ; the achievement—seventy pages of lamentation
on lamentation—a prodigy.

The ' Winterreise ' brings to mind the ' Müllerin ' now by
analogy and again by contrast. The texture of the music
remains simple, for there was still nothing that was ambitious
or anything but simple in Müller's verse. The whole interest
lay in the depth of feeling, not in psychological refinements.
The lover is tortured by regrets, by dreams, by frustration,
rather than by thought. He struggles longer and more
desperately with his feelings than the little miller ; and hence
the pages and pages of drear minor harmonies in the
' Winterreise ' (sixteen of the songs are in minor keys, against
six in the ' Müllerin '). The miller was more pathetic. He
simply gave in, gave up. The winter wanderer is more
agonizing. He probes his wounds deeper, and drives himself
to madness. But the case remained plain, and its appeal
was solely to sympathy. As it possessed no point of
intellectual subtlety, so there is none in Schubert's music.
The cycle is a succession of states of pure emotion. Schubert's
single-heartedness here can be appreciated by us to-day
perhaps better than ever. Hardly one of the later musicians
of his century would in the circumstances have so cleanly
avoided sentimentality ; and it is marvellous that in the course
of the twenty-four songs Schubert should never have been
tempted to call up reminiscences of foregoing motives, a device
which here would have spelt self-consciousness and would have
spoilt the temper of the whole. Neither the miller nor the
wanderer is a sentimentalist—they do not compose their
states of emotion, but directly face, all unprepared, the blasts
of the different and surprising hours of life. The recurrence
of old themes would have granted the victims relief from
strain and action ; for in the active life of sentiment there are
no recurrences, and no hour is like another. Schubert knew
it so well that not even *Rückblick* turns back towards any
earlier song. The device, which would have been so facile
and so touching, is completely absent from both cycles, and
this is something we cannot be too grateful for. The new
hour strikes its own note, how truly let *Der Leiermann*
witness, which is come upon at the last turning of the
wintry road—a chance encounter to which no purpose

had led, but there, and so not refused by our poet and musician.

The two expeditions of 1823 and 1827 are youthfully alike in that both start off without a plan. Neither wanderer has a glimpse of the future or any protection of experience. *Das Wandern* cheerfully adopts chance as guide. *Gute Nacht* at the beginning of the ' Winterreise ' bids farewell with some dignity, with some irony, with some tenderness, and there is no knowing what is to get the upper hand. The jilted lover, reeling under his blow, is momentarily concerned to keep some sort of footing. He does not think of what he may have to feel. The thrumming D minor harmonies are drear enough but balanced. The general movement recalls the processional threnodies in some of the instrumental works, for instance the C minor Andante of the E*b* pianoforte trio, and the A minor movement of the symphony in C. This first, although more nearly a purely strophic song than any other in the ' Winterreise,' comes like the rest of the cycle into the ' modified strophic ' category. The melody droops wearily in the first two stanzas, then in the third it tries to pluck up courage with a slight variation, and in the fourth, with a certain gentleness in the farewell, into the major. The postlude, however, relapses into the funereal D minor.

The mood does not last. The sight of the weathercock whips up a fury. The vane swings in the music, the wind whistles mockingly in the pianoforte's trills. The song taunts. There could not be a better example of Schubert's graphic effects, made with the smallest handful of notes. But if the general quality of vividness is typical, the actual spitfire expression here is quite peculiar. Schubert, bending so over the text, has found something unexpected in his own art, a sting, a point of mockery and malice, (notably in the lines about the vane's being the true emblem of the house, with the quick, excited rising modulations, G, A minor, and so on to D). But while the lover mocked, he has without knowing it wept. *Gefror'ne Thränen* moves heavily and desolately. The characteristic bass has a syncopated limp and falling octaves. The wanderer drags his steps. He is all fever within, yet the tears that gushed have frozen before they fell. The music half submits to this congealing by the cruel air. But then comes a flickering of memories and fancies in *Erstarrung*, a song of agitated movement with incessant quaver triplets. Cannot his tears melt the snow that the track may be disclosed where two lovers once walked together ? It must be that his heart is frozen ! But that

heart's ice at least retains her image. What of the precious
image when the ice thaws? 'Mein Herz ist wie *erstorben*'
(in the last stanza) in the popular editions is a mistake for
'erfroren,' dating from the first edition of the 'Winterreise'
and due to Schubert's hastiness. 'Dead' for 'frozen'
upsets the sense; but Schubert had, before coming to that,
got from the text all he needed for his fine song—a new wave
of feeling and stirring of old desires that allowed the composer the contrast of a quick, almost rushing movement.

Der Lindenbaum, the fifth song, is the only one in the
'Winterreise' which is very commonly sung separately from
the rest and which is universally familiar. It is a midwinter
glimpse of the ghost of spring. Only in the song's place in
the cycle is the suavity of the E major harmonies fully realized.
It is as though the memory of an old tune haunted the wanderer, while in the whispering sixths of the prelude he hears
in fancy the wind rustling the linden's leaves. The figure
of broken sixths turns into the minor, and becomes a chilly
gust. And yet the tone of dreaminess prevails. A delicious
fancy lulls the unfortunate; and the music ends with a return
of the mirage of the friendly foliage. The admiration that
has never failed *Der Lindenbaum* in a hundred years has not
been overdone. No music is more poetic. It is almost
too beautiful to be sung; and it should certainly be for-
bidden ground to any singer not possessing the dreamy
quality of the finest *mezza voce*.

The flood of sorrow breaks out in *Wasserflut*, whose melody
streams to and fro over the E minor arpeggio and scale,
covering nearly two octaves. There is another fancy here—
of the torrent of tears that will be released in the spring
thaw. Schubert gives it desperation by a brusque return to
F♯ minor and an hallucinated repetition of the last line, after
the A major middle section. The setting of the word 'Weh'
is positively a sob. In the next song, *Auf dem Flusse*, winter
closes down rigorously again. The text contains some of
Müller's rather unfortunate conceits, conceits so much below
the music that non-German audiences perhaps have some
compensation if they miss the words when Schubert is sung.
The verses are about the graving of the jilt's name on the ice
of the frozen river. Schubert has set them to the music of a
funeral march in E minor, with a 'trio' in the major, and
muffled drums in the last section—a march for the obsequies
of dead love. The sentiment is lifted up to a degree of
passionate mourning. The song is remarkable for the
extended compass (nearly two octaves, low A♯ to high A)

of the vocal part. The publisher, Haslinger, is thought to have pressed Schubert to supply the optional notes in *Auf dem Flusse*. What kind of voice had Schubert in mind for the ' Winterreise ' ? Not an ordinary lyric tenor, certainly, who would render phrase after phrase of the ' Winterreise ' ineffective. More often than in ' Die schöne Müllerin ' the writing keeps to the barytone tessitura. The *Lindenbaum* is a typical barytone song. Schubert perhaps had in mind Vogl, who was a barytone with an exceptional compass. But again he may have written without a strictly practical regard. The autograph shows him beginning *Frühlingstraum* in G, and at the end of the prelude starting it over again in A. Even in that key the song takes the voice no higher than F natural. Schubert may, then, have written the several songs at the pitch suggested by the moment's mood, not thinking primarily of the whole. The ' Winterreise ' has not a formal key-scheme, any more than it has a reminiscent elaboration of themes.

The eighth song, *Rückblick*, veers between G minor and major, between an agitated syncopation and an even ripple of semiquavers, between a chromatic and a diatonic bass, between a hastening and delaying, between the harassing present and the happy past. The stormy pianoforte part with its strong triple beat cuts remarkably across the stumbling rhythm of the voice whose opening phrases are really in alternating bars of four and of five beats. All this warring is blandly resolved in the G major section, with its evocation of the linden's flowering-time. *Irrlicht* presents a changed landscape. The musician has been taken not by the mention of the will-o'-the-wisp but by the cavernous and echoing gully where the wanderer, following the frozen river, has strayed. The singular and impressive song is characterized by solemn and rather bare B minor harmonies, above which the voice soars and swoops. The bold echoing phrases help to create the craggy scene. Characteristic too are the abrupt shifts, in the last stanzas, to and from the remote keys of B and C. In *Rast*, the next song, there are again striding vocal phrases, sometimes ranging over as much as a twelfth, such as we had in *Wasserflut* and *Irrlicht*.

Frühlingstraum begins with an amiable, old-fashioned tune in tripping 6-8 movement. The wanderer has slept and has dreamt of the flowers of spring ; then the cock's crow wakes him to the dark and freezing winter morning. There perhaps is in the 6-8 tune the only suggestion of parody to be found in all Schubert's music. It is sweetly pretty ; it is redolent of simple old provincial Germany. As a boy Schubert wrote such tunes in all seriousness, and from that type sprang the *Schäfers Klagelied*. In 'Die schöne Müllerin' the *Frühlingstraum* air would not have caused a suspicion. *Des Müllers Blumen* is nearly related to it. But appearing with its charming, faded colours in the midst of the tragic 'Winterreise' music it conveys a mockery of the conventional songs of spring. A faint mockery. The tune is too graceful to be a caricature. But the *Lindenbaum* gave us the winter wanderer's true tone of tenderness. On this dark morning he tells his idyllic dream in another mood, with just a hint of irony. The tone quickly changes. The dreamer has not irony enough to protect him from the shiver of his awakening.

In *Einsamkeit* he stares at the blank and windless winter day, and would prefer the angry weather that shouts down the grumblings of his pain. The song is a secondary one, but it exemplifies Schubert's flexible style in the alternations between the two-note sighing phrase and the muttering of the storm in the pianoforte part. There comes the sound of the posthorn from the road. This twelfth song, *Die Post*, is the problem of the 'Winterreise.' We hear the horn's cheerful call on the notes of the Eb chord ; it is a merry piece, or at least it has to be very cautiously treated not to become one. Schubert may turn into Eb minor, but the rhythm remains jaunty. The difficulty is that with all the vivid depiction of the scenes of the journey, everything has hitherto been seen from the angle of the lover's vision, and he at this hour is all too far from the illusion of hope to take up the postman's tune so lightly. He has indulged in dreams, but never (it is a distinction of the 'Winterreise') in false hopes. The 'Winterreise' was from the beginning a monody of despair. *Die Post* does well enough in Müller's sequence. Schubert's setting would be perfect as a detached song. But as it stands, its lightness is out of keeping with the tragic wanderer who is soon to say, ' Ich bin zu Ende mit allen Träumen.' The song is dated October 1827. With it Schubert took up again the cycle whose first part he had composed in February. Perhaps he did not call to mind at once the passion and significance with which he had been charging the songs. Or again (for the problem is one of sentiment rather than music proper), he may have simply grasped at the excuse to relieve the series of lamentations with a gay song for the sake of musical contrast, much as Bach did with the bass's G major aria in the ' St. Matthew Passion.' The exaggeration of singers have a good deal to do with the false impression made by *Die Post*. The tactful singer and pianist can help to bring it into relation. The horn should fall dully on the ear ; the possibility of the postman's knock is to be felt as an idle fancy, and the relief never really believed in.

Schubert is now more than ever filled with his subject, and image after image makes a succession of vivid songs. *Der greise Kopf* plays on a simple fancy—the rime on his hair sets the wanderer thinking for a moment that grief has made him old in a night. Whence, then, comes Schubert's superb and tragic musical phrase that climbs with large stride up a minor thirteenth (an eleventh in the voice part) and falls like a breaking wave ? There is no clue at the beginning of the song. The first lines of the last stanza, ' Between night-fall and daybreak many a head has turned white as old age,' give the clue. Schubert has felt a great arching theme wanted to convey the extension and awfulness of the night ; and we see how well it carries the words (' Vom Abendrot zum Morgenlicht,' etc.) of the tragic statement. When applied to the beginning of the poem it carries the words less well, and a preposition unfortunately falls to the note at the crest. The grim song of the crow, *Die Krähe*, follows on in the same key, C minor. It has been seen how Schubert renders the idea of loneliness by a unison of voice and piano-forte. While this song tells of the wanderer's companion crow, the music rather ironically takes up the ' lonely ' device between the voice and the left hand, while the semiquaver triplets keep to a dogged movement, as much as to say, ' Every step forward is a step towards the grave.'

Letzte Hoffnung is the song of the dead leaf, hope's symbol. The poet says that here and there a leaf still clings to the twig. Schubert has too hastily transcribed ' many a one ' (' manches ' for ' noch ein '). The music is vivid and poignant. The first part is full of falling two-note figures that drift, so to say, across the bar-lines. The wanderer takes one trembling leaf as an omen. As he stares, it falls ; and the music follows it to earth in sombre E*b* minor. ' Weep, weep,' says the song, ' over hope's grave,' to the most passionate of Schubert's lamenting phrases. A few more leaves fall in the ending of the piece. From now the wanderer seems to feel less the first burn of his sorrow ; he no longer mentions the past, and begins to be consumed with the thought of escape. In *Im Dorfe*, the wonderful song of the night, we hear in the roll of the bass semiquavers the low, growling of the village watchdogs, with long, nocturnal pauses, and then the wanderer's slow and dispassionate reflections on mankind and its illusions, in which he no longer has part. The music is strangely suggestive of the emptiness of night and the wanderer's weary composure.

Day breaks in a rage in *Der stürmische Morgen*, and the man is bitterly glad of the wild weather. Schubert seizes the opportunity for a strongly animated movement, with a jagged vocal line, bare unisons, and a crash of diminished sevenths.

The final songs of the ' Winterreise ' are indicative of the overwrought mind's derangement. In *Irrlicht* the man had followed the will-o'-the-wisp defiantly. In *Täuschung*, to a light tune, he dances after it half irresponsibly, cf. Troila's song, *Alfonso und Estrella*, Act II (*Monthly Musical Record*, June 1949). From this false A major gleam there is a drop into sheer melancholia in the G minor *Wegweiser*. How is the proud spirit reduced in this patient moaning, with its modest creeping movement ! The broken man would find a hole to hide in. He is not like the other unfortunate in ' Die schöne Müllerin ' in instinctively seeking refuge in suicide, but he creeps near the doors of death, waiting to be invited in. Towards the end of *Der Wegweiser* the voice in a curious passage is set half muttering while the alto and bass parts in the pianoforte slowly move towards each other by chromatic steps, to find their resolution in G minor. *Das Wirthshaus*, the song of the graveyard, moves gently and wearily in F major, rather in the manner of an evensong hymn-tune or organ voluntary. As such it has indeed been made to serve at times. The progressions are extremely sweet and suggest Mendelssohn. It is tempting to fancy some faint intention of irony on Schubert's part in associating the strains of homely devotion with the crazed lover who peers through the graveyard fence ; but it might be far-fetched. Another would have given the pitiable scene a touch of the macabre. The distraught man longs for hospitality at the silent inn, but the crowded mounds do not move to make place for him ; he fancies himself rejected even by death, and totters on. What Schubert's evensong music tells us is simply that his sympathy has ruled out every other thought. We should remember that the *Wirthshaus* harmonies, with their bland sevenths, had not in 1827 been hackneyed in the daily wear and tear of generations. The song is only to be thought of fairly in its place. After so much passion Schubert knew what he was at in accepting, when the occasion offered, a short truce.

A new note, one of cynical defiance, is struck in *Mut*, and

Schubert makes the most of it for an effect of energy. The music's violence is of desperation ; so much the singer must be convinced of by the wanderer's predicament, and by the song's coming like a gesture of futile revolt between two moods of resignation. Taken separately, *Mut* would appear simply a fine, bluff song. It ranks next to *Der Lindenbaum* as a favourite excerpt from the 'Winterreise.' In its place in the cycle it is to be sung with a certain wildness and hint of frenzy. *Die Nebensonnen* is a relapse into melancholy and the weariness that follows weeping. The simple but touching melody is of only four bars' length and is contained within a fourth. The strange winter phenomenon of 'mock suns' is addressed by the crazed man. 'No, you are not my suns ! I once had three suns. But the two best have set, and the sooner the third does the better, for then I shall lie down and be quiet.' Fox Strangways suggested that the lost suns are Love and Hope, and the third one Life.

A wonder is reserved for the last page of the 'Winterreise.' Given a thousand guesses, no one could have said that the last song would be at all like this. Müller must be given his due. *Der Leiermann* was an inspired ending. The madman meets a beggar, links with him his fortune ; and the two disappear into the snowy landscape. Schubert must be given his due. He realized the beauty of the proffered subject. No one else would have taken it quite like this. Almost anyone else would have overdone it. We say that such a man was worthy of any gift. How this one was compensated in the acceptance ! The result is pure poetry. The lamentations of seventy pages have died away. We may read any-thing or nothing much into the cleared scene. All that happens is the drone and tinkling of the hurdy-gurdy. The bass A and its fifth sound throughout the piece (a device here renewed from Schubert's use of it in the Pastoral Melody in 'Rosamunde '). The hurdy-gurdy's two-bar tune enters intermittently between the wanderer's half-numb sentences, which strike us strangely after all that has gone before. Only near the end is there a glimmer of warmth.

An almost toneless song. But what a task to set a singer at the end of an hour and half ! *Der Leiermann* has had unforgettable interpreters, like George Henschel and Plunket Greene. The 'Winterreise ' as a whole awaits one. A fine voice is wanted to hold the attention for so long, but the most musical tone will pall here if it is not the servant of the imagination. The singer must have sympathy with the passionate temper. For the dry of heart, the 'Winterreise ' might as well not exist.

The cycle was Schubert's Op. 89. It was published in two parts, the first in January 1828, the second—the proofs of which Schubert, as was said, corrected on his death-bed— in January 1829.

XIV

SONGS OF 1827–1828 :
'THE SWAN SONG'

THE events of 1828, the accomplishments and the catastrophe, still seem to us staggering. There had been wonderful years before, but 1828 surpassed them. It was the year of the C major symphony, of the quintet, of choral works and pianoforte sonatas, it was the year of the ' Schwanengesang.' The beautiful genius was young, was gaining every year, was still only at the beginning.

The Schubert of 1828 makes his contemporary world look paltry. Was there no one to appreciate what he meant to the world ? There was no one. The publishers were unconscionable. And in the light of to-day how inadequate seem the hearty friends and fellows of the Schubertian circle ! Poetasters and bohemians, pretentious painters and æsthetes borrow life for a time from Schubert's light. But the light burns too bright for them. In 1828 they look paltry. It goes out ; and after 1828 they are nobodies. What sort of Schubertians were they, that in 1828 Schubert could not afford a holiday—that it was left for Schumann ten years later to unearth the 1828 symphony—that the quintet remained unknown for twenty-two years ? The gay friends were a feeble crew. Yet Bauernfeld risked infection by visiting the dying Schubert, so let us try to think kindly of him ; and remember Schubert's stepsister Josefa, his ' dear little thirteen-years-old nurse.' Schubert's relations were decent, ordinary, penurious people who did what they could.

We hear nothing in the earlier part of the year to cause alarm. The tale then was one of bursting activity. The C major symphony was composed in March. Schumann found it at Ferdinand Schubert's in the autumn of 1838. It was first played at Leipzig in 1839. In March 1828 also was composed *Mirjams Siegesgesang* for soprano solo, chorus, and pianoforte, on a text by Grillparzer, published as Op. 136 in 1838. On March 26 Schubert gave his one and only concert. It was a success, and Schubert was at last able to buy himself a pianoforte. The programme of the concert included the first movement from one of the new string quartets and the new pianoforte trio ; the following songs, *Der Kreuzzug, Die Sterne, Der Wanderer an den Mond, Fragment aus dem Æschylus, Die Allmacht* (sung by Vogl), and *Auf dem Strom* (sung by Tietze) ; and the choral pieces *Ständchen* (i.e. Grillparzer's ' Leise klopf' ich '), with Josephine Fröhlich as soloist, and the 1827 setting of Klopstock's *Schlachtgesang*.

The string quintet in C was composed in the autumn. It was first performed in 1850 and was published as Op. 163 in 1854. It is a direct utterance of the spirit of music. In June 1828 there came Schubert's sixth mass, in Eb. It was published in 1865.

In this summer Schubert received invitations from friends both at Steyr and at Graz. All had to be declined for lack of money. Passing over several compositions of the summer, we come to the three pianoforte sonatas written in September. They are Nos. 13, 14, and 15, in C minor, A major, and Bb. Diabelli published them in 1838, dedicating them to Schumann.

At the end of August Schubert, who had been lodging with Schober, moved to take up quarters with his brother Ferdinand. In September he was not well, but early in October he undertook a three days' excursion into the country with his brother. His illness and breakdown are mysterious. He was unwell throughout October, but seems not to have been particularly apprehensive or to have suffered such depression as in 1823. On October 31 at supper he could not eat—food tasted to him like poison. On November 3 he was still able to go to church to hear a Requiem of his brother's composition. On November 4 he went to see the theorist Sechter with a view to taking a course of counterpoint. He talked hopefully to Lachner at this time about his opera, ' Der Graf von Gleichen.' On November 12 he wrote his last letter to Schober. Spaun visited him. He painfully corrected proofs of the ' Winterreise.' On November 16, a Sunday, typhoid was diagnosed. On Monday, the 17th, Bauernfeld visited him. He was himself, and talked of the opera, but that evening he was delirious. On the 18th the family apprehended the worst. Schubert died on Wednesday, November 19, 1828, at three in the afternoon.

* *

*

There are a number of 1827 songs in Mandyczewski's ninth volume to be mentioned before we come to those of the last

year of all. Thus the last two of his Walter Scott songs.
The *Lied der Anne Lyle* is a version of ' Wert thou, like me,
in life's low vale,' (taken by Scott from Andrew Mac-
Donald's comedy ' Love and Loyalty ') sung in ' A Legend of
Montrose ' by Annot Lyle in her obscurity, before her reinstate-
ment as the Knight of Ardenvohr's lost daughter. Schubert has
composed it without a special picturesque element, but has
made of it simply a contemporary love song. As before when a
text offered no remarkable visual suggestion, Schubert has
here backed up a charming melody with pianoforte writing
derived from his purely instrumental style. It calls to
mind the *Suleika* songs and *Delphine*. The characteristic
pianoforte figure is one of those that in Schubert pursue
delightful harmonic ways. The opening bars might be the
beginning of one of his pianoforte Andantes. With trifling
adjustment the music fits Scott's text, as does that of *Gesang
der Norna*. This is a version of Norna's ' For leagues along
the watery way ' in the nineteenth chapter of ' The Pirate.'
' Norna the Fitful Head ' (Ulla Troil) is the unhappy daughter
of Erland Troil, and mother of Clement Cleveland, the
pirate. Schubert has set the song in the 6-8 quaver-crotchet,
quaver-crotchet movement characteristic of much of his
water-music. It was evidently thrown off lightly, and the
pirate's mother sings in effect a rather jovial ditty, hardly in
keeping with Scott's weird ' sovereign of the seas and winds.'
These two songs were published by Diabelli in March 1828
as Op. 85. Likewise from Scotland came the subject of
Eine altschottische Ballade, a setting of ' Edward,' translated
from Percy by Herder. It was composed during the Graz
holiday in September. It is a strophic song with a minimum
of notes, the field being left to the narrator to present the
grim dialogue between the mother and son. In this
small room Schubert spoke characteristically. The mother's
questions begin in G minor and end on a B*b* cadence.
Edward's answers begin in B*b* minor and return to G minor.
The melody can be fitted to the original ballad, which has
an advantage over the German in our monosyllables ' your '
and ' my.' ' Deines ' and ' meinen ' in the German bring
into the melody semiquavers, which rather hamper the movement. In the version which was published as Op. 165,
No. 5 (there is another, very slightly different, in
Mandyczewski), someone, we hope not Schubert, wrote
' female voice ' and ' male voice ' over the question and
answer. Brahms actually set ' Edward ' as a duet (Op. 75,
No. 1) for alto and tenor. Both Brahms and Loewe (whose

well-known setting was composed before Schubert's) treat
the conventional ' O ! ' at the end of the lines expressively.
Schubert appreciated the convention, and of the three his
setting comes nearest to true ballad style.

The favourite of the songs of 1827, apart from the ' Winterreise,' is *Das Lied im Grünen* (Reil) :

> ' Spring ! Some young god has said the word ; and
> out of the earth daffodils and bluebells come crowding up
> madly, and blackbirds and larks in crowds are mad with
> a mixture of business and pleasure. And something sets
> us laughing and talking nineteen to the dozen, and more
> than half believing we have only to say the word to get
> anything in life we choose to ask for. Spring, spring !
> Where is the young god ? If I can't see him I can hear
> plainly what he says : " Gather ye rosebuds, rosebuds,
> rosebuds ! " '

It is the happiest of the songs of spring. A bewitching
tunefulness emerges from the pianoforte's incessant rippling
quavers ; and bewitching vocal melodies, three of them,
are thrown off with a sort of birdlike rapture. The song is
in simple rondo form. The first two stanzas are set to
melody *a* in A major ; the third and fourth to *b* in D ; the
fifth returns to *a* ; the sixth and seventh to *c*, which is a variant
of *a* in A major and F♯ minor ; the eighth to *a* again ; and
the coda is in D minor and A. The song is usually sung
from Friedländer's edition, which makes it shorter by omit-
ting repetitive stanzas. The fourth stanza in Mandyczewski,
set to *b*, is in Friedländer the fifth, set to *c*. It is suggested
that Schubert did not mean the whole of Reil's poem to be
sung, but that someone else, poet or publisher, inserted the
omitted stanzas. *Das Lied im Grünen* was published with two
earlier songs as Op. 115 in 1829.

Heimliches Lieben (Caroline Louise von Klenke) was one
of the Graz songs of September 1827. It is not a very
characteristic piece. Nothing cries out ' Schubert ' when
the page is opened. The song is in the nature of a ' period
piece,' but the elegance and the sentiment are charming.
Behold Schubert in the drawing-room ! He must have
heard much young ladies' music at *biedermeierisch* parties ;
and now, perhaps, he said he would show how, with just as
thin a texture, the thing might be done delightfully. The
song, composed for the Graz friends (it was dedicated to
Marie Pachler), has the merit of preserving the atmosphere

of the drawing-rooms of the 1820's with some poetic idealization ; and, moreover, it is most gratefully vocal. The melody that sails above the pianoforte's undulations is an irresistible invitation to the singer. How is it that the song is ignored ? A graceful tenor should still find *Heimliches Lieben* a piece to charm his audience.

In 1827-28 Schubert composed a group of Leitner songs. The modest poet was first met with in the 1823 song *Drang in die Ferne*. The new songs are for the most part secondary. Schubert might as well not have attempted *Vor meiner Wiege*. Leitner begs his mother to survive him so that she may soothe him at the last as she did in his infant hours. Such sentiments are either false—falsely simplified—or, if genuine, feeble minded. Schubert's music for *Vor meiner Wiege* flowed in a moment of no great control. Two other Leitner songs are in what was called the composer's ' evensong ' vein. *Das Weinen* sings the praise of tears to a gentle hymnlike strain, and *Der Kreuzzug*, pious and mild, tells of a monk's meditations as he observes a departing company of crusaders. German romanticism simplified and idealized the crusaders ; and Schubert accepted the poet's description of the expeditionary force as ' a beautiful and earnest choir, chanting sacred songs.'

Der Wallensteiner Lanzknecht beim Trunk is a racy drinking song. The Lanzknecht (who is not a lancer, as might perhaps be thought, but an infantryman) drinks from his helmet, which for all the knocks it had on Lützen's field is still serviceable for this and other uses. The song is very interesting for the reckless way in which it veers between G minor and B♭. Archaicism was no part of Schubert's art ; and yet this remarkable tune suggests to English ears our seventeenth-century country dances. The whole effect is bold and rollicking. *Des Fischers Liebesglück* is the fifth of the group :

> ' A light twinkles among the willows. It is the sign ! Quick, my oars, and light ; soft and quick ! She is there in the dimness, she is here ! And now my boat is adrift between earth and heaven, with us two together. The world has vanished, and all is mist and the wash of waters and our kisses, unending kisses.'

This barcarolle is a charming piece, rather in the vein of *Auf dem Wasser zu singen*, but a slighter song. The syncopations of the 6-8 movement are its special characteristic. It is the song for a light and ingratiating tenor.

Der Winterabend (Leitner) is the first of the 1828 songs :
a long piece of seven pages in which the patter of soft semiquavers never ceases. The look of the song is attractive,
the pages are true Schubert, and yet *Der Winterabend* does
not hold the field. The poem is a description of the quiet
pleasures of a solitary's winter evening, but the mood needed
more defining. The memories and the sighs, towards the
end, seem perfunctory. Schubert found little to grasp, and
fell back on accompanying the poem line by line with a
vaguely sympathetic murmur of music. To the same time,
January 1828, belongs *Die Sterne* :

'Often and often do I stand star-gazing. Surely they are
holy and benign, those high, twinkling dancers. We,
who know not all their mystery, know them as guides of
the belated traveller, and we divine in them a portent of
the life beyond life. Stars, be propitious to my love and
me ! '

The last of the Leitner songs is a piece of entrancing music.
Rhythmically it recalls the Allegretto of Beethoven's seventh
symphony—a light and airy relation, of course, the mode
being major and the pace just twice as fast as Beethoven's.
It dances softly and as though it might perpetually, and the
singer is left long pauses in which to contemplate the divine
choreography. The part-writing almost visibly presents a
dance by the way in which Schubert sets one couple marking
time while another moves from the position and back again :

An effect of untrammelled elfin play is made by Schubert's
darting modulations in the third line of each stanza. The
key is E♭. In the first stanza there is a shift into C major
for the third line. The next time, in the corresponding place,
the shift is into C♭, and the third time into G major. The
last stanza returns to the scheme of the first. *Die Sterne*
was published in the summer of 1828 as Op. 96, No. 1, dedicated to Princess Kinsky.

Herbst (Rellstab) is a strophic song in E minor, with a broad arpeggio melody over a stormy pianoforte part. It was written in the album of Heinrich Panofka, a Viennese lawyer, musical amateur, and member of Schubert's circle. *Auf dem Strom* (Rellstab) was composed for Schubert's concert on March 26, 1828, when it was sung by Tietze, with Levy as horn obbligato. It is a matter of fourteen pages. The voice bids passionate farewells, while the horn gives free imitations of the melodies, above the pianoforte's arpeggios. The music flows with animation, but the sentiment is really only formal. This sort of composition belongs to the ' copious ' Schubert of the legend. Longer still is *Der Hirt auf dem Felsen* (text partly by Müller and partly by Wilhelmine von Chézy),[1] which was composed in October 1828, and may possibly have been Schubert's last song, although, unless this can be actually proved, the Schubertian will prefer to believe that the *Taubenpost* was the real farewell. The piece hardly belongs to Schubert's true songs. It was composed as a vehicle of display for the Berlin singer Anna Milder-Hauptmann, who liked Schubert's best music, but at the same time kept asking him for something that would give full scope to her remarkable organ. *Der Hirt auf dem Felsen* has a clarinet obbligato. There is no interest in the pianoforte part, but it is certainly a good test-piece for a singer. It demands an extended compass, and some of the phrases include leaps of ninths and tenths. The final allegretto is a brilliantly gay movement, deriving a little from Rossini. A copy of the song was sent to the diva by Ferdinand Schubert a year after the composer's death. *Lebensmut* (Rellstab) is an unfinished song that stopped short when on the way to being a delightful thing. Again *Auf dem Wasser zu singen* is recalled by the movement of the slurred semiquavers ; but here the spirit is more vehement and challenging. The setting ends with Rellstab's first stanza.

* *

*

The songs of the ' Schwanengesang ' are not a cycle like the two Müller cycles, but are a collection of settings of seven poems by Rellstab and six by Heine, composed in August 1828, together with Seidl's *Taubenpost*, which was composed

---

[1] The first four stanzas are from Müller's *Dor Berghirt*, and the last from his *Liebesgedanken*. The rest is by Wilhelmine von Chézy.

in October and was ' unquestionably Schubert's last song.' [1]
The title ' Schwanengesang,' with which we need not quarrel,
was given to the set of songs by Haslinger the publisher, who
issued them six months after Schubert's death. Except
perhaps two, they are extremely well known and of the highest
interest.

The mind that conceived this music was never more alert
or inventive. When the procedure was familiar the detail
was fresh. When a new departure was called for, Schubert
found the way, as it seems without an instant's uncertainty,
to untrodden ground. Such songs as *Die Stadt*, *Am Meer*,
and *Der Doppelgänger* astonish us with a new vision. The
Heine songs have a special intensity. The music of the three
just mentioned matches the concentration of the poems. It
was not that Schubert now refrained on principle from
repeating the poet's phrases. In two of the Heine songs he
did so repeat them. But he could also meet Heine on his
own ground of economical statement. The newness of the
last songs is our wonder and despair. What was impossible
to the music that could so launch out on the fresh poetry ?
Schubert, says our regret, had but made a beginning. We
think of Purcell and Mozart, Shelley and Keats ; but none
even of them struck out in his last months on anything so
new as the music of the *Doppelgänger*.

The Rellstab songs come first. The last of Schubert's
brooks ripples in *Liebesbotschaft* :

' Hurry, tumble down the valley, little brook ! You are
a living link between me and her. Freshen her flowers.
And ah ! if she is by the bank, murmur my messages as
you pass.'

The last of the brooks is one of the most amiable and most
placid. Those demisemiquavers, for all their black look on
the page, are not to sound hurried. The brook is softly slip-
ping by, the lover is perfectly happy and assured. His song
is a tender compliment, turned almost as much to his own
happiness as to the maiden downstream. Three melodies
spring up like flowers beside the equable stream. Schubert
uses them in the order *a b c a*. The eloquent modulations in
the third stanza introduce as much emotion as is suitable on
a lazy afternoon. The lover's promise that he will not be
long away leads the music from A minor into the brightness
of B major. But the brook's demisemiquavers keep on,

[1] Grove.

neither faster nor slower, and the singer will hardly raise his voice above mezzo-piano even on ' Geliebte,' with its F♯. The key sinks down again into G for the fourth stanza, and the end is a sleepy murmuring. The lovely song represents Schubert's second thoughts. A sketch exists for a quite different setting with a melody in 9-8 and 4-4 times.

Kriegers Ahnung (Rellstab) :

> ' The very eve of battle, and all the men asleep !—all but me. I shall sleep soon enough, but not tonight. My heart is thudding, my brain seems on fire. I shall sleep, but not as once I slept, locking love in my arms with mine locked in love. This is unendurable. I must try to bear up. But what sleep will be mine ? Goodbye, life, love, white arms, goodbye ! '

For the last time Schubert uses the form of compressed operatic scena, of the old type of the Schmidt *Wanderer* and so many of his early pieces. The C minor exordium is charged with tragedy. This, and the crescendo of despair which works its way from F♯ minor to F minor, are the best parts of the song. Why, with all the fine music that is in it, is not *Kriegers Ahnung* quite irresistible ? Because there is a point at which Schubert's treatment is felt to be if not perfunctory at least exterior. The song is unequal. The A♭ movement (' time was, when I lay me down in the warmth of my love's bosom ') seems to be too easily complacent on a sudden. The charming drooping phrase in which the man tells his foreboding of the cold last sleep (' Bald ruh' ich ') is hardly characteristic enough. Poet and composer strike us as having dealt rather lightly with a specially poignant case. ' A soldier, and afeard ! ' There is here a peculiar torment ; and it is insensitive to approach with the ordinary expressions of sympathy a case in which such shame is involved.

The song is for barytone voice. Its great range calls for a practised singer. The thing to note is that for all the variety of the music and all the anguish of the mood there is no *ff*. The drama of the song is wholly an inner drama. In his cold sweat of apprehension and homesickness the wretched man hardly raises his voice. He is a soldier still, he manages to hold to his sanity, and the end is resignation. The sense of his torment is to be conveyed by intensity, not by explosiveness. The singer is all the time to be aware of the sleeping camp about him.

Frühlingssehnsucht (Rellstab) sings the praise of the sweet

season and pleads that among its blessings may be included
a remedy for the yearnings and desires that leave the poet
no rest. The thought of spring sets Schubert racing along
gaily. Only after four stanzas does the poet's insistence on
the heart's unrest switch him, perhaps perfunctorily, into
the minor mode. The woe is not very serious. The music
is thoroughly sanguine, but the song is not a first favourite.
    The fourth of the Rellstab songs is the *Ständchen* :

> ' Listen, you have only to listen. My voice and the un-
> sleeping leaves and that beseeching nightingale—every
> sound to-night quivers with desire. You cannot but listen,
> you cannot but come—come, and give me love.'

No song of Schubert's is more celebrated. It is not a formal
serenade, but an effusion of youth's desire. In the pauses
between the sentences, while the lover strains his ears for an
answer, the voices of the night echo the cadences of his song.
The song is composed of two strophes with an *Abgesang*
or ' afterstrain ' such as Sachs recommended to Walther von
Stolzing. To hear the *Ständchen* is as a rule to remark how
much the singer has forgotten of heady youth and the intoxication of the summer night. Every attempt has been made to
murder this music. A merely pretty performance is not
right. Ardour and imagination are required. How the song
revives and flowers again in Chaliapin's art ! Not to be
forgotten is his ' Komm', beglücke mich '—wheedling, antici-
pative, irresistible. After the song of desire, the song of
despair, Rellstab's *Aufenthalt* :

> ' Howl, wind. Roar, river. Wilderness, my wilderness,
> your fury of rain matches my tears. As your woods creak
> and the strong branch is rent, so is my heart breaking.
> Roar, river ! Break, heart ! '

It is the despair of youth, all effervescent with rage. The
fine bass theme breaks through the E minor triplets like an
overflowing torrent. The declamatory vocal phrase is a
translation into music of ' Rauschender Strom, brausender
Wald,' a translation so direct that it is impossible to find in
English an exactly fitting rendering of the German words.
The pianoforte bass follows the voice in deep imitations. It
is to be noted how moderate are all Schubert's dynamic
directions, except the one *fff* on the last page. Here, if the
crescendo has been well prepared, the tone may be of all

possible volume. In its last wail the voice takes up for the
first time and into its highest range the bass theme of the
prelude. In performance it is important to preserve the
squareness of the 2-4 subjects against the unceasing triplets—
to maintain one's foothold, so to say, against the beating of
wind and rain.

In der Ferne (Rellstab) is an expression of curiously mixed
melancholy and rapture. The poem means little or nothing.
It indicates passionate homesickness, but its essence is a kind
of Swinburnian revel of triple rhymes. The woeful exile
is passionate and exuberant. The dance of the rhymes has
caught Schubert's ear and waked his melody. The sense of
delight can hardly be kept out, and when the words hint
at winds and streams and sunlight the major mode comes in
and there is an invasion of arpeggios that will not hear of
moping. For all the beauty of the music the piece is felt
to be lacking in purpose and it is not much sung.[1]

Abschied is a student's song :

'Goodbye, friendly town, friendly folk ! You never
saw me glum and you won't now. How jolly it was to be
here, how jolly too to be off and away ! The girls blow
kisses. Goodbye ! There is one window that it's hard
to say goodbye to. How jolly it was here ! Still, how
jolly to be going ! Goodbye !'

The rhythm of this debonair song suggests the trotting of
the horse ; the general effect of the music is of a student's
ditty, accompanied by a twanging mandoline. There are
six stanzas, set to alternating but similar tunes in E*b* and
A*b* until we come to the last, which is not quite like either
of the others, and which begins as far from the main key
as C*b*. The pianist's spirit counts for nearly everything
in this song. There is to be no flagging. The youth
is not slowing down or turning round for anyone. The part
wants playing with steadiness, gaiety and delicacy. *Abschied*

---

[1] A curious contemporary criticism was called forth by this song (in
particular by the progression at the words ' Mutterhaus hassenden ') in
the ' Allgemeine Musikalische Zeitung ' : ' If such unseemlinesses, such
insolently placed harmonic distortions, could find, in defiance of all common-
sense; their impudent swindlers, who would foist them as surplus originality
upon patient admirers of extravagance, we should, supposing that the
egregious thing were to succeed, soon be removed into the most blissful
of all states, a state of anarchy similar to that of the days of the interregnum.'
(Quoted by M. Bauer, *op. cit.*)

is farewell to Rellstab.   The first of the Heine songs is
Der Atlas :

> 'Atlas I, the damned. My burden, the world and the
> world's woe, a burden not to be borne ; and my heart is
> breaking.   Heart ! thy proud will it was to scorn all between
> heaven and hell ; and fate said hell.'

The song begins like a symphony, so charged and tragic
is the musical thought.   A powerful G minor theme appears
in the bass, and the giant when he lifts up his voice in complaint seems to feel the drag of its octaves.   They may
represent the load from which he vainly tries to shake himself.
At the words ' I bear the unbearable ' his effort consists
in clearing G minor by way of a diminished seventh and
mounting a scale, with a wrenching augmented second, into
B minor.   But the implacable octaves dog him.   The swinging middle section is Atlas's admission.   The recapitulation
is somewhat condensed (thirteen bars for sixteen).   The voice
is brought in to overlap the bass octave theme, with yet heavier
effect ; and on the *ff* it reaches a minor third higher than
before.   And the awful answer remains :

Ihr Bild (Heine) is a song of quiet sorrow and touching
memories :

> ' Her face in the portrait seemed to stir as I peered, her
> lips to smile, her eyes to gleam with tears.   My tears came
> too.   Ah, this is hard, to believe the unbelievable, that
> she, she is lost to me.'

Nothing in Schubert could more easily be taken for Schumann.   It anticipates the intimate, domestic tone of the
later German song-writers.   The grief expressed is gentle,
as though mitigated by time.   The economy of Schubert's
writing is insurpassable.   Not a note could be subtracted.
Schubert appreciated in a flash Heine's condensed style,
and here gave the precise musical equivalent.   The bare
octaves reflect the loneliness of the bereaved speaker.   When
he pauses there is heard in the emptiness a muffled echo of
his cadence.   In the next strain the bare theme becomes

clothed, as it were, in the harmonies of his tender thoughts. The return in the third stanza of the hollow music of the beginning is an example of repetitions being more than ' mere ' repetition. The fancy of the movement of life in the picture has died away, and the reality is left of the speaker's loneliness and pain. The Bb minor melody then returns with identical notes, yet (such is the peculiarity of musical expression) saddened as though by experience and intensified in effect. The whole piece is a consummate little picture ; if not one of Schubert's greatest songs, one that wonderfully speaks of his ever fresh sympathies and responsiveness.

Schubert on the other hand perhaps missed something of Heine's intention in *Das Fischermädchen*, which comes next :

' Come, you so bold, out there in your boat in all weathers ! If the sea cannot frighten you, why should you fear love, mermaid ? Love is like the sea. It can rage, it can soothe ; and in its depths there are pearls.'

Schubert goes back for the last time to the 6-8 barcarolle movement, in which he was always happy. It is all delight-fully pretty and carefree, and the appearance of the middle stanza in Cb (the main key being Ab) is one of Schubert's happy surprises. But in the music there is not the equivalent of something in Heine's invitation of which the fishergirl had better beware. The poet is not a suitable humble lover, but, we rather fear, a philanderer from the town. Think twice, O maid, of those pearls ! But in the musician there is no cynical strain to suspect.

The next three songs are the purest masterpieces. They begin with *Die Stadt* :

' The mist is rising and veils the city. The breeze that wrinkles the water is chill, and the oars beat a mournful rhythm. Ah, that last gleam of day ! It shows up a place I know, the place where I lost love and all.'

There is a shiver in the bass octaves. The scurrying diminished seventh in the right-hand part, which recurs seventeen times without resolution, is the gusty wind. The city and its towers, solemn in the twilight, are depicted by deep C minor harmonies. It is a picture such as before Schubert was never composed in music. The vocal line, like that of *Atlas* and the *Doppelgänger*, combines elements which in early Schubert had been separated in recitative and

air. It is melodious, yet the words are hugged, and the
accentuation (an improvement over that of *Atlas*) is without
a fault. Schubert repeats no word. The cry of loss on the
6-4 minor chord is uttered wildly ; but lost is lost, and there
is no more to be said. Whither was Schubert tending ?
These last Heine songs hint at changes, at new depths, at
Schubert's maturity. Were unimaginable developments
latent ? or is the new quality in this last music only an innocent
reflection of the new-found, different poet ? Heine, the deep
Jew, was never young in the manner of the native German
poets. There is a world of experience and old bitterness in
his sentiment. In contact with him Schubert began to
assume, by his strange force of sympathy, a tone of knowledge
and of disillusionment.

The writing of *Die Stadt* throws some light on the question
of Schubert's appoggiaturas. He did not as a rule trouble
to make his notation plain on this point, and the singer has
to form his own judgment whether the appoggiatura is
' crushed ' (acciaccatura) or is weightier than the note on
which it leans. Dr. Ernest Walker, discussing Schubert's
appoggiaturas,[1] suggests a third interpretation when the
appoggiatura is followed by repeated notes, and that is the
complete elimination of the first of the repeated notes, the
appoggiatura taking up the whole of the strong beat. This
interpretation, if we have a right to it, is sometimes most
attractive. Dr. Walker thinks it is nearly always most to be
favoured. But *Die Stadt* raises a doubt. In the first stanza
Schubert writes :

Ho - ri - zon - te

According to Dr. Walker's interpretation the appoggiatura
would be precisely what Schubert has written out in the
corresponding place in the third stanza :

sich noch ein - mal

If he is right we are left wondering at Schubert's variation of
style in so short a composition ; and in fact it is not so easy
to follow him as could be wished.

[1] *Music and Letters*, April 1924.

Am Meer (Heine):

'The sea took on the last hues of the sunset. We two, sitting there by the fisherman's hut, stared and said nothing. It grew misty, the tide crept in, and gulls flew to and fro. I saw that she was quietly weeping. Those tears! I fell on my knees and kissed them away from her hand where they had fallen. Those tears! My lips still burn with them, they have set fire to my blood. Body and soul are wasted by the fatal drink.'

The low sighing of wind and wave is heard in the German sixths of the prelude. The voice is lifted up in a broad but most quiet melody above serious C major harmonies. All is as diatonic as can be. At the end of eight bars the voice leaves off, and the pianoforte softly, softly echoes the cadence, as is the Schubertian way. Then with a shiver there is a turn into C minor (the mist, the rising tide, the gulls). The music sobs on a diminished seventh, it sinks again, and there comes the line about the falling tears—softly, softly. So do hearts break. The second stanza repeats this music, only with the difference of a slight heightening of the plaint in the last line. At the end the sixths of the prelude are again heard faintly sighing. We stare at the miracle, we stare and cannot think what the hour was like, that gave all this into the artist's grasp. Nothing else, nothing, is like it.

Am Meer is the most difficult song in Schubert. The tessitura is high; and twice there are stretches of eight bars of Adagio Molto to be sung extremely smoothly in *mezza voce*. In brief, it puts the finest technics to the test. The least fault of quality is discovered. The C major melody cannot be too slow and the tone must be a kind of whisper, yet without a trace of breathiness, and, in fact, controlled to the last degree. *Am Meer* is rarely well sung, and in C practically never. It is safest with a lyric barytone, in B♭.

Der Doppelgänger is the last of the Heine songs:

'This must be what they call the dead of night. Heart, do you remember that empty house? Do you remember who used to live there? Ha! somebody here! A man, wringing his hands. Horrible! It is myself. I can see my own face now that the moon comes out. Hi! Signor Ghost! What is the meaning of it? What are you doing,

mocking the torments I went through here all those years
ago ? ' [1]

The chimes of the hour, Hamlet's hour, reverberate with a
hint of ' Dies Iræ ' in the four-bar phrase :

The pianoforte part consists wholly of this phrase and
variants (in the first form it recurs six times), except for two
echoes of the singer's cadences which quaver weirdly in the
deserted scene.   The persistent tolling is to be taken as sounding in the half-conscious fancy of the speaker.   When his
excitement rises it swells in his ears to a brazen roar.   One
of the considerations in performance is that for all the slow-
ness of the movement and the apparent freedom of the voice
part this tolling is to be kept going rigorously in time.   Once
we have learnt to listen for its knell, the song is no longer
itself if only a vague recitative accompaniment is heard.   The
vocal writing represents the culmination of Schubert's art
in setting quasi-dramatic lyrical verse to measured and
melodious recitative.   It is strictly metrical—it falls into
simple four-bar sections—and yet the effect is of free declamation.   This was Schubert's new lyric style.   The economy
of the *Doppelgänger* is austere.   The song is one of the

---

[1] The *Doppelgänger* presents one of the classic problems of the song
translator.   The version offered here is meant for the singer, not the reader.
It involves slight changes in note values, justifiable in view of the nature of
Schubert's vocal line :

' THE SPECTRAL SELF '

' How still the night.   The streets are deserted.
In that house yonder one I loved did dwell.
She is far away.   The place is forsaken,
And there stands the house dark and lone and chill.

' And there is a man stands staring at her window,
He shakes and shudders in agony.
Saints in heaven !   He turns his face towards me.
The moon comes out—'tis myself I see !

' Thou ghostly double, no man but a shadow,
What dost thou, aping my old cry
And all the pangs that here I suffered
So many a night in time gone by ? '

barest in Schubert. We feel him to have been all self-for-getting as he strained to delineate the subject. The heavy persistence of B minor is to be observed. There is no modu-lation till the third stanza, where in the address to the spectre there is a wrenching chromatic progression to D♯ minor. The composition is the finest of all achievements in the matching of music and verse. It is transparently simple. To the singer it does not present just the same technical difficulties as *Am Meer* ; but what gifts of passion and imagina-tion does it not demand ? In point of purely technical requirements the *pp* calls for the art of speaking tonefully and tunefully ' on the breath.' This pianissimo lies rather low. The *fff* rises an octave and a minor sixth above the lowest note. Transposition to A minor is reasonable. But the peculiar demands of the song are not so much technical as visionary. They place the *Doppelgänger* out of reach of the ordinary singer. The uncanny scene and the mingling of distress and irony in the man's mood (for it is not a simpleton's ghost story, and Heine while he suffered sneered)—these things require a touch of genius in the rendering.

Schubert's last song was *Die Taubenpost* (Seidl) :

> ' The faithfullest of carrier-pigeons is mine. It wings its way without tiring to a certain house, to a certain person, with messages by the thousand ; and day and night are all the same. And my messenger's name ? Love-longing ? '

The last song is a return to Schubert's homeliest style. There is no trace of the adventures just recorded. By this time we should know Schubert's resilience well enough ; but the *Taubenpost* comes all the same as a surprise with its sunny ingenuousness and almost jaunty lilt. The last song of that fatal autumn ! It is enough to prove that Schubert's death was casual, a stroke of chance, and not, as some of the bio-graphers suggest, the determined event of conspiring circum-stances.

The syncopated, dancing pianoforte part carries us away to village life. Like the finale of the C major quintet of the same year, it is a reminder of the dance rhythms of the Slav and Magyar peoples, whose territories begin at so short a distance from Vienna and whose national traits can be made to account for much in Viennese musical idiom. Vienna was in the great musical period the capital of an empire that was largely Slavonic. Schubert's father was Moravian. The *Taubenpost* dance brings to mind the polka-like measures in

Smetana's and Dvořák's music. It is countrified, and all
the same nothing could be daintier. There are all manner
of charming details. One is the escape of the lilting pianoforte part into B (from G) at the end of the singer's first
eight-bar period—whence it returns suddenly as though
called to order at the re-entry of the voice. Another detail
is the saucy little flute-like scale figure which comes in four
or five times in the right-hand part. The form is *a b a* and
coda, this last being composed of broken vocal phrases, coy
pauses, tender questions, and triumphant repetitions. The
same amiable dance rhythm is kept up regularly, except that
once or twice the right hand feels compelled to join in the
lover's tune.

Schubert, thus flirting and sonneteering, ended the page,
which another day was to be turned and the next piece written.
The song ends ; but as for its being itself an end, nothing is
farther from the suggestion. The day is young, we have
been at play ; there is time in plenty, there is all the future,
for other thoughts and works—that is the impression remaining. But the time was already over ! There is nothing to
explain such things—that Schubert should have been
Schubert—that this should have been the end.

APPENDIX I

THE COLLECTED SONGS

THE following is a list of the songs as they appear in the ten volumes of Mandyczewski's edition (Breitkopf & Härtel). 'B.H.P.' stands for Breitkopf & Härtel's Popular edition; 'P' for Peters's edition (Friedländer). N.B.—In the various reprints of Peters's edition there are sometimes differences in the pagination of 2, more rarely 4 pages.

VOL. 1, 1811–1814

1. *Hagars Klage*, Schücking (B.H.P. II. 1).—2. *Des Mädchens Klage* (I.), Schiller (B.H.P. II. 2).—3. *Eine Leichenphantasie*, Schiller (B.H.P. V. 1).—4. *Der Vatermörder*, Pfeffel (B.H.P. VI. 1).—5. *Der Jüngling am Bache* (I.), Schiller (B.H.P. VI. 2).—6. *Klaglied*, Rochlitz (B.H.P. II. 3, P. IV. 156).—7. *Totengräberlied*, Hölty (B.H.P. X. 1).—8. *Die Schatten*, Matthisson (B.H.P. VI. 3).—9. *Sehnsucht* ('Ach, aus dieses Thales') (I.), Schiller (B.H.P. X. 2).—10. *Verklärung*, Pope (B.H.P. V. 2, P. V. 86).—11. *Thekla: Eine Geisterstimme* (I.), Schiller (B.H.P. II. 4).—12. *Der Taucher*, Schiller (B.H.P. X. 3, P. V. 49).—13. *Don Gayseros*, Fouqué: I. *Don Gayseros, Don Gayseros*; 14. II. *Nächtens klang die süsse Laute*; 15. III. *An dem jungen Morgenhimmel* (B.H.P. V. 3, 4, 5).—16. *Andenken*, Matthisson (B.H.P. V. 6). —17. *Geisternähe*, Matthisson (B.H.P. V. 7).—18. *Totenopfer*, Matthisson (B.H.P. V. 8).—19. *Trost an Elisa*, Matthisson (B.H.P. VI. 4).—20. *Die Betende*, Matthisson (B.H.P. II. 5, P. V. 171).—21. *Lied aus der Ferne*, Matthisson (B.H.P. VI. 5).—22. *Der Abend*, Matthisson (B.H.P. II. 6, P. IV. 142).— 23. *Lied der Liebe*, Matthisson (B.H.P. VI. 6).—24. *Erinnerungen*, Matthisson (B.H.P. VI. 7, P. IV. 117).—25. *Adelaïde*, Matthisson (B.H.P. VI. 8, P. VI. 33).—26. *An Emma*, Schiller (B.H.P. VI. 9, P. II. 118).—27. *Romanze*, Matthisson (B.H.P. V. 9).—28. *An Laura*, Matthisson (B.H.P. VI. 10, P. V. 173).—29. *Der Geistertanz* (II), Matthisson (B.H.P. V. 10, P. II. 237).—30. *Das Mädchen aus der Fremde* (I), Schiller (B.H.P. VI. 11).—31. *Gretchen am Spinnrade*, Goethe (B.H.P. II. 7, P. I. 176).—32. *Nachtgesang*, Goethe (B.H.P. VI. 12, P. VI. 54).—33. *Trost in Thränen*, Goethe (B.H.P.

VI. 13, P. II. 230).—34. *Schäfers Klagelied*, Goethe (B.H.P. *a*. VI. 14, *b*. V. 11, P. I. 225).—35. *Sehnsucht* (' Was zieht mir '), Goethe (B.H.P. VI. 15, P. VI, 8).—36. *Am See*, Mayrhofer (B.H.P. VI. 16, P. VII. 42).—37. *Scene aus Goethe's ' Faust* ' (B.H.P. XII. 1, P. V. 108).—38. *Ammenlied*, Lubi (B.H.P. II. 8).

VOL. 2, 1815, JANUARY TO JULY

39. *Auf einen Kirchhof*, Schlechta (B.H.P. VI. 17, P. VI. 69). —40. *Minona*, Bertrand (B.H.P. II. 9).—41. *Als ich sie erröthen sah*, Ehrlich (B.H.P. VI. 18, P. VI. 16).—42. *Das Bild* (B.H.P. VI. 19, P. V. 88).—43. *Der Mondabend*, Ermin (B.H.P. VI. 20, P. IV. 154).—44. *Lodas Gespenst*, Ossian (B.H.P. V. 12, P. IV. 177).—45. *Der Sänger*, Goethe (B.H.P. VI. 21, P. III. 94).—46. *Die Erwartung*, Schiller (B.H.P. VI. 22, P. III. 84).—47. *Am Flusse* (I.), Goethe (B.H.P. VI. 23).— 48. *An Mignon*, Goethe (B.H.P. V. 13, P. II. 49).—49. *Nähe des Geliebten*, Goethe (B.H.P. II. 10, P. III. 3).—50. *Sängers Morgenlied* (I.), Körner (B.H.P. VI. 24).—51. *Sängers Morgenlied* (II.), Körner (B.H.P. VI. 25).—52. *Amphiaraos*, Körner (B.H.P. X. 4).—53. *Trinklied vor der Schlacht*, Körner (B.H.P. XII. 2).—54. *Schwertlied*, Körner (B.H.P. VI. 26).—55. *Gebet während der Schlacht*, Körner (B.H.P. X. 5, P. II. 214).—56. *Das war ich*, Körner (B.H.P. VI. 27, P. VI. 20).—57. *Die Sterne*, Fellinger (B.H.P. VI. 28).—58. *Vergebliche Liebe*, Bernard (B.H.P. VI. 29, P. VI. 112).—59. *Liebesrausch*, Körner (B.H.P. VI. 30).—60. *Sehnsucht der Liebe*, Körner (B.H.P. II. 11).—61. *Die erste Liebe*, Fellinger (B.H.P. VI. 31, P. V. 202).—62. *Trinklied*, Zettler (B.H.P. X. 6, P. VII. 69).—63. *Stimme der Liebe* (I.), Matthisson (B.H.P. II. 12).—64. *Naturgenuss*, Matthisson (B.H.P. II. 13, P. VII. 86).—65. *Die Sterbende*, Matthisson (B.H.P. II. 14).— 66. *An die Freude*, Schiller (B.H.P. VI. 32, P. IV. 126).— 67. *Des Mädchens Klage* (II.), Schiller (B.H.P. V. 14, P. I. 210).—68. *Der Jüngling am Bache* (II.), Schiller (B.H.P. VI. 33, P. VII. 90).—69. *An den Mond* (' Geuss nicht '), Hölty (B.H.P. VI. 34, P. II. 116).—70. *Die Mainacht*, Hölty (B.H.P. VI. 35).—71. *Amalia*, Schiller (B.H.P. II. 15, P. VI. 104).— 72. *An die Nachtigall*, Hölty (B.H.P. II. 16, P. VI. 98).— 73. *An die Apfelbäume, wo ich Julien erblickte*, Hölty (B.H.P. VI. 36, P. VI. 74).—74. *Seufzer*, Hölty (B.H.P. VI. 37).—75. *Liebeständelei*, Körner (B.H.P. VI. 38).—76. *Der Liebende*, Hölty (B.H.P. VI. 39).—77. *Die Nonne*, Hölty (B.H.P. II. 17). —78. *Die Liebe* (Clärchen's Lied, ' Freudvoll und leidvoll '),

Goethe (B.H.P. II. 18, P. II. 236).—79. *Adelwold und Emma*,
Bertrand (B.H.P. VI. 40).—80. *Der Traum*, Hölty (B.H.P.
VI. 41, P. VI. 94).—81. *Die Laube*, Hölty (B.H.P. VI. 42,
P. VI. 96).—82. *Meeresstille*, Goethe (B.H.P. V. 15, P. II. 3).—
—83. *Kolmas Klage*, Ossian (B.H.P. II. 19, P. II. 207).—84.
Grablied, Kenner (B.H.P. II. 20, P. VI. 32).—85. *Das Finden*,
Kosegarten (B.H.P. VI. 43, P. VI. 30).—86. *Lieb Minna*,
Stadler (B.H.P. II. 21, P. VII. 31).—87. *Wanderers Nachtlied*
(' Der du von dem Himmel bist '), Goethe (B.H.P. II. 22,
P. II. 8).—88. *Der Fischer*, Goethe (B.H.P. II. 23, P. II. 9).
—89. *Erster Verlust*, Goethe (B.H.P. II. 24, P. II. 11).—90.
Idens Nachtgesang, Kosegarten (B.H.P. II. 25, P. VII. 22).—
91. *Von Ida*, Kosegarten (B.H.P. II. 26).—92. *Die Ercheinung*,
Kosegarten (B.H.P. VI. 44).—93. *Die Täuschung*, Kose-
garten (B.H.P. VI. 45, P. VI. 91).—94. *Das Sehnen*, Kose-
garten (B.H.P. II. 27, P. VI. 99).—95. *Der Abend*, Kosegarten
(B.H.P. II. 28).—96. *Geist der Liebe*, Kosegarten (B.H.P. II.
29, P. IV. 140).—97. *Tischlied*, Goethe (B.H.P. VI. 46, P.
IV. 143).—98. *Der Liedler*, Kenner (B.H.P. VI. 47, P. IV.
33).—99. *Ballade*, Kenner (B.H.P. II. 30, P. IV. 148).—100.
Abends unter der Linde (I), Kosegarten (B.H.P. II. 31).—
101. *Abends unter der Linde* (II), Kosegarten (B.H.P. II. 32).—
102. *Die Mondnacht*, Kosegarten (B.H.P. VI. 48).—103.
Huldigung, Kosegarten (B.H.P. VI. 49).—104. *Alles um Liebe*,
Kosegarten (B.H.P. II. 33).

VOL. 3, 1815, AUGUST TO DECEMBER

105. *Das Geheimnis* (I), Schiller (B.H.P. VI. 50).—106. *Hoff-
nung* (I), Schiller (B.H.P. II. 34).—107. *An den Frühling* (I),
Schiller (B.H.P. VI. 51, P. VII. 34).—108. *Das Mädchen
aus der Fremde* (II), Schiller (B.H.P. II. 35, P. VII. 92).—
109. *Die Bürgschaft*, Schiller (B.H.P. V. 16, P. V. 11).—110.
Punschlied. ' Im Norden zu singen,' Schiller (B.H.P. XII. 3,
P. VII. 93).—111. *Der Gott und die Bajadere*, Goethe (B.H.P.
V. 17, P. VII. 106).—112. *Der Rattenfänger*, Goethe (B.H.P.
VI. 52, P. VI. 52).—113. *Der Schatzgräber*, Goethe (B.H.P.
X. 7, P. VII. 102).—114. *Heidenröslein*, Goethe (B.H.P. II.
36, P. I. 182).—115. *Bundeslied*, Goethe (B.H.P. VI. 53).—
116. *An den Mond* (I), Goethe (B.H.P. II. 37, P. VI. 55).—
117. *Wonne der Wehmuth*, Goethe (B.H.P. VII. 54, P. IV.
137).—118. *Wer kauft Liebesgötter*, Goethe (B.H.P. VII. 55,
P. VI. 50).—119. *Die Spinnerin*, Goethe (B.H.P. II. 38, P.
IV. 147).—120. *Liebhaber in allen Gestalten*, Goethe (B.H.P.
VII. 56, P. VII. 97).—121. *Schweizerlied*, Goethe (B.H.P. II.

39, P. VII. 36).—122. *Der Goldschmiedsgesell*, Goethe (B.H.P. X. 8, P. VI. 64).—123. *Cora an die Sonne*, Baumberg (B.H.P. II. 40, P. VI. 31).—124. *Der Morgenkuss nach einem Ball*, Baumberg (B.H.P. VII. 57, P. VI. 45).—125. *Abendständchen*, Baumberg (B.H.P. VII. 58).—126. *Morgenlied*, Stolberg (B.H.P. VII. 59, P. II. 4).—127. *An die Sonne*, Baumberg (B.H.P. II. 41, P. IV. 146).—128. *Der Weiberfreund* (B.H.P. VII. 60).—129. *An die Sonne* (B.H.P. VII. 61).—130. *Lilla an die Morgenröthe* (B.H.P. II. 42).—131. *Tischlerlied* (B.H.P. X. 9, P. VI. 65).—132. *Todtenkranz für ein Kind*, Matthisson (B.H.P. II. 43).—133. *Abendlied*, Stolberg (B.H.P. II. 44).— 134. *Die Fröhlichkeit*, Prandstetter (B.H.P. VII. 62).—135. *Lob des Tokayers*, Baumberg (B.H.P. VII. 63, P. IV. 144).—136. *An den Frühling* (II), Schiller (B.H.P. VII. 64, P. VI. 101).—137. *Lied*, Schiller (B.H.P. II. 45).— 138. *Furcht der Geliebten*, Klopstock (B.H.P. VII. 65, P. VII. 24).—139. *Das Rosenband*, Klopstock (B.H.P. VII. 66, P. V. 160).—140. *Selma und Selmar*, Klopstock (B.H.P. XII. 4, P. V. 158).—141. *Vaterlandslied*, Klopstock (B.H.P. II. 46).— 142. *An Sie*, Klopstock (B.H.P. VII. 67).—143. *Die Sommernacht*, Klopstock (B.H.P. VII. 68).—144. *Die frühen Gräber*, Klopstock (B.H.P. II. 47, P. V. 162).—145. *Dem Unendlichen*, Klopstock (B.H.P. *a. b.* V. 18, *c.* VII. 69, P. V. 31).—146. *Shilrik und Vinvela*, Ossian (B.H.P. XII. 5, P. IV. 188).— 147. *Ossians Lied nach dem Falle Nathos'* (B.H.P. V. 19, P. IV. 196).—148. *Das Mädchen von Inistore*, Ossian (B.H.P. II. 48, P. IV. 198).—149. *Lambertine*, Stoll (B.H.P. II. 49, P. VI. 3).—150. *Labetrank der Liebe*, Stoll (B.H.P. VII. 70).— 151. *An die Geliebte*, Stoll (B.H.P. VII. 71, P. VII. 108).— 152. *Wiegenlied*, Körner (B.H.P. II. 50).—153. *Mein Gruss an den Mai*, Ermin (B.H.P. II. 51).—154. *Skolie*, Deinhardstein (B.H.P. VII. 72).—155. *Die Sternenwelten*, Fellinger (B.H.P. II. 52).—156. *Die Macht der Liebe*, Kalchberg (B.H.P. II. 53).—157. *Das gestörte Glück*, Körner (B.H.P. VII. 73).—158. *Sehnsucht* (I) ('Nur wer die Sehnsucht kennt'), Goethe (B.H.P. II. 54).—159. *Hektors Abschied*, Schiller (B.H.P. XII. 6, P. IV. 53).—160. *Die Sterne*, Kosegarten (B.H.P. VII. 74).—161. *Nachtgesang*, Kosegarten (B.H.P. V. 20, P. VII. 88).—162. *An Rosa* (I), Kosegarten (B.H.P. VII. 75).—163. *An Rosa* (II), Kosegarten (B.H.P. X. 10).—164. *Idens Schwanenlied*, Kosegarten (B.H.P. II. 55).—165. *Schwanengesang*, Kosegarten (B.H.P. V. 21).—166. *Luisens Antwort*, Kosegarten (B.H.P. II. 56).—167. *Der Zufriedene*, Reissig (B.H.P. VII. 76).—168. *Mignon* ('Kennst du das Land?'), Goethe (B.H.P. II. 57, P. II. 221).—169.

Hermann und Thusnelda, Klopstock (B.H.P. XII. 7, P. V. 154).
—170. *Liane*, Mayrhofer (B.H.P. II. 58).—171. *Augenlied*,
Mayrhofer (B.H.P. X. 11, P. VI. 78).—172. *Klage der Ceres*,
Schiller (B.H.P. II. 59).—173. *Harfenspieler* (' Wer sich der
Einsamkeit ') (I), Goethe (B.H.P. VII. 77).—174. *Geistes-
gruss*, Goethe (B.H.P. X. 12, P. IV. 82).—175. *Hoffnung*,
Goethe (B.H.P. VII. 78, P. VII. 62).—176. *An den Mond*
(II), Goethe (B.H.P. II. 60, P. VII. 50).—177. *Rastlose Liebe*,
Goethe (B.H.P. VII. 79, P. I. 222).—178. *Erlkönig*, Goethe
(B.H.P. III. 61, P. I. 170).—179. *Der Schmetterling*, Schlegel
(B.H.P. III. 62, P. IV. 49).—180. *Die Berge*, Schlegel (B.H.P.
VII. 80, P. IV. 51).—181. *Genügsamkeit*, Schober (B.H.P. X.
13, P. IV. 122).—182. *Das Grab* (I), Salis (B.H.P. V. 22).

VOL. 4, 1816

183. *An die Natur*, Stolberg (B.H.P. V. 23).—184, *Lied*,
Fouqué (B.H.P. V. 24).—185. *Klage*, Hölty (B.H.P. VII. 81).
—186. *Das Grab* (II), Salis (B.H.P. V. 25).—187. *Der Tod
Oscars*, Ossian (B.H.P. XII. 8, P. IV. 200).—188. *Cronnan*,
Ossian (B.H.P. XII. 9, P. IV. 170).—189. *Morgenlied* (B.H.P.
VII. 82).—190. *Abendlied* (B.H.P. III. 63).—191. *Ritter
Toggenburg*, Schiller (B.H.P. VII. 83, P. V. 103).—192. *Der
Flüchtling*, Schiller (B.H.P. VII. 84).—193. *Laura am Clavier*,
Schiller (B.H.P. VII. 85).—194. *Des Mädchens Klage* (III),
Schiller (B.H.P. III. 64).—195. *Die Entzückung an Laura* (I),
Schiller (B.H.P. VII. 86).—196. *Die vier Weltalter*, Schiller
(B.H.P. X. 14, P. IV. 130).—197. *Pflügerlied*, Salis (B.H.P.
X. 15).—198. *Die Einsiedelei* (I), Salis (B.H.P. VII. 87, P.
VI. 12).—199. *Gesang an die Harmonie*, Salis (B.H.P. VII.
88).—200. *Die Wehmuth*, Salis (B.H.P. III. 65, P. VII. 12).—
201. *Lied* (' In's stille Land '), Salis (B.H.P. III. 66, P. VI.
23).—202. *Der Herbstabend*, Salis (B.H.P. VII. 89).—203.
Der Entfernten, Salis (B.H.P. VII. 90, P. VII. 40).—204.
Fischerlied (I), Salis (B.H.P. X. 16).—205. *Lebensmelodieen*,
Schlegel (B.H.P. XII. 10, P. IV. 128).—206. *Die verfehlte
Stunde*, Schlegel (B.H.P. III. 67).—207. *Sprache der Liebe*,
Schlegel (B.H.P. VII. 91, P. IV. 138).—208. *Abschied von der
Harfe*, Salis (B.H.P. X. 17, P. VII. 83).—209. *Daphne am
Bach*, Stolberg (B.H.P. V. 26, P. VII. 87).—210. *Stimme der
Liebe*, Stolberg (B.H.P. VII. 92, P. III. 200).—211. *Ent-
zückung*, Matthisson (B.H.P. VII. 93).—212. *Geist der
Liebe*, Matthisson (B.H.P. III. 68).—213. *Klage*, Matthisson
(B.H.P. V. 27).—214. *Stimme der Liebe* (II), Matthisson
(B.H.P. X. 18).—215. *Julius an Theone*, Matthisson (B.H.P.

VII. 94).—216. *Klage* (' Dein Silber schien '), Hölty (B.H.P.
VII. 95, P. VI. 60).—217. *Frühlingslied*, Hölty (B.H.P. III.
69, P. VII. 89).—218. *Auf den Tod einer Nachtigall*, Hölty
(B.H.P. III. 70).—219. *Die Knabenzeit*, Hölty (B.H.P. VII.
96).—220. *Winterlied*, Hölty (B.H.P. III. 71).—221. *Minne-
lied*, Hölty (B.H.P. VII. 97, P. VII. 10).—222. *Die frühe
Liebe*, Hölty (B.H.P. VII. 98).—223. *Blumenlied*, Hölty
(B.H.P. VII. 99, P. VII. 100).—224. *Der Leidende*, Hölty
(B.H.P. VII. 100, P. VI. 77).—225. *Seligkeit*, Hölty (B.H.P.
VII. 101).—226. *Erntelied*, Hölty (B.H.P. III. 72, P. VI.
58).—227. *Das grosse Halleluja*, Klopstock (B.H.P. III. 73).
—228. *Schlachtgesang*, Klopstock (B.H.P. VII. 102).—229.
Die Gestirne, Klopstock (B.H.P. VII. 103, P. V. 35).—230.
Edone, Klopstock (B.H.P. VII. 104, P. V. 161).—231. *Die
Liebesgötter*, Uz (B.H.P. VII. 105, P. VII. 98).—232. *An
den Schlaf*, Uz (B.H.P. III. 74).—233. *Gott im Frühlinge*, Uz
(B.H.P. III. 75, P. VII. 94).—234. *Der gute Hirt*, Uz (B.H.P.
III. 76).—235. *Die Nacht*, Uz (B.H.P. X. 19, P. VI. 38).—
236. *Fragment aus dem Æschylus*, Mayrhofer (B.H.P. VII.
106, P. V. 78).—237. *An die untergehende Sonne*, Kosegarten
(B.H.P. III. 77, P. IV. 45).—238. *An mein Clavier*, Schubart
(B.H.P. III. 78, P. VII. 23).—239. *Grablied auf einen Soldaten*,
Schubart (B.H.P. X. 20).—240. *Freude der Kinderjahre*,
Köpken (B.H.P. VII. 107, P. VII. 84).—241. *Das Heimweh*,
Hell (B.H.P. III. 79, P. VII. 64).—242. *Aus Diego Manazares*
(B.H.P. III. 80).—243. *An den Mond* (' Was schauest du '),
Hölty (B.H.P. VII. 108).—244. *An Chloen*, Jacobi (B.H.P.
VII. 109).—245. *Hochzeitlied*, Jacobi (B.H.P. V. 28).—
246. *In der Mitternacht*, Jacobi (B.H.P. V. 29).—247. *Trauer
der Liebe*, Jacobi (B.H.P. III. 81, P. VII. 26).—248. *Die Perle*,
Jacobi (B.H.P. III. 82).—249. *Liedesend*, Mayrhofer (B.H.P.
XII. 11, P. V. 139).—250a. *Lied des Orpheus, als er in die
Hölle ging*, Jacobi (B.H.P. VII. 110).—250b. *Orpheus*, Jacobi
(B.H.P. X. 21, P. V. 98).—251. *Abschied*, Mayrhofer (B.H.P.
V. 30, P. VII. 18).—252. *Rückweg*, Mayrhofer (B.H.P. X.
22).—253. *Alte Liebe rostet nie*, Mayrhofer (B.H.P. VII. 111).
—254 (*a* and *b*), 255 (*a* and *b*), 256, 257, 258. *Gesänge des
Harfners*, Goethe. As follows : 254. ' Wer sich der Ein-
samkeit ' (II) (B.H.P. VII. 114, P. II. 27) ; 255. ' An die
Thüren ' (B.H.P. VII. 116, P. II. 33) ; 256. ' Wer nie sein
Brod ' (I) (B.H.P. VII. 112) ; 257. ' Wer nie sein Brod ' (II)
(B.H.P. VII. 113) ; 258. ' Wer nie sein Brod ' (III) (B.H.P.
VII. 115, P. II. 30).—259. *Lied der Mignon* (' Nur wer die
Sehnsucht kennt ') (II), Goethe (B.H.P. III. 83).—260. *Lied
der Mignon* (' Nur wer die Sehnsucht kennt ') (III), Goethe

(B.H.P. III. 84).—261. *Der König in Thule*, Goethe (B.H.P. VII. 117, P. II. 12).—262. *Jägers Abendlied*, Goethe (B.H.P. VII. 118, P. I. 228).—263. *An Schwager Kronos*, Goethe (B.H.P. X. 23, P. II. 44).—264. *Der Sänger am Felsen*, Pichler (B.H.P. VII. 119).—265. *Lied*, Pichler (B.H.P. III. 85).— 266a. *Der Unglückliche*, ' Werner '—266b. *Der Wanderer*, Schmidt of Lübeck (B.H.P. X. 24, P. I. 184).—267. *Der Hirt*, Mayrhofer (B.H.P. VII. 120).—268. *Lied eines Schiffers an die Dioskuren*, Mayrhofer (B.H.P. VII. 121, P. III. 32).—269. *Geheimnis. An Fr. Schubert*, Mayrhofer (B.H.P. III. 86, P. VII. 46).—270. *Zum Punsche*, Mayrhofer (B.H.P. X. 25, P. VI. 40).—271. *Abendlied der Fürstin*, Mayrhofer (B.H.P. V. 31).—272. *Am Bach im Frühling*, Schober (B.H.P. V. 32, P. IV. 120).—273. *An eine Quelle*, Claudius (B.H.P. VII. 122, P. IV. 124).—274. *Bei dem Grabe meines Vaters*, Claudius (B.H.P. III. 87, P. VII. 28).—275. *Am Grabe Anselmos*, Claudius (B.H.P. VII, 123, P. II. 14).—276. *An die Nachtigall*, Claudius (B.H.P. III. 88, P. IV. 96).—277. *Wiegenlied*, Claudius (B.H.P. III, 89, P. II. 194).—278. *Abendlied*, Claudius (B.H.P. III. 90, P. VII. 30).—279. *Phidile*, Claudius (B.H.P. III. 91).—280. *Lied* (I) Claudius (B.H.P. VII. 124). —281. *Lied* (II), Claudius (B.H.P. X. 26).—282. *Herbstlied*, Salis (B.H.P. III. 92).—283. *Skolie*, Matthisson (B.H.P. X. 27).—284. *Lebenslied*, Matthisson (B.H.P. V. 33, P. VI. 14).— 285. *Leiden der Trennung*, Metastasio, trans. Collin (B.H.P. III. 93).—286. *Licht und Liebe*, Nachtgesang, Collin (B.H.P. XII. 12).—287. *Alinde*, Rochlitz (B.H.P. VII. 125, P. II. 154). —288. *An die Laute*, Rochlitz (B.H.P. VII. 126, P. IV. 62).

Vol. 5, 1817 and 1818

289. *Frohsinn* (B.H.P. X. 28, P. VI. 42).—290. *Jagdlied*, Werner (B.H.P. X. 29).—291. *Die Liebe*, Leon (B.H.P. III. 94).—292. *Trost* (' Nimmer lange ') (B.H.P. V. 34, P. VII. 9). —293. *Der Schäfer und der Reiter*, Fouqué (B.H.P. X. 30, P. III. 7).—294. *Lob der Thränen*, Schlegel (B.H.P. III, 95, P. I. 187).—295a. *Der Alpenjäger*, Mayrhofer (B.H.P. X. 31, P. II. 35).—295b. *Der Alpenjäger*, Mayrhofer.—296. *Wie Ulfru fischt*, Mayrhofer (B.H.P. X. 32, P. IV. 16).—297. *Fahrt zum Hades*, Mayrhofer (B.H.P. X. 33, P. V. 94).—298. *Schlaflied*, Mayrhofer (B.H.P. V. 35, P. II. 66).—299. *Die Blumensprache*, Platner (B.H.P. III. 96, P. VI. 188).—300. *Die abgeblühte Linde*, Széchenyi (B.H.P. III. 97, P. IV. 7).—301. *Der Flug der Zeit*, Széchenyi (B.H.P. X. 34, P. IV. 10).— 302. *Der Tod und das Mädchen*, Claudius (B.H.P. XII. 13, P. I. 221).—303. *Das Lied vom Reifen*, Claudius (B.H.P. VII.

127).—304. *Täglich zu singen*, Claudius (B.H.P. VII. 128).—
305. *Die Nacht*, Ossian (B.H.P. XII. 14, P. IV. 158).—306.
Am Strome, Mayrhofer (B.H.P. III. 98, P. II. 25).—307.
Philoktet, Mayrhofer (B.H.P. X. 35, P. V. 45).—308. *Memnon*,
Mayrhofer (B.H.P. X. 36, P. III. 4).—309. *Antigone und
Oedip*, Mayrhofer (B.H.P. XII. 15, P. IV. 3).—310. *Auf dem
See*, Goethe (B.H.P. III. 99, P. II, 172).—311. *Ganymed*,
Goethe (B.H.P. III. 100, P. III. 11).—312. *Der Jüngling und
der Tod*, Spaun (B.H.P. XII. 16, P. VII. 56).—313. *Trost im
Liede*, Schober (B.H.P. VII. 129, P. VI. 81).—314. *An die
Musik*, Schober (B.H.P. V. 36, P. II. 166).—315. *Pax vobis-
cum*, Schober (B.H.P. V. 37, P. II. 213).—316. *Hänflings
Liebeswerbung*, Kind (B.H.P. III. 101, P. IV. 12).—317. *Auf
der Donau*, Mayrhofer (B.H.P. X. 37, P. IV. 14).—318. *Der
Schiffer*, Mayrhofer (B.H.P. X. 38, P. II. 52).—319. *Uraniens
Flucht*, Mayrhofer (B.H.P. V. 38).—320. *Nach einem Gewit-
ter*, Mayrhofer (B.H.P. III. 102).—321. *Fischerlied* (II), Salis
(B.H.P. X. 39).—322. *Die Einsiedelei* (II), Salis (B.H.P. VII.
130, P. VII, 72).—323. *Das Grab* (III), Salis (B.H.P. XI. 40).
—324. *Der Strom*, Stadler (B.H.P. XI. 41, P. VII. 65).—325.
Iphigenia, Mayrhofer (B.H.P. III. 103, P. IV. 97).—326. *An
den Tod*, Schubart (B.H.P. XI, 42, P. V. 84).—327. *Die
Forelle*, Schubart (B.H.P. III. 104, P. I. 197).—328. *Gruppe
aus dem Tartarus*, Schiller (B.H.P. XI. 43, P. II. 61).—329.
Elysium, Schiller (B.H.P. VII. 131, P. IV. 211).—330. *Atys*,
Mayrhofer (B.H.P. VII. 132, P. V. 124).—331. *Erlafsee*,
Mayrhofer (B.H.P. III. 105, P. II. 19).—332. *Der Alpenjäger*,
Schiller (B.H.P. VII. 133, P. IV. 28).—333. *Der Kampf*,
Schiller (B.H.P. XI. 44, P. VI. 162).—334. *Thekla* (II),
Schiller (B.H.P. III. 106, P. II. 168).—335. *Der Knabe in der
Wiege*, Ottenwalt (B.H.P. VII. 134).—336. *Auf der Riesen-
koppe*, Körner (B.H.P. VII. 135, P. VI. 66).—337. *An den
Mond in einer Herbstnacht*, Schreiber (B.H.P. VII. 136, P. V.
88).—338. *Grablied für die Mutter* (B.H.P. III. 107, P. V.
170).—339. *Einsamkeit*, Mayrhofer (B.H.P. VIII. 137, P. V.
175).—340. *Der Blumenbrief*, Schreiber (B.H.P. VIII. 138,
P. II. 225).—341. *Das Marienbild*, Schreiber (B.H.P. III. 108,
P. V. 38).—342. *Litanei auf das Fest Aller Seelen*, Jacobi
(B.H.P. V. 39, P. II. 212).—343. *Blondel zu Marien* (B.H.P.
VIII. 139, P. V. 200).—344. *Das Abendroth*, Schreiber (B.H.P.
XI. 45, P. VI. 121).—345. *Sonett I*, Petrarca (B.H.P. VIII
140).—346. *Sonett II*, Petrarca (B.H.P. VIII. 141).—347.
Sonett III, Petrarca (B.H.P. VIII. 142).—348. *Blanka*,
Schlegel (B.H.P. III. 109, P. VII. 44).—349. *Vom Mitleiden
Mariä*, Schlegel (B.H.P. III. 110, P. V. 39).

VOL. 6, 1819–1821

350. *Die Gebüsche*, Schlegel (B.H.P. III. 111, P. VII. 3).—
351. *Der Wanderer*, Schlegel (B.H.P. XI. 46, P. IV. 58).—
352. *Abendbilder*, Silbert (B.H.P. VIII. 143, P. III. 134).—
353. *Himmelsfunken*, Silbert (B.H.P. V. 40, P. II. 218).—354.
Das Mädchen, Schlegel (B.H.P. III. 112, P. III. 211).—
355. *Berthas Lied in der Nacht*, Grillparzer (B.H.P. III, 113,
P. VI. 24).—356. *An die Freunde*, Mayrhofer (B.H.P. VIII.
144, P. VI. 26).—357. *Sehnsucht* (' Ach, aus dieses Thales ')
(II), Schiller (B.H.P. XI, 47, P. II. 86).—358. *Hoffnung* (II)
Schiller (B.H.P. V. 41, P. IV. 75).—359a. *Der Jüngling am
Bache* (III), Schiller (B.H.P. III. 114, P. II. 158).—359b. *Der
Jüngling am Bache* (III), Schiller (B.H.P. VIII. 145).—360.
Hymne (I), Novalis (B.H.P. VIII, 146).—361. *Hymne* (II),
Novalis (B.H.P. VIII. 147).—362. *Hymne* (III), Novalis
(B.H.P. VIII. 148).—363. *Hymne* (IV), Novalis (B.H.P. VIII.
149).—364. *Marie*, Novalis (B.H.P. VIII, 150).—365. *Beim
Winde*, Mayrhofer (B.H.P. III. 115, P. V. 129).—366. *Die
Sternennächte*, Mayrhofer (B.H.P. VIII. 151, P. VI. 86).—
367. *Trost*, Mayrhofer (B.H.P. VIII. 152, P. VI. 36).—368.
Nachtstück, Mayrhofer (B.H.P. VIII. 153, P. II. 82).—369.
Die Liebende schreibt, Goethe (B.H.P. III. 116, P. VI. 83).—
370. *Prometheus*, Goethe (B.H.P. XI. 48, P. III. 212).—371.
Fragment aus Schillers Gedicht ' Die Götter Griechenlands '
(B.H.P. VIII. 154, P. VI. 28).—372. *Nachthymne*, Novalis
(B.H.P. III. 117).—373. *Die Vögel*, Schlegel (B.H.P. III. 118,
P. VI. 102).—374. *Der Knabe*, Schlegel (B.H.P. VIII. 155).—
375. *Der Fluss*, Schlegel (B.H.P. III. 119).—376. *Abendröte*,
Schlegel (B.H.P. III. 120, P. V. 7).—377. *Der Schiffer*,
Schlegel (B.H.P. VIII. 156, P. V. 190).—378. *Die Sterne*,
Schlegel (B.H.P. V. 42, P. VI. 56).—379. *Morgenlied*, Werner
(B.H.P. III. 121, P. II. 4).—380. *Frühlingsglaube*, Uhland
(B.H.P. *a.* VIII. 157, *b.* III. 122, P. I. 194).—381. *Liebes-
lauschen*, Schlechta (B.H.P. VIII. 158, P. III. 151).—382.
Orest auf Tauris, Mayrhofer (B.H.P. XI. 49, P. V. 40).—383.
Der entsühnte Orest, Mayrhofer (B.H.P. XI. 50, P. V. 42).—
384. *Freiwilliges Versinken*, Mayrhofer (B.H.P. XI. 51, P. V.
47).—385. *Der Jüngling auf dem Hügel*, Hüttenbrenner (B.H.P.
III. 123, P. II. 16).—386. *Sehnsucht* (' Der Lerche '), Mayr-
hofer (B.H.P. VIII. 159, P. II. 22).—387. *Der zürnenden
Diana*, Mayrhofer (B.H.P. VIII. 160, P. II. 75).—388. *Im
Walde*, Schlegel (B.H.P. V. 43, P. III. 159).—389. *Die gefan-
genen Sänger*, Schlegel (B.H.P. III. 124, P. V. 193).—390.
Der Unglückliche, Pichler (B.H.P. VIII. 161, P. IV. 70).—

391. *Versunken*, Goethe (B.H.P. VIII. 162, P. III. 207).—
392. *Geheimes*, Goethe (B.H.P. VIII. 163, P. I. 232).—393.
Grenzen der Menschheit, Goethe (B.H.P. XI. 52, P. III. 144).
—394. *Mignon* (I) (' Heiss mich nich reden ') (I), Goethe
(B.H.P. III. 125).—395. *Mignon* (II) (' So lasst mich schei-
nen ') (I), Goethe (B.H.P. III. 126, P. VI. 62).—396. *Suleika*
(I), Goethe (B.H.P. III. 127, P. II. 38).—397. *Suleika* (II),
Goethe (B.H.P. III. 128, P. II. 68).—398. *Der Jüngling an der
Quelle*, Salis (B.H.P. VIII. 164, P. VI. 2).—399. *Der Blumen
Schmerz*, Mailath (B.H.P. III. 129, P. VI. 114).—400. *Sei mir
gegrüsst*, Rückert (B.H.P. VIII. 165, P. I. 190).

VOL. 7, 1822 TO ' DIE SCHÖNE MÜLLERIN,' 1823

401. *Der Wachtelschlag*, Sauter (B.H.P. III. 130, P. II. 134).
—402. *Ihr Grab*, Roos (B.H.P. VIII. 166, P. VI. 6).—403.
Nachtviolen, Mayrhofer (B.H.P. VIII. 167, P. VII. 60).—
404. *Aus ' Heliopolis '* (I), Mayrhofer (B.H.P. V. 44, P. III.
33).—405. *Aus ' Heliopolis '* (II), Mayrhofer (B.H.P. X.
53, P. III. 204).—406. *Selige Welt*, Senn (B.H.P. XI.
54, P. IV. 19).—407. *Schwanengesang*, Senn (B.H.P. IV.
131, P. IV. 21).—408. *Die Rose*, Schlegel (B.H.P. *a*. IV. 132,
b. V. 45, P. II. 140).—409. *Du liebst mich nicht*, Platen (B.H.P.
a. V. 46, *b*. VIII. 168, P. II. 120).—410. *Die Liebe hat gelogen*,
Platen (B.H.P. VIII. 169, P. II. 60).—411. *Todesmusik*,
Schober (B.H.P. VIII. 170, P. IV. 112).—412. *Schatzgräbers
Begehr*, Schober (B.H.P. XI. 55, P. IV. 22).—413. *Schwestergruss*, Bruchmann (B.H.P. VIII. 171, P. V. 135).—414. *An
die Leier*, Bruchmann (B.H.P. XI. 56, P. II. 110).—415. *Im
Haine*, Bruchmann (B.H.P. IV. 133, P. II. 114).—416. *Der
Musensohn*, Goethe (B.H.P. VIII. 172, P. IV. 78).—417. *An
die Entfernte*, Goethe (B.H.P. VIII. 173, P. VII. 54).—418.
Am Flusse (II), Goethe (B.H.P. XI. 57).—419. *Willkommen
und Abschied*, Goethe (B.H.P. VIII. 174, P. III. 25).—420.
Wanderers Nachtlied (' Ueber allen Gipfeln '), Goethe (B.H.P.
IV. 134, P. I. 229).—421. *Der zürnende Barde*, Bruchmann
(B.H.P. XI. 58, P. V. 26).—422. *Am See*, Bruchmann (B.H.P.
IV. 135, P. V. 29).—423. *Viola*, Schober (B.H.P. IV. 136, P.
III. 110).—424. *Drang in die Ferne*, Leitner (B.H.P. VIII.
175, P. II. 136).—425. *Der Zwerg*, Collin (B.H.P. XI. 59,
P. II. 55).—426. *Wehmuth*, Collin (B.H.P. V. 47, P. III. 15).
—427. *Lied*, Stolberg (B.H.P. IV. 137, P. V. 164).—428.
Auf dem Wasser zu singen, Stolberg (B.H.P. IV. 138, P. I.
216).—429. *Pilgerweise*, Schober (B.H.P. VIII. 176, P. III.
175).—430. *Vergissmeinnicht*, Schober (B.H.P. VIII. 177, P.

V. 112).—431. *Das Geheimnis* (II), Schiller (B.H.P. VIII. 178, P. VI. 107).—432. *Der Pilgrim*, Schiller (B.H.P. VIII. 179, P. IV. 24).—433–452. *Die schöne Müllerin*, Müller (B.H.P. I. 1–20).—433. *Das Wandern* (P. I. 4).—434. *Wohin?* (P. I. 6).—435. *Halt!* (P. I. 10).—436. *Danksagung an den Bach* (P. I. 12).—437. *Am Feierabend* (P. I. 14).—438. *Der Neugierige* (P. I. 18).—439. *Ungeduld* (P. I. 20).—440. *Morgengruss* (P. I. 22).—441. *Des Müllers Blumen* (P. I. 24).—442. *Thränenregen* (P. I. 26).—443. *Mein!* (P. I. 28).—444. *Pause* (P. I. 32).—445. *Mit dem grünen Lautenbande* (P. I. 35). —446. *Der Jäger* (P. I. 36).—447. *Eifersucht und Stolz* (P. I. 38).—448. *Die liebe Farbe* (P. I. 41).—449. *Die böse Farbe* (P. I. 43).—450. *Trockne Blumen* (P. I. 46).—451. *Der Müller und der Bach* (P. I. 49).—452. *Des Baches Wiegenlied* (P. I. 52).

VOL. 8, FROM ' DIE SCHÖNE MÜLLERIN ' TO THE ' WINTER-REISE,' 1823–1827

453. *Dass sie hier gewesen*, Rückert (B.H.P. VIII. 180, P. III. 30).—454. *Du bist die Ruh'*, Rückert (B.H.P. IX. 181, P. I. 212).—455. *Lachen und Weinen*, Rückert (B.H.P. IV. 139, P. II. 122).—456. *Greisengesang*, Rückert (B.H.P. XI. 60, P. II. 124).—457. *Dithyrambe*, Schiller (B.H.P. XI. 61, P. II. 128).—458. *Der Sieg*, Mayrhofer (B.H.P. XI. 62, P. V. 122).—459. *Abendstern*, Mayrhofer (B.H.P. IX. 182, P. V. 133).—460. *Auflösung*, Mayrhofer (B.H.P. IX. 183, P. V. 196). —461. *Gondelfahrer*, Mayrhofer (B.H.P. XI. 63).—462. *Glaube, Hoffnung und Liebe*, Kuffner (B.H.P. IV. 140, P. II. 190).—463. *Im Abendrot*, Lappe (B.H.P. IV. 141, P. II. 219).—464. *Lied eines Kriegers* (B.H.P. XI. 64, P. V. 204).— 465. *Der Einsame*, Lappe (B.H.P. IX. 184, P. II. 92).—466. *Des Sängers Habe*, Schlechta (B.H.P. XI. 65, P. V. 2).—467. *Totengräbers Heimweh*, Craigher (B.H.P. XI. 66, P. V. 143). —468. *Der blinde Knabe*, Colley Cibber (trans. Craigher) (B.H.P. IX. 185, P. II. 196).—469. *Die junge Nonne*, Craigher (B.H.P. IV. 142, P. I. 201).—470. *Nacht und Träume*, Collin (B.H.P. IV. 143, P. II. 97).—471. *Ellens Gesang* (I) (' Soldier, rest!'), Scott (B.H.P. IV. 144, P. III. 16).—472. *Ellens Gesang* (II) (' Huntsman, rest!'), Scott (B.H.P. IV. 145, P. III. 22).—473. *Normans Gesang* (' The heath this night'), Scott (B.H.P. IX. 186, P. II. 99).—474. *Ellens Gesang* (III) (' Ave Maria '), Scott (B.H.P. IV. 146, P. I. 206).—475. *Lied des gefangenen Jägers* (' My hawk is tired of perch '), Scott (B.H.P. XI. 67, P. II. 106).—476. *Im Walde*, Schulze (B.H.P. IX. 187, P. III. 57).—477. *Auf der Bruck*, Schulze (B.H.P.

IX. 188, P. II. 176).—478. *Das Heimweh*, Pyrker (B.H.P. IX. 189, P. II. 142).—479. *Die Allmacht*, Pyrker (B.H.P. IX. 190, P. II. 150).—480. *Fülle der Liebe*, Schlegel (B.H.P. IX. 191, P. III. 193).—481. *Wiedersehn*, Schlegel (B.H.P. IX. 192).—482. *Abendlied für die Entfernte*, Schlegel (B.H.P. IX. 193, P. III. 52).—483 and 484. *Zwei Scenen aus ' Lacrimas*,' Schütz : I. *Florio* (B.H.P. IX. 194, P. III. 132) ; II. *Delphine* (B.H.P. IV. 147, P. III. 126).—485. *An mein Herz*, Schulze (B.H.P. IX. 195, P. V. 73).—486. *Der liebliche Stern*, Schulze (B.H.P. IV. 148, P. III. 140).—487. *Tiefes Leid*, Schulze (B.H.P. XI. 68, P. III. 202).—488-491. *Gesänge aus ' Wilhelm Meister*,' Goethe.—488. *Mignon und der Harfner* (' Nur wer die Sehnsucht ') (IV) (B.H.P. XII. 17).—489. *Lied der Mignon* (' Heiss mich nicht ') (II) (B.H.P. IV. 149, P. II. 130).—490. *Lied der Mignon* (' So lasst mich ') (II) (B.H.P. IV. 150, P. II. 132).—491. *Lied der Mignon* (' Nur wer die Sehnsucht ') (V) (B.H.P. IV. 151, P. I. 214).—492. *Am Fenster*, Seidl (B.H.P. IX. 196, P. III. 77).—493. *Sehnsucht*, Seidl (B.H.P. IX. 197, P. IV. 100).—494. *Im Freien*, Seidl (B.H.P. IX. 198, P. III. 39).—495. *Fischerweise*, Schlechta (B.H.P. XI. 69, P. II. 186).—496. *Totengräberweise*, Schlechta (B.H.P. V. 48, P. III. 155).—497. *Im Frühling*, Schulze (B.H.P. IX. 199, P. II. 227).—498. *Lebensmut*, Schulze (B.H.P. IX. 200, P. IV. 80).—499. *Um Mitternacht*, Schulze (B.H.P. IX. 201, P. II. 162).—500. *Über Wildemann*, Schulze (B.H.P. IX. 202, P. III. 80).—501. *Romanze des Richard Löwenherz*, Scott (B.H.P. IX. 203, P. III. 45).—502. *Trinklied* (' Come, thou monarch of the vine '), Shakespeare (B.H.P. IX. 204, P. VI. 61).—503. *Ständchen* (' Hark, hark, the lark '), Shakespeare (B.H.P. IX. 205, P. I. 234).—504. *Hippolyts Lied*, Gerstenbergk (B.H.P. IX. 206, P. V. 5). —505. *Gesang : An Silvia* (' Who is Silvia ? '), Shakespeare (B.H.P. IX. 207, P. II. 202).—506. *Der Wanderer an den Mond*, Seidl (B.H.P. IX. 208, P. IV. 59).—507. *Das Zügenglöcklein*, Seidl (B.H.P. IV. 152, P. III. 36).—508-511. *Vier Refrainlieder*, Seidl.—508. *Die Unterscheidung* (B.H.P. IV. 153, P. IV. 83).—509. *Bei dir* (B.H.P. IX. 209, P. III. 66).—510. *Die Männer sind méchant* (B.H.P. IV. 154, P. IV. 88).—511. *Irdisches Glück* (B.H.P. IX. 210, P. IV. 91).—512. *Wiegenlied*, Seidl (B.H.P. IV. 155, P. III. 72).—513. *Das Echo*, Castelli (B.H.P. IV. 156, P. II. 204).—514. *Der Vater mit dem Kind*, Bauernfeld (B.H.P. V. 49, P. III. 172).—515. *Jägers Liebeslied*, Schober (B.H.P. XI. 70, P. III. 70).—516. *Schiffers Scheidelied*, Schober (B.H.P. XI. 71, P. III. 181).

VOL. 10

I. Songs with Two Instruments

568. *Auf dem Strom*, Rellstab (B.H.P. IX. 217, P. III. 100).
—569. *Der Hirt auf dem Felsen*, Müller (B.H.P. IV. 172, P. VI. 132).

II. Songs with Italian Text

570. *Misero pargoletto*, Metastasio (B.H.P. IV. 161).—571. *Pensa, che questo istante*, Metastasio (B.H.P. XI. 75, P. VI. 178).—572. *Son fra l'onde*, Metastasio (B.H.P. IV. 162).— 573. *Aria* (' Vedi, quanto adoro '), Metastasio (B.H.P. IV. 163).—574. *La pastorella*, Goldoni (B.H.P. IV. 164).—575-578. *Quattro Canzoni*, Metastasio : I. *Non t'accostar all'urna* (B.H.P. IV. 165, P. VI. 169) ; II. *Guarda, che bianca luna* (B.H.P. IV. 166, P. VI. 170) ; III. *Da quel sembiante apresi* (B.H.P. IV. 167, P. VI. 174) ; IV. *Mio ben ricordati* (B.H.P. IV. 168, P. VI. 176).—579-581. *Tre Canti*, Metastasio.— 579. *L'incanto degli occhi* (B.H.P. XI. 76, P. VI. 144), *Die Macht der Augen.*—580. *Il traditor deluso* (B.H.P. XI. 77, P. VI. 148), *Der getäuschte Verräther.*—581. *Il modo di prender moglie* (B.H.P. XI. 78, P. VI. 155), *Die Art ein Weib zu nehmen.*

III. Occasional Songs

582. *Zur Namensfeier des Herrn Andreas Siller.*—583. *Auf den Sieg der Deutschen.*—584. *Die Befreier Europas in Paris.* —585. *Lied* (' Brüder, schrecklich brennt ').—586. *Abschied*, Schubert (B.H.P. IX. 215, P. V. 169).—587. *Namenstagslied*, Stadler (B.H.P. IV. 169).—588. *Herrn Joseph Spaun*, Collin (P. VI. 45).—589. *Herbst*, Rellstab (B.H.P. IX. 216).

IV. Fragments

590. *Der Geistertanz* (I), Matthisson.—591. *Die drei Sänger.* —592. *Lorma*, Ossian (B.H.P. IV. 170).—593. *Pflicht und Liebe*, Gotter (P. VII. 37).—594. *Gesang der Geister über den Wassern*, Goethe.—595. *Mahomets Gesang* (I), Goethe.— 596. *Gretchen*, Goethe (P. V. 166).—597. *Die Entzückung an Laura* (II), Schiller.—598. *Lied eines Kindes.*—599. *Über allen*

Zauber Liebe, Mayrhofer.—600. *Mahomets Gesang* (II), Goethe.—601. *Johanna Sebus*, Goethe.—602. *Lebensmut*, Rellstab (P. VII. 58).

V. Melodrama

603. *Abschied von der Erde*. Pratobevera (B.H.P. IV. 171, P. VII. 109).

'ADIEU!'

AN appendix is the only place in which to mention the notorious song *Adieu!* which for generations enjoyed a vogue along with the most popular of Schubert's compositions, and which still appears, without a hint of its spuriousness, in a number of editions (e.g. Augener's and Boosey's). Even Friedländer includes it (Peters, VI, 128), no doubt to please old admirers, while not allowing that it is genuine. He ascribes it to Weyrauch, and prints it with a French text (' Voici l'instant suprême '). Augustus Heinrich von Weyrauch, whose acknowledged songs (settings of Rückert), were long ago forgotten, has thus curiously come to be remembered by a mere pastiche. *Adieu!* faintly recalls *Im Abendroth* and *Der Wegweiser* ; but the writing is wooden.

APPENDIX II

THE POETS OF THE SONGS

₊ The numbers in parentheses refer to the Collected edition.

EDUARD VON BAUERNFELD.—1. *Der Vater mit dem Kind* (514).

GABRIELE VON BAUMBERG.—1. *Cora an die Sonne* (123). 2. *Der Morgenkuss* (124). 3. *Abendständchen* (125). 4. *An die Sonne* (127). 5. *Lob des Tokayers* (135).

JOSEF CARL BERNARD.—*Vergebliche Liebe* (58).

JOHANN GUSTAV BERTRAND.—1. *Minona* (40). 2. *Adelwold und Emma* (79).

FRANZ VON BRUCHMANN.—1. *Schwestergruss* (413). 2. *An die Leyer* (414). 3. *Im Haine* (415). 4. *Der zürnende Barde* (421). 5. *Am See* (422).

FRANZ VON CASTELLI.—*Das Echo* (513).

COLLEY CIBBER.—*Der blinde Knabe* (trans. J. N. Craigher) (468 *a* and *b*).

MATTHIAS CLAUDIUS.—1. *An eine Quelle* (273). 2. *Bei dem Grabe meines Vaters* (274). 3. *Am Grabe Anselmos* (275). 4. *An die Nachtigall* (276). 5. *Wiegenlied* (277). 6. *Abendlied* (278). 7. *Phidile* (279). 8. *Lied* (*Ich bin vergnügt*) (280 and 281). 9. *Der Tod und das Mädchen* (302). 10. *Das Lied vom Reifen* (303). 11. *Täglich zu singen* (304).

HEINRICH VON COLLIN.—*Leiden der Trennung* (*Metastasio*) (285).

MATTHÆUS VON COLLIN.—1. *Licht und Liebe* (286). 2. *Der Zwerg* (425). 3. *Wehmut* (426). 4. *Nacht und Träume* (470). 5. *Herrn Josef Spaun* (588).

ABRAHAM COWLEY.—*Der Weiberfreund* (trans. J. F. Ratschky).

JAKOB NICOLAUS CRAIGHER.—1. *Totengräbers Heimweh* (467). 2. *Der blinde Knabe* (*Colley Cibber*) (468 *a*, *b*). 3. *Die junge Nonne* (469).

LUDWIG DEINHARDSTEIN.—*Skolie* (154).

EHRLICH.—*Als ich sie erröthen sah* (41).

ERMIN (J. G. KUMPF).—1. *Der Mondabend* (43). 2. *Mein Gruss an den Mai* (153).

JOHANN GEORG FELLINGER.—1. *Die Sterne* (57). 2. *Die erste Liebe* (61). 3. *Die Sternwelten* (155).

FRIEDRICH DE LA MOTTE-FOUQUÉ.—1–3. *Don Gayseros* (13, 14, 15). 4. *Lied* (*Mutter geht*) (184). 5. *Der Schäfer und der Reiter* (293).

FRIEDRICH VON GERSTENBERGK.—*Hippolyts Lied* (504).

from ' *Didone* ' (573). 5. *Guarda che bianca luna* (576). 6. *Da quel sembiante appresi* (577). 7. *Mio ben ricordati* (578). 8. *L'incanto degli occhi* (579). 9. *Il traditor deluso* (580). 10. *Leiden der Trennung* (trans. H. von Collin) (285).

WILHELM MÜLLER.—1-20. *Die schöne Müllerin* (433-452). 21-44. *Winterreise* (517-540). 45. *Der Hirt auf dem Felsen* (569).

FRIEDRICH NOVALIS.—1-4. *Hymnen* (360-363). 5. *Marie* (364). 6. *Nachthymne* (372).

OSSIAN.—1. *Lodas Gespenst* (44). 2. *Kolmas Klage* (83). 3. *Shilrik und Vinvela* (146). 4. *Ossians Lied nach dem Falle Nathos*' (147). 5. *Das Mädchen von Inistore* (148). 6. *Der Tod Oskars* (187). 7. *Cronnan* (188). 8. *Die Nacht* (305). 9. *Lorma* (592).

ANTON OTTENWALT.—*Der Knabe in der Wiege* (335).

PETRARCA.—1. *Sonett* (I) (*Apollo, lebet noch*) (345). 2. *Sonett* (II) (*Allein nachdenklich*) (346). 3. *Sonett* (III) (*Nunmehr, da Himmel*) (347) (trans. Gries).

PFEFFEL.—*Der Vatermörder* (4).

CAROLINE VON PICHLER.—1. *Der Sänger am Felsen* (264). 2. *Lied* (*Ferne von der grossen Stadt*) (265). 3. *Der Unglückliche* (390 *a, b*).

AUGUST PLATEN.—1. *Du liebst mich nicht* (409 *a, b*). 2. *Die Liebe hat gelogen* (410).

EDUARD PLATNER.—*Die Blumensprache* (299).

ALEXANDER POPE.—*Verklärung* (trans. Herder) (10).

MARTIN JOSEPH PRANDSTETTER.—*Die Fröhlichkeit* (134).

ADOLF VON PRATOBEVERA.—*Abschied von der Erde* (*Melodrama*) (603).

LADISLAUS PYRKER.—1. *Das Heimweh* (478 *a, b*). 2. *Die Allmacht* (479).

FRIEDRICH REIL.—*Das Lied im Grünen* (543).

CHRISTIAN LUDWIG REISSIG.—*Der Zufriedene* (167).

LUDWIG RELLSTAB.—1. *Liebesbotschaft* (554). 2. *Kriegers Ahnung* (555). 3. *Frühlingssehnsucht* (556). 4. *Ständchen* (557). 5. *Aufenthalt* (558). 6. *In der Ferne* (559). 7. *Abschied* (560). 8. *Auf dem Strom* (568). 9. *Herbst* (589). 10. *Lebensmut* (602).

FRIEDRICH ROCHLITZ.—1. *Klaglied* (6). 2. *Alinde* (287). 3. *An die Laute* (288).

RICHARD ROOS (Carl August Engelhardt).—*Ihr Grab* (402).

FRIEDRICH RÜCKERT.—1. *Sei mir gegrüsst* (400). 2. *Dass sie hier gewesen* (453). 3. *Du bist die Ruh'* (454). 4. *Lachen und Weinen* (455). 5. *Greisengesang* (456).

JOHANN GAUNDENZ VON SALIS.—1. *Das Grab* (182, 186, 323).
2. *Pflügerlied* (197). 3. *Die Einsiedelei* (198, 322). 4. *Gesang
an die Harmonie* (199). 5. *Die Wehmut* (200). 6. *Lied* (*In's
stille Land*) (201 a, b). 7. *Der Herbstabend* (202). 8. *Der
Entfernten* (203). 9. *Fischerlied* (204, 321). 10. *Abschied
von der Harfe* (208). 11. *Herbstlied* (282). 12. *Der Jüngling
an der Quelle* (398).

S. F. SAUTER.—*Der Wachtelschlag* (401).

FRIEDRICH VON SCHILLER.—1. *Des Mädchens Klage* (2, 67 a,
b, 194). 2. *Eine Leichenphantasie* (3). 3. *Der Jüngling am
Bache* (5, 68, 359 a, b). 4. *Sehnsucht* (9, 357 a, b). 5.
Thekla (11, 334 a, b). 6. *Der Taucher* (12, a, b). 7. *An Emma*
(26 a, b, c). 8. *Das Mädchen aus der Fremde* (30, 108). 9.
Die Erwartung (46). 10. *An die Freude* (66). 11. *Amalia*
(71). 12. *Das Geheimnis* (105, 431). 13. *Hoffnung* (106),
358). 14. *An den Frühling* (107 a, b, 136). 15. *Die Bürgschaft* (109). 16. *Punschlied* (110). 17. *Lied* (*Es ist so ange-
nehm*) (137). 18. *Hektors Abschied* (159 a, b). 19. *Klage
der Ceres* (172). 20. *Ritter Toggenburg* (191). 21. *Der
Flüchtling* (192). 22. *Laura am Klavier* (193 a, b). 23. *Die
Entzückung an Laura* (195, 597). 24. *Die vier Weltalter* (196).
25. *Gruppe aus dem Tartarus* (328). 26. *Elysium* (329).
27. *Der Alpenjäger* (332). 28. *Der Kampf* (333). 29. *Die
Götter Griechenlands, Fragment* (371 a, b). 30. *Der Pilgrim*
(432). 31. *Dithyrambe* (457).

FRANZ VON SCHLECHTA.—1. *Auf einen Kirchhof* (39). 2. *Aus
Diego Manazares* (242). 3. *Liebeslauschen* (381). 4. *Des
Sängers Habe* (466). 5. *Fischerweise* (495 a, b). 6. *Toten-
gräberweise* (496). 7. *Widerschein* (553).

AUGUST WILHELM SCHLEGEL.—1. *Lebensmelodien* (205). 2.
Die verfehlte Stunde (206). 3. *Sprache der Liebe* (207). 4.
Lob der Thränen (294). 5–7. *Sonette* (trans. from Petrarca)
(345–346). 8. *Die gefangenen Sänger* (389). 9. *Wiedersehen*
(481). 10. *Abendlied für die Entfernte* (482).

FRIEDRICH SCHLEGEL.—1. *Der Schmetterling* (179). 2. *Die
Berge* (180). 3. *Blanka* (348). 4. *Vom Mitleiden Mariä*
(349). 5. *Die Gebüsche* (350). 6. *Der Wanderer* (351). 7.
Das Mädchen (354). 8. *Die Vögel* (373). 9. *Der Knabe*
(374). 10. *Der Fluss* (375). 11. *Abendröte* (376). 12. *Der
Schiffer* (377). 13. *Die Sterne* (378). 14. *Im Walde* (388).
15. *Die Rose* (408 a, b). 16. *Fülle der Liebe* (480).

GEORG PHILIPP SCHMIDT.—*Der Wanderer* (266 a, b).

FRANZ VON SCHOBER.—1. *Genügsamkeit* (181). 2. *Am Bach
im Frühling* (272). 3. *Trost im Liede* (313). 4. *An die Musik*
(314 a, b). 5. *Pax vobiscum* (315). 6. *Todesmusik* (411). 7.

CHRISTOPH AUGUST TIEDGE.—*Au die Sonne* (129).

LUDWIG UHLAND.—*Frühlingsglaube* (380 *a, b*).

JOHAN PETER UZ.—1. *Die Liebesgötter* (231). 2. *An den Schlaf* (232). 3. *Gott im Frühlinge* (233). 4. *Der gute Hirt* (234). 5. *Die Nacht* (235).

ZACHARIAS WERNER.—1. *Jagdlied* (290). 2. *Morgenlied* (379).

MARIANNE VON WILLEMER.—*Suleika* (11) (51).

ALOIS ZETTLER.—*Trinklied* (62).

UNKNOWN AUTHORS.—*Das Bild* (42). *Lilla an die Morgenröthe* (130). *Tischlerlied* (131). *Klage* (185). *Morgenlied* (189). *Abendlied* (190). *Frohsinn* (289). *Trost* (292). *Grablied für die Mutter* (338). *Blondel zu Marien* (343). *Lied eines Kriegers* (464). *Zur Namensfeier des Herrn Andreas Siller* (582). *Auf den Sieg der Deutschen* (583). *Die Befreier Europas in Paris* (584). *Lied (Brüder, schrecklich brennt die Thräne)* (585). *Die drei Sänger* (591). *Lied eines Kindes* (598).

INDEX TO NAMES

INDEX OF SONGS

INDEX OF WORKS OTHER THAN SONGS